PRAISE FOR
BACK FROM THE DEAD

"Bill Walton won at every level with extraordinary skill and intelligence. Yet more importantly, he continues to win in the game of life."

—Bill Russell, Bill Walton's favorite player ever

"Elegaic yet exuberant. . . . A celebration of a life in sports that is also a frank assessment of the toll basketball took on his body. . . . [Walton] writes with admirable candor."

—John Swansburg, *The New York Times Book Review*

"A remarkable journey of resilience, reinvention, and ultimate triumph told in the unique voice of one of the great pundits—and players—of our generation."

—David J. Stern, NBA Commissioner Emeritus

"This isn't a basketball story, it's a story of victory over adversity and the Tao of positive thinking. Quitters never win and winners never quit. Bill Walton is a winner."

—Mickey Hart, drummer/percussionist, Grateful Dead

"An astounding book. . . . A book of sadness, of incredible pain, and yet great joy. . . . [Walton] really didn't have to go ahead and write a book. But it's good that he did, all by himself. Because he's Bill Walton, and there is no copy."

—Nick Canepa, *San Diego Union-Tribune*

"Bill Walton played the game of life with the same verve as he did the game of basketball, even in the face of crippling injuries and withering pain. Funny, poignant, and inspiring, *Back from the Dead* is a rollicking, riveting memoir, told with characteristic honesty by one of America's most compelling personalities."

    —David Axelrod, author of *Believer: My Forty Years in Politics*

"Larger than life, with a heart and soul to match his reach and accomplishments, Bill Walton has written a compelling autobiography, *Back from the Dead*. This is Walton at his best, a great friend who helps you overcome even the most brutal setback."

    —Roger McNamee, tech investor, musician, Deadhead

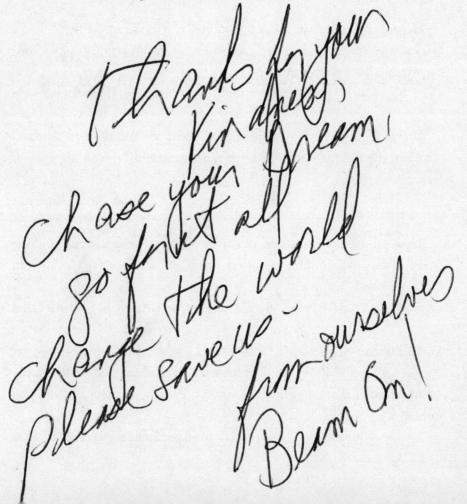

Thanks for your Kindness, chase your dream, go for it all, change the world, please save us — from ourselves. Beam On!

BACK
FROM THE
DEAD

Gratefully

BILL WALTON

Bill Walton

SIMON & SCHUSTER PAPERBACKS

New York London Toronto Sydney New Delhi

Simon & Schuster Paperbacks
An Imprint of Simon & Schuster, Inc.
1230 Avenue of the Americas
New York, NY 10020

First Simon & Schuster paperback edition March 2017

SIMON & SCHUSTER PAPERBACKS and colophon are registered
trademarks of Simon & Schuster, Inc.

For information about special discounts for bulk purchases,
please contact Simon & Schuster Special Sales at 1-866-506-1949
or business@simonandschuster.com.

The Simon & Schuster Speakers Bureau can bring authors to your
live event. For more information or to book an event, contact the
Simon & Schuster Speakers Bureau at 1-866-248-3049 or visit
our website at www.simonspeakers.com.

Manufactured in the United States of America

10 9 8 7 6 5 4 3 2 1

The Library of Congress has cataloged the hardcover edition as follows:

Walton, Bill, 1952– author.
Back from the dead / Bill Walton.
First Simon & Schuster hardcover edition. | New York : Simon &
    Schuster, 2016. | Includes index.
LCCN 2015031712 | ISBN 9781476716862 (hardcover) | ISBN
    9781476716886 (ebook)
LCSH: Walton, Bill, 1952– | Basketball players—United
    States—Biography. | Sportscasters—United States—Biography.
LCC GV884.W3 A3 2016 | DDC 796.323092—dc23
LC record available at http://lccn.loc.gov/2015031712

ISBN 978-1-4767-1686-2
ISBN 978-1-4767-1687-9 (pbk)
ISBN 978-1-4767-1688-6 (ebook)

CONTENTS

One Way or Another
This Darkness Got to Give

Summer 2009, San Diego

I can't do this anymore. It's just too hard. It hurts too much. Why should I continue? What's the point in going on? I have been down so long now, I have no idea which way anywhere is anymore. There's no reason to believe that tomorrow is going to be any better.

If I had a gun, I would use it.

The light has gone out of my life, and there's no sound, either. Not even in my spirit and soul, where at least there has always been music.

I have been living on the floor for most of the last two and a half years, unable to move, unable to get up. I've cut myself off from Jerry, Bob, Neil, and the rest, just as I've disconnected from most everybody and everything else. The only people I see, talk to, or hear from are the few who refuse to leave me alone—my wife, Lori; my brother Bruce; our four sons; the most obstinate of my closest friends, like Andy Hill, Jim Gray, my guys in the Grateful Dead—and the one person *I* refuse to leave alone, John Wooden, now almost one hundred years old. Everybody else has been turned away. My mom doesn't even know about any of this. She only gets the good news.

Lori always says my mind is like a slot machine: you never know how the spinning wheels are going to align.

> *The wheel is turning and you can't slow down,*
> *You can't let go, and you can't hold on,*
> *You can't go back, and you can't stand still,*
> *If the thunder don't get you, then the lightning will.*

I've lived with pain for most of my life, but pain has never been my entire life. It's in my spine now, and radiating everywhere from it. It has taken me down like never before. And it just won't let me be.

What to some is pain, to me is really just fatigue. I love and live for that fatigue and the soreness that comes with it, when you've pushed yourself relentlessly up and over another long, hard climb—the longer and harder the better—and met the toughest challenges imaginable, fighting against gravity and exhaustion, even when one more push seems impossible, until you reach the top, and the destination of euphoria, and you throw your arms over your head in a wild explosion of ecstasy and celebration—a high-altitude climax that you're sure will last forever. There is nothing like it.

But this time is different—real different.

I was inspired early on by George Bernard Shaw, who challenged us all, as we approach the scrap heap of life, to become "a force of nature instead of a feverish, selfish little clod of ailments and grievances, complaining that the world will not devote itself to making you happy."

That's the way it has always gone for me, as a young boy growing up in San Diego, chasing my basketball dreams at UCLA, then Portland, with my hometown Clippers, and finally in Boston. It was more of the same later on, out on the broadcasting and business road for more than twenty years. It's why I've gone to more than 859 Grateful Dead shows.

It's really all been one show that never ends. It's also why, when I'm not at a Dead show, or not involved with basketball or business, I am at my happiest and best when riding high, up on my bike, dripping and soaking with sweat under the hot, burning sun, turning the crank and pushing the wheel endlessly over, time after time after time. Mile after countless mile across the warm, dry desert, along the twisting, jagged coast, or winding up a mountain, spinning, twirling, rolling, drifting, dreaming, celebrating—the chance of being on yet another long, hard climb, the longer and harder the better.

I can't count the number of these long, hard climbs I've made over the years. But I do know that while the longest and hardest have taken me the highest, I never was able to get that euphoria to last very long. Every time, way too soon after I'd reached the top—so tantalizingly close to perfection—the dancing, dreaming, and celebrating that I was sure would never end would come to a crashing halt. Somehow, some way, my wheels would stop turning; I'd lose control and wind up skidding or skulking off the road, collapsing into a crumpled, helpless, hopeless heap—where everything would end up broken.

But with every inevitable catastrophic collapse, at least I always had the music—the one thing that never stopped. The songs, the stories, the dreams, the hope, would always get me through.

I realized at a very early age that all the songs of my heroes were really just songs of my own. And that they were written for me, to me, about me, and about everything that happened in my life. Somehow, some way, they all knew. About everything. The Dead, Dylan, Neil, the Johns—Lennon and Fogerty—Crosby, Stills & Nash, the Stones, Carlos, the Beach Boys, the Beatles, Jimmy Cliff, Jackson Browne, and ultimately the Eagles and Bruce Springsteen.

It fell apart, and it breaks my heart to think about how close we came.

So close, so many times. It all could have been so perfect but for the fiery crash that would ruin everything, every time. UCLA and the 88-game winning streak that should have been a perfect 105—what could and should have been, ultimately ending in disappointment, shame, and embarrassment. The Trail Blazers, Clippers, Celtics—more of the same. It all could have been so right; it all should have been so perfect.

When life looks like Easy Street, there is danger at your door.

It's never a good idea, Coach Wooden preached, to measure yourself by what you have done rather than by what you could or should have been able to do.

But at least my crashes—painful, miserable, and frequent as they were—always eventually led to new beginnings and the next long, hard climb. And on each new climb, I had to try to remember to learn perspective, relativity, patience, and tolerance, and remind myself of the fragility of it all. You'd think I would know by now. But the pattern kept repeating. Each new challenge filled me with new confidence that this time would be different. And that the joys of this long, hard climb would finally last forever.

Coach Wooden was presciently brilliant on so many fronts. Sadly it took me too long to realize it. When I played for him, I was a teenager—seventeen, eighteen, nineteen years old. Most of what he said in those days seemed ridiculous. He would constantly remind me then, and continue to tell me over the next four decades, "Walton, you are the slowest learner I have ever had!"

Coach Wooden was an English teacher by profession; he had young men under his athletic supervision in the afternoon. Coach was charged by his father, Joshua, to "make each day your masterpiece." Coach dutifully passed that wisdom on to all of his students. For his certificate of currency, relevancy, and authenticity, he wrote his master's thesis on how to teach poetry. And while Coach had his poets—Shakespeare, Tennyson, Frost, Longfellow, Whitman, Dailey—I have mine: Jerry Garcia, John Lennon, Neil Young, Bob Dylan. Maybe if Coach had listened more closely, he would have realized that my guys were singing the same songs as his. I'm sure he felt the same way about me—listening more closely and all.

These days, it feels like none of them are singing anymore at all—Coach's masters or mine. The music has finally, unexpectedly, tragically, totally stopped. I am buried too far down. It's just too dark down here. And the climb is finally too long and too darn hard.

By the numbers, I am the most injured athlete in the history of sports. My injuries are not the gravest, but they are mine. They never go away. Sadly, they are the kinds of injuries that no one could see happen or ultimately understand—the way the world witnessed Joe Theismann's leg snapping like a twig, endlessly replayed on TV.

And while I am a fighter and a player in the game of life, I am not much more than that. The true champions and heroes in our world are the freedom fighters struggling for truth and justice, the ones who through the ages gave up everything—their limbs, their minds, their freedom, their lives—so that all of us could have a chance to chase our dreams.

For me, the dream has too often devolved into the nightmare of endlessly repetitive and constant pain, agony, and guilt. Thirty-seven orthopedic surgeries, nearly all stemming from my malformed feet—my faulty foundation, which led to the endless string of stress fractures, which ultimately brought on the whole mess I'm in now. The insidious, ever-widening fractures in my feet, made so much worse by the fact that they were undetectable, even by machines, so that practically everyone had doubts that they ever even really existed. Confusing and confounding doubts that even consumed me.

> The band was packed and gone
> Were they ever even here at all?

I was born with structural, congenital defects in my feet, something that I learned way too late in life. My feet were not built to last—or to play basketball. My skeletal, structural foundation—inflexible and rigid—could not absorb the endless stress and impact of running, jumping, turning, twisting, and pounding for twenty-six years. Those fractures, tiny at first, were buried deep inside the bones, breaking from the inside out. Those bones in my feet and legs would ultimately fail just from playing the game I lived and loved, forced apart like earth's tectonic plates, scraping and torqueing along a fault line.

I eventually ground my lower extremities down to dust.

As each long, hard climb became more impossibly difficult, the pain that I always thought was just part of life and the price of commitment and perfection would ultimately send me limping off the road into that miserable, useless scrap heap.

Yes, the external pressures on me to play—when the crippling pain in my feet would tell me to stop—were enormous and very real. But ultimately the fault was mine. I was too weak to stand up for myself.

> *Won't you try just a little bit harder? Couldn't you try just a little bit more? . . .*
> *Tryin' to get just a little bit farther than you've gone before.*

Chasing my dreams was devolving into the deteriorating state of tormented conflict that has come to define my life.

—

I grew up in San Diego. It was perfect. My life was wonderful—great families; excellent schools, teachers, and coaches; it was sunny and eighty degrees every day. I assumed it was the same everywhere, for everyone.

Cursed with my bad feet and a lifelong speech impediment, I grew up thinking that everybody's feet hurt all the time and that only the lucky ones were able to talk. I was twenty-one before it ever occurred to me that there might be people who didn't have my best interests at heart.

And then I joined the NBA.

I was totally unprepared for a professional life outside the shelter of my family, my friends, my teachers, my coaches, and California. My parents loved me more than they cared about themselves. They taught my two brothers, my sister, and me to speak up and out, and to take action to make things better and right. It never crossed my mind that this could ever lead to problems.

Both my parents were college graduates and professionals. My dad was a social worker, adult educator, and music teacher; my mom was our town's librarian. I was a top student. I loved school. But because of my profound, limiting, and shamefully embarrassing stuttering problem, I learned to live and love life by myself. I loved to read, study history, write, and immerse my spirit and soul in all kinds of music. For the longest time we didn't have a TV, couldn't afford one. When finally we saved up enough money to buy one, my mom, who was in charge of the finances, declared under relentless pressure from the children that while we did now have enough money to buy a TV, she had done extensive research at the library and determined that there was nothing on TV worth watching—so we weren't going to get one.

When I was twelve I discovered, at a friend's house, that basketball was on TV. With that revelation came the staggering conclusion that my mom was not right about everything.

I had started playing basketball when I was eight and immediately fell in love with it because of my first coach, Rocky—our local fireman. When I was ten, I discovered the Lakers and the NBA on the radio, brought to life by Chick Hearn. Rocky and Chick were God to me. They defined my reality, creating a world that was not only fun but incredibly exciting. They had the ability to paint a masterpiece every night. And they delivered.

Basketball is the most perfect of all games. All you have to do is wait for the opening tip; then it's, Who's got a game? Who's in shape? Who can play? Who really wants this? It also allows someone who might be less naturally gifted than another to always have the chance to win, by outthinking and working smarter than the other guy, especially if teamed with equally smart, dedicated, and determined dreamers.

Rocky ultimately turned out to be my best coach. Rocky—like John Wooden, Denny Crum, Lenny Wilkens, Jack Ramsay, Gene Shue, Paul Silas, Don Chaney, K. C. Jones, and Red Auerbach—never really coached basketball. They all coached life. I learned early on that basketball was life, and that every possession of the ball provided unlimited opportunities to make a powerful, positive impact and contribution to our goal, a realization that I try to apply to everything I do in my life.

In basketball—like life—if your team is well coached, well condi-tioned, reasonably intelligent, and totally determined to make a posi-tive, consistent contribution, you just might be able to find a way to beat anybody, maybe everybody. Or at least to have the chance to suc-ceed on any long, hard climb.

Despite my bad feet and cursed speech, things were going fine for me until I was fourteen. I was 6'1", maybe 110 pounds, and playing basketball every minute that I could. Then one day in the summer of '67, down at the Helix High gym, I was playing against some really old guys—they must have been in their thirties. I was having a big day, just torching them, and they didn't like it. So they took me down with a high-low, tearing up my left knee. They stood over me, laughing.

Bob Dylan wrote: "When I was down, you just stood there grin-ning."

After a few months of rest and rehabilitation during which my knee didn't get any better, I was wheeled into surgery in the early fall for my first operation. I was fourteen years old. Afterward the doctor told me, "We don't know how this is going to play out, Billy. Just go home and lie down for a few months and we'll hope and pray for the best."

Things were never the same again. I dutifully went to bed, and when I got up three months later I was six and a half inches taller—but only five pounds heavier. My parents were aghast; none of my clothes fit anymore. But my coach, now Gordon Nash, was ecstatic.

I loved basketball from the very beginning—because of Rocky, be-cause of the nature of the game, the speed, strategy, execution, repetition, running, jumping, and sweating. And I really loved the results—like winning.

In my first varsity season as a Helix junior in 1968–69, we won our last sixteen games. The next time my team lost was about five and a half years later, midway through my senior season at UCLA.

I lived to play on winning teams. At UCLA, I was All-America, Academic All-America, and College Player of the Year three times each. In the NBA, I was the league's No. 1 draft pick, its Most Valu-able Player, was part of two championship teams, NBA Finals MVP,

NBA Sixth Man of the Year, and was named to the NBA's All Time Team as one of the 50 Greatest Players in NBA History. I got to know and work with some of the most important people of the second half of the twentieth century. I've had the greatest adventures and lived the most wonderful life imaginable. But I also carry the burdens of my failures—every day.

Just as there was a stretch over six seasons when I didn't play in a losing game, there were another six seasons over which I could hardly play in any games at all. I am responsible for the failure of my hometown Clippers to succeed in San Diego. I was an NBA player for fourteen seasons, but when you add up all the games I could not play because of injuries—mostly those disastrously frustrating foot fractures that so many fans, reporters, announcers, coaches, cheerleaders, teammates, team owners, trainers, league officials, team doctors, and even I at times thought were imaginary—I missed the equivalent of nine and a half of those fourteen seasons. That I let down so many people because of injuries that no one could see caused me incredible pain and despair that was almost as overwhelming as the pain I'm feeling now.

On May 10, 1993, the night I was inducted into the Naismith Memorial Basketball Hall of Fame, it all came full circle. I was part of the Hall of Fame class that includes Julius Erving, Calvin Murphy, Ann Meyers, Walt Bellamy, Dan Issel, Dick McGuire, and Uljana Semjonova (the 7' Latvian woman who played eighteen years without losing a game in international competition). Each of us was asked to speak for five minutes, and I went last, at the bottom of the alphabet. By this time in my life, I had learned to speak a little bit—another long, hard climb—and as my remarks passed the sixteen-minute mark of my allotted five, Brian McIntyre, monitoring the proceedings on behalf of the NBA, stood up and interrupted me midsentence, yelling, "Come on, Walton, let's wrap this thing up! Your speech is lasting longer than your career did!"

People who suffer learn to laugh about their sadness in public. But in retrospect today, I understand now that I let down every team I ever played on. It's hard not to think of those moments that could have been.

On the night Coach Wooden was honored as the greatest coach

in the history of the world—not simply the greatest college coach, not merely the greatest basketball coach, but the greatest of all coaches in all sports for all time—Wooden, then ninety-nine years old, wrapped up his speech, the last of his life, by saying, "Finally, I want to say that I'm sorry to each and every one of you. I am sorry that I wasn't able to do more to help you."

While Wooden was and is my coach, Bill Russell is my hero, my favorite player ever—on and off the court—and the greatest winner in the history of sports. His college teams won back-to-back championships, and his Boston Celtics won eleven NBA championships in thirteen seasons. And yet, Russell only wants to talk about the two years he didn't win. One of the reasons he is my hero is that for Bill Russell, success is limited by the things that don't get done.

My failures lurk in the dates that have become daggers to my heart: January 7, January 19, and March 23, 1974; April 21, 1978; September 27, 1979; June 14, 1987; February 1, 1990.

And then in late February 2008—the day my spine collapsed and failed. The day I staggered down into this crumpled, wretched heap on the floor from which I no longer have the strength or the will to get up.

All the things I planned to do but did only halfway.

I live to be part of a special team, which is why my forty-three-year relationship with Coach Wooden was so perfect, despite the fact that when we first came together at UCLA in 1970—he was sixty-one and I just seventeen—we saw things so differently. Everything but basketball. In what was then the most serious contest under way in America, the Battle for the Soul and Future of our Country, we had opposite views on almost every subject, from the length of my hair to my lifestyle, politics, and choice of friends to my idea of writing a letter to President Nixon demanding he resign—on Coach Wooden's personal stationery. I made Coach's life miserable. And here at the end, he's the one saying he's sorry.

Life puts you on all sorts of teams, in all sorts of games. One of the best teams that I got to be part of never lost a game, and came the closest of all to reaching that endless and perfect wave that stretches to eternity.

But it sadly did end for Jerry Garcia in 1995, and it has ended now for me. The music of the Grateful Dead that ran through my head nonstop for more than forty years has inexplicably now stopped. I am desperate, empty of hope, empty of dreams, empty of everything. I live—if you can call it life—on the floor, and I can't take it anymore.

My spine will no longer hold me. After spending more than forty years on the road—half as a player, half as a broadcaster, all as a proud Dead Head, logging two hundred nights and often six hundred thousand air miles each and every year—I can't go anymore. I can't get up off the floor.

The pain I'm feeling now is worse than anything I could have ever imagined. Unrelenting, debilitating, and excruciating—the pain has destroyed me. Imagine being submerged in a vat of scalding acid with an electric current running constantly through it. A burning, stinging, pulsating, punishing pain that you can never escape. Ever.

There are times when I'm lying here—with nothing. Lori, the most beautiful and wonderful of angels, as fine as anything's fine, comes to me. As she gets ever closer, it is just too much. And I cry out, in whimpering pain, "STOP. Don't come any closer. YOU'RE PUSHING THE AIR ONTO ME! It's too much. STOP!!!"

My life is over. I can do nothing. I eat my meals stretched out prone on the floor. I have to crawl like a snake to the bathroom, and use all my strength to climb up to the toilet. I don't think I am going to make it. I tell Lori that it's time for her to go, to get out while the getting is good.

Not wanting to leave her with a big mess, we've put our longtime family home—the dream of a lifetime for the past thirty-six years—up for sale and moved into the small cottage next door. I can't think. I can't sleep, except when my neighbor Danny comes over and starts explaining his insurance company workers' comp legal defense work, which puts me straight out, but only for a moment.

One day I am on the floor, as always, and Lori has just put some food down in front of me, so that I can slurp something in. I hear the front door open at the other end of the house and know it's our youngest son, Chris, dropping in for a visit with his new dog, Cortez, a huge, rambunctious bullmastiff that must weigh three or four hundred pounds, and is still just a puppy. I can hear Chris release Cortez, and the giant, panting beast begins to roam. On the prowl, Cortez comes around a corner and wanders over to where I am lying facedown on the floor and stares at me, transfixed, as I try to nibble or slurp some food off the plate, just inches in front of my mouth. The giant dog looks at the meal in front of my face, marches right up to it, and wolfs down every morsel in a single bite—and there is nothing I can do about it.

Cortez turns to leave, and as he rounds the corner, he belches and passes gas, never looking back. It is the lowest point imaginable.

I've run the gamut from thinking I am going to die to wanting to die to the worst of all possible places—being afraid that I am going to live—and this is what I am going to be stuck with. I have given up. I am standing on the edge of a bridge, measuring, knowing full well that it would be better to jump than to go back to what is left of my life. It is time to go.

Knocked down—it gets to wearing thin,
They just won't let you be.

Two and a half years I have spent on the floor. When I was at my lowest, I was fired from my broadcasting job—right in the middle of Lori's birthday party. I didn't have the heart to tell her for several days. There went our income, our health insurance, my dignity, my self-respect. We would lose our home.

Johnny Cash and Merle Haggard could have written a song.

I no longer have the strength to fight back. The mind-numbing, spirit-sapping, life-draining drugs they tell me are supposed to help eventually just become more of what I desperately need to get away from. If only this were a game and I could look to Maurice Lucas, my greatest teammate, the strongest, gentlest, and toughest friend anybody could ever ask for, who, anytime anything needed to be done—move somebody out of the way, punch someone in the face—would stand tall and convincingly say, "I'll take care of this." But Maurice can't help here—he's dying of cancer himself. Where is Larry Bird to shoot us out of trouble, now that the game is really on the line? What can Coach Wooden tell me now? Where is the band? Please, Jerry, just one more time—take me safely home.

Turn on your light, let it shine on me.

But there is no light at all now, and no sound, either, not even in my mind. It is all so terribly dark. The music has been gone for months, years now. If only I could float and bathe, one more time, in the Dead's flesh-eating, low-end beam, maybe it could breathe life into me—one more time.

The music has stopped. The pain digs in ever deeper and devours more and more of me for days, weeks, months, years—with no end in sight. Only I can end this.

I ask Lori to drive me to my beloved Balboa Park, where my glorious childhood memories live—of picnic dinners with our family, of running wild through the playgrounds with my brothers and sister, of one day discovering magical Muni Gym, my personal Shangri-la where endless games of pickup basketball changed and made my life.

I struggle to pull myself out of the car and take a few agonizing steps along the beautifully ancient Cabrillo Bridge, which spans the park and the freeway, hundreds of feet below. I stand, peer, and ponder.

Later I hear a friend on my voice mail: "Hey, Bill—I was driving to work this morning and I saw you standing on the bridge. I was going to yell 'Don't jump!' but I didn't want to scare you. It was great to see you out in the sunshine, though!"

Comes a time, when the blind man takes your hand,
Says: Don't you see? Got to make it somehow, on the dreams you still
*   believe*
Don't give it up, you've got an empty cup, only love can fill.

—

I have lost everything, the last possession being the will to live.

But then. Just before the final fade-out . . .

I know I don't control it, but somewhere deep inside, there is still a faint spirit fighting for life, for the light, trying to escape the darkness and evil that is strangling me. I try to reach one last time for some strength to give this fighting spirit some room to move, to breathe, but it's harder and requires more of everything than I've ever given to anything in my life.

I can't do it alone. I need help to push through the pain and the sadness. I need Maurice with all his strength to clear the space and pull me through. I keep working and searching and fighting, calling for help from everyone I've encountered along the road—from my family and friends, from my teammates, my heroes, my teachers and coaches—searching to find that way out . . . and back.

The effort exhausts me, and I am ready to give it all up when I begin to sense something. It's more than just the dull, numb, lifeless, joyless pulse I've had now for all these interminable months. Something is swelling up and bulging out from the depths.

> *Did you hear what I just heard? There seems to be a beat now,*
> *I can feel it in my feet now, listen, here it comes again!*

I can't believe it, but I'm faintly hearing a beat. And slowly that beat is getting stronger and louder. And now there is energy and a current of electricity. Now a vamp. A rising tide of anticipation. More sound and more tension, turning into a rhythm, about to become a frenzy. And now I can feel it.

The fans are on their feet. They know what's coming next.

And then . . .

The band is starting up again! The music plays, the wheel begins to turn again, and to my complete astonishment, the total darkness of death and the fog of despair are beginning to lift. Can I really hold on? Is there a chance I can take more trips, make an impact, play in the game of life one more time?

> *Every time that wheel turns around, bound to cover just a little more
> ground. . . .*
> *Round, round, robin run round, got to get back where you belong.*

—

Could it be that Coach Wooden's slowest learner ever has finally figured out a way to make that last long, hard climb—one more time? The one that will take me all the way to heaven?

Old man, take a look at my life, I'm a lot like you were.

CHAPTER 2

My Time Comin' Any Day, Don't Worry 'Bout Me, No!

California, preaching on the burning shore;
California, I'll be knocking on the golden door
Like an angel, standing in a shaft of light;
Rising up to paradise, I know I'm gonna shine.

That's just the way it was—perfect.

San Diego. What more could anyone ask for in life?

I was lucky that my parents chose San Diego as the place to build their lives and chase their dreams. When I was born into California's golden sunshine on November 5, 1952, San Diego was bursting with dizzying possibilities and potential. Its vibrancy as our country's primary West Coast Navy port and a budding educational and technological hub has consistently drawn huge waves of dreamers and visionaries for more than a century.

My mom, Gloria, was a Brooklyn girl growing up in the 1920s and '30s. When she was thirteen her dad died, and her mom announced, "We're out of here. We're going to San Diego." They first lived in a beautiful house downtown near the bay and the train station. But when World War II came, the city's population blew up. Downtown was made over by the military and related industries, much more space was needed, and her house—like dozens of others—was in the way. So they jacked it up, put it on the back of a truck, hauled it a mile up the hill on Third Avenue just south of Hawthorne, and replanted it three blocks west of Balboa Park, that magnificent treasure where so many of my dreams—good and bad—would play out over the next six decades.

My dad, Ted, grew up in California's Central Valley town of Taft, just west of Bakersfield. He went to college at UC Berkeley—finishing second in his class academically—got drafted into the Army, and fought in the "Good War" in Europe. When he got back, he dedicated the rest of his life to convincing people to get along. He first spent some time in Sebastopol and Eureka, both in Northern California, trying his hand as a writer. When he realized that the morning dew and the cold rain and snow there were not lifting or drying out for him, it took only a few dreary months before he announced, "I'm out of here. I'm going to San Diego."

If you were in San Diego today, you would understand why they came. I still thank my mom every day for having come to San Diego. I thanked my dad, too, every day up until the day he passed on in 2004.

Gloria and Ted met at a social event, soon got married, and quickly started their family. My brother Bruce came first, and I followed eighteen months later. We were living originally in Mission Hills near Presidio Park, but my parents wanted more room to move around, and more children were soon to come. Mom and Dad bought a lot and built a house on a hill in La Mesa—"the Jewel of the Hills"—a few blocks from Lake Murray, about ten miles to the east of the city. My sister, Cathy, and brother Andy came along quickly.

My dad loved the outdoors, plants, and gardening. When each child was born, my parents planted a special tree at our house: Bruce (avocado), me (Brazilian pepper), Cathy (golden acacia), Andy (tangerine).

We didn't have much in the way of material possessions, but

really—we had it all. My mom was a librarian and my dad worked as a social worker, adult educator, and music teacher. Our worlds were built on music, radio, newspapers, and books. Those forces shaped and gave me my life.

My brothers and sister and I are all totally different. We were then, as we are today. We each went our own way from the very beginning, each with different interests, each chasing our own dreams. Bruce and I were especially close, but not necessarily in a friendly way. Bruce was a bully, and he stole my food. But he was also my protector whenever anyone tried to mess with me. He was sensitive to my stuttering and always tried to help me get words out. When we played together on the same sports teams, frustrated opponents who couldn't beat me within the rules would simply try to beat me up. Anybody who wasn't already familiar with Bruce would eventually end up on the ground gasping for breath after one of Bruce's strategically delivered elbows would connect with the guy's windpipe or groin. The only person Bruce would allow to beat me up was Bruce.

All my life, I have been a stutterer, and it has caused me terrible pain and endless embarrassment. I was extremely shy in school and almost never spoke. I simply couldn't do it. Thankfully, my teachers never called on me in class. It helped that I was a straight-A student and could express myself happily and prolifically in essays, letters, and journals throughout my life. I took refuge in the things I did well, and could enjoy doing alone—reading, music, nature, riding my bike—and playing basketball.

We didn't have a TV, but I was one of the first kids around to have a skateboard, which I built myself. Our house on the hill was at an intersection, the northeast corner of which formed a perfect natural half-pipe. There was only one road in and out of our neighborhood, and there were no sidewalks, just asphalt that flowed seamlessly to the front yards. That skateboard kept my adrenaline stoked for a while. Then one day my dad took me to a police auction and bought me my first bike, a well-used one, for five dollars. In about a week I outgrew it and was devastated. I rode that little bike back to the next police auction. They must have remembered me, because one of the officers said, "Come on in here, Billy. Take any bike you want. And please come back anytime you need a bigger one. We'll take care of you." I have been biking, passionately, ever since. I love my bike.

When I was nine, the Los Angeles Chargers of the American Football League (AFL) moved to San Diego and fantastically selected for their practice field Sunset Park, a sacred and free public, open green space less than half a mile from our home. I would ride my bike or my skateboard up to that park every day and just hang on the fence, watching these larger-than-life heroes up close. Among a myriad of future Hall of Famer players like Ron Mix and Lance Alworth, they also had the brilliant, innovative coach Sid Gillman and a dazzling wonder running back, Paul Lowe, who, on the very first play of the very first game in the very first exhibition season for the brand-new AFL at the Los Angeles Coliseum in 1960, ran back the opening kickoff 105 yards for a touchdown. I learned to love fast and explosive starts.

I'd watch the Chargers practice all week and then on Sundays I would go, often on my bike, down to Balboa Stadium, the 30,000-seat cement horseshoe south of Balboa Park on the northeast edge of downtown, where the Chargers played their home games (and where a few years later I'd find another home in the purple haze of Hendrix, the Doors, and Crosby, Stills & Nash concerts). We never had any money, but we never had any trouble doing whatever we wanted. You could always put the sad, soft eyes on a ticket taker and he'd inevitably say, "Okay, come on in." We'd find seats anywhere and everywhere, constantly on the move throughout the stadium. Going to the show—first in and last out: there was, and still is, nothing quite like it.

Later, when I got into high school and started experiencing expanded success of my own, I got to meet all my Charger idols, and they were even friendlier, kinder, gentler, nicer, and more interesting than I ever dreamed possible. What could be better in life than to dream of something fantastic and then discover down the road that the reality is even greater than the imagined? That's what my life has been like—first in San Diego, then at UCLA, in Portland, in Boston, and beyond—but then, sadly, eventually, ultimately, and unrelentingly, everything would fall through each time.

Things changed for me big-time when I became such a good basketball player in high school that everything I did was being publicly recognized, acknowledged, analyzed, and ultimately scrutinized. People wanted to know everything about me. But that was not my thing. I didn't want to be impolite, but I just was never comfortable trying to give answers to people I didn't know. My personal thoughts and values, even my "true" height, became constant, burning obsessions. The local newspaper reported, "Walton is somewhere between 6'10½" and seven feet tall, depending on whom you ask." So they asked my dad, who told the paper, "I don't even know how tall he is for sure. All I know is we got him an eight-foot bed and when he's in it there's very little room at either end."

I made an early and conscious decision that I was not going to let all the attention and focus on me negatively impact my life, or define me. I have never liked to read about myself, from those first early years to this very day. Even when I couldn't speak and was so self-conscious and embarrassed when strangers approached me, I never felt bothered, as their intentions were invariably good—or so I thought. Anyway, how can you ever get tired of people being nice to you?

My parochial elementary school, Blessed Sacrament, was fantastic. The only drag there was the "Sisters of Perpetual Misery" who ran the joint. The nuns somehow had the misguided notion that suffering, deprivation, austerity, and repentance were the dominant themes by which to lead one's life. That is not my idea of the world as it could be. I opted early on to have fun in this lifetime. Dressed in their long black habits, they were strange, strict, and dour—the absolute antithesis of everything that defined our California of the 1950s and '60s. Here I was, little Billy, living in a place filled with sunshine, pretty girls in bikinis dancing in our daydreams and in the streets, endless summers on the beach, guys with surfboards, burgeoning tropical gardens, exotic flavors and smells, and rock 'n' roll pounding out delicious rhythms everywhere. And I'm spending my school day in a beat-down world darkened by black-robed crones!

Other than that, Blessed Sacrament had a lot of solid things going for it, but nothing better, more important, or longer lasting than Rocky. Rocky was my first coach. Like me, Rocky was born in San Diego—or National City, really, the seamless first suburb south of town. It started for Rocky in 1928. After he graduated from Sweetwater High, Rocky decided, "I'm going to be a fireman and take care of things when they all go wrong."

Rocky was our fireman, at Engine Company No. 10. He and his life-long sweetheart, Bernice, had three children of their own, who were the same age as Bruce and me, and we all went to the same school. In 1956, when I was just four, Rocky was dissatisfied with the lack of opportunities for young children when school let out at three o'clock each day. So as a volunteer, he started an athletic program at Blessed Sacrament— every day, every sport, every grade, every student, all year long. I started playing for Rocky when I was eight, in 1960. Today, almost sixty years after he started, Rocky is still there at Blessed Sacrament, every day, every sport, every student. In all these years, Rocky never took a penny. He has to be the richest guy I've ever known.

Rocky was everything to us. We couldn't wait to get through the school day so we could go play with, and for, Rocky. We had flag football in the fall, basketball in the winter, baseball and track and field in the spring. Rocky kept everything moving, always in perfect order.

This was all great, but it wasn't enough for me. I wanted more, I wanted everything, and I wanted it all the time. You couldn't play football and baseball without a lot of other guys. But basketball you could play all by yourself—shooting, dribbling, running, dreaming. Rocky taught me how to do all those things, and I was fantastically lucky to have him in my life as my first coach. How different my life would have played out if my first coach had been Bob Knight. I would have quit. There would have been nothing there to love.

I first met Rocky because of my brother Bruce. I loved to follow Bruce around, much to his dismay. Every day at the end of school I would search him out and follow him to the bus that would take us home. One day after school Bruce was going someplace different. It wasn't the bus. "Where are you going?" I asked him. He shrugged and said, "Come on."

He was going to a game—with Rocky. I didn't even know what a basketball game was. Bruce was out there playing, and I sat down at the end of the bench and watched, fascinated by the intricate action and by Rocky, standing like a commanding general on the sideline: orchestrating, dictating, coaching the game of life. Rocky kept looking down at me and began asking everybody, "Who's the little guy with the red hair, big nose, and freckles who can't talk?"

Somebody said, "Oh, that's Billy—Bruce's little brother."

Eventually Rocky came over to me and said, "Okay, Billy, get in there. Let's see what you've got."

Immediately upon entering my very first game, I was standing, bewildered, at midcourt when somebody threw me the ball. The ball was bigger than my head. I looked up-court and saw a teammate wide open, far down under the basket. I wound up and threw that ball as hard, high, and far as an eight-year-old possibly could, and the ball, flying from half-court, swished through the basket. Yeah! I never looked back.

As we walked off after that first game, Rocky came up to me, put a reassuring arm around my scrawny shoulder, and said, "Billy, you looked like you had some talent out there, but I never thought that the game would come quite that easily to you."

But it did. And it came very quickly. Basketball and school were always the easiest things in my life.

—

My dad was to sports what the Sisters of Perpetual Misery were to California cool. My parents are the most unathletic people ever. I never shot a basket with my dad. I saw him run one time at a church picnic, and I fell over laughing. The most spirited competition in our relationship was over who could get up earliest in the morning to get first crack at the freshly printed and delivered *Los Angeles Times,* my parents' choice as our primary printed daily news source. My dad, a devoted humanitarian, was very particular, selective, proud, and protective.

My basketball fever spiked when I learned that the family next door to our school was dismantling their backboard and basket—for reasons that

I could not possibly fathom. I talked my dad into helping me go get it. We brought the pieces home and I found some scrap lumber lying around and we rebuilt the whole thing. I scrounged up a long support beam and dug a hole in the backyard, and we jammed it down in there, stabilizing it by nailing and wiring it to the side of a little playhouse we had.

I was in heaven. I could now play whenever I wanted, and I did, for hours on end, winning every game I played—in my imagination. But, as always, I soon wanted more. I wanted to beat a real person. Fortunately there was a boy Bruce's age a few houses up the hill. He thought himself a basketball player as well, so I eagerly invited him over. But I beat him so badly that after five or six thrashings he told me he was through and going home, unless we could play a game to 100 points by ones—and I would spot him 99. Which I did. And I'm not sure that I ever lost.

When he finally gave up, I would beg Bruce to come out and play, which was not fun, nor a good idea. But I was bored. Bruce was nearly twice my size, and his game was not built on speed, quickness, or agility. Bruce was tough, big, and rugged—he would grow into a 6'6", 300-pound star offensive lineman for Helix High, UCLA, and the Dallas Cowboys. Big as he was, Bruce didn't like playing basketball against me, because I would torch him every time. But I would beg him to play, and eventually he'd come out.

The games would always go the same way. Each time, as I would get further and further ahead, he would get madder and madder. He'd start using his hips, knees, and elbows to try to slow me down. He'd grab my shirt, or dig in even harder to get some flesh. But I'd keep scoring. On drives to the right he would lower a shoulder and smash me into the wall of the playhouse. But I kept coming, and the harder I came the harder he hit me. The violence would escalate into the inevitable climax. I would go to my favorite move—fake right and drive left for my bank shot—and Bruce would go to his favorite: grab me with both hands and, using my momentum, push and throw me into an enormous pampas grass bush that grew just off the left side of the court. That bush was like a medieval torture weapon, loaded with razor-sharp serrated fronds. It was no problem going in, but coming out, the thousands of tiny razors would tear the flesh off your bones. I would emerge dripping with blood and go running into the house crying to my mom, and she'd come out threatening to call the police on Bruce.

This saga repeated itself endlessly. Ultimately Coach Wooden was right: Walton, you ARE the slowest learner I've ever had!

The game that Rocky taught me became my life. When I wasn't playing it, I was thinking it or dreaming it, until it became much more than a game to me. Growing up without a television, and never going to the movies—that cost money and it was indoors—my imagination was driven by books that my mom, our town's librarian, would bring home. I loved *Two Years Before the Mast,* a young man's fantastically dramatic sailing adventure on an 1830s voyage from Boston to California, around South America and Tierra del Fuego. I devoured John Steinbeck, Jack London, Leon Uris, Irving Stone, James Clavell, the Sinclairs—Upton Sinclair and Sinclair Lewis—and couldn't get enough about the Civil and Revolutionary Wars and the great explorers, adventurers, and naturalists. And then one day my mom brought home a book about a sports figure whom I had known of but not about. It was Bill Russell's first book, *Go Up for Glory,* through which I went with Russell on the trip of a lifetime, as he battled the relentless racism that followed him from his childhood in 1930s Louisiana all the way into his days as the greatest winner in the history of sports. During an era of hopeless and depressing racism and segregation, Russell always stood tall and proud, demanding to be treated with dignity and respect. I just kept reading it over and over again. Bill Russell became my hero—but my mom was mad as can be because I wouldn't let her return *Go Up for Glory* to the library.

From the beginning I was never into stuff. But I did have a basketball, a bike, and a skateboard. And then there was my ticket to ride beyond all physical limits: my transistor AM radio. San Diego has always been about the opportunity of tomorrow, and tomorrow needs rest tonight. So when my parents insisted on early lights-out and doors closed shortly after dark, I willingly agreed, self-assured that once the coast was clear and I was safe at home under the covers of my nice long, warm bed, I could then turn to my little transistor. I love—and live—to be exhausted.

School and play all day, dinner every night at precisely 6:15. And you'd better be on time. Or your big brother would eat all your food, and you would face the extremely serious but never explained repercussions of being late. Are you kidding—who would ever do that? Then homework and reading; and then early to bed—or so my parents thought.

But that's when the real action would begin for me, under the covers with my $9.95 transistor. I'd go tripping across the universe. I'd listen to talk-radio bullies like Joe Pyne screaming at peaceniks or telling UFO nuts to "go gargle with razor blades," to Paul Harvey and Bishop Sheen, to Vin Scully calling Dodger baseball. But it all changed for me forever the first night I heard Chick Hearn.

One night in 1962, when I was ten, I stumbled across this voice, the most interesting and exciting one I'd ever heard. At first I didn't even realize that the subject was basketball. I was mesmerized by the sound of Chick, his intelligence, wit, energy, enunciation, tone, and perfect rapid-fire delivery. As I listened that first time, I couldn't keep from smiling and laughing. There I was, little Billy, who couldn't talk at all, listening to this guy who could talk faster than I could think. His brain and mouth were synced in perfect melody.

And . . . he's talking about a basketball game! This was the symphony orchestra come to life.

"He did the bunny hop in the pea patch . . ."

"If that shot goes in, I'm walking home . . ."

"He jumped so high his head came down wet . . ."

"If there's really eighteen thousand here tonight, a lot of them are dressed like seats . . ."

"This game's in the refrigerator! The door's closed, the lights are out, the eggs are cooling, the butter's getting hard, and the Jell-O is jiggling . . ."

Rocky had been the first to begin teaching me how to play basketball. But Chick taught me how to think about the game, ultimately showing me how to love a world that became my life. It wasn't until I was in my late twenties and beginning to learn things I was so sure I already knew that I realized Chick had been teaching me the game of life the whole time. There was nothing better than growing up with the comforting solace that Chick was your best friend, knowing that at the end of the day, Chick would always be there with more. He never missed, and he never failed to deliver. The creativity, the excitement, the intensity, the exuberance, the vibrancy, the joy, the openness, the honesty, the personal touch. I always knew that he was speaking directly to me.

There was nothing that Chick could not do with his voice. He was the perfect artist who could take the darkness out of nighttime or paint the daytime black. My stomach would clench when the game went badly and Chick would cry, "Oh, I've never seen the Lakers play worse!" And then three minutes later, after an Elgin Baylor–Jerry West scoring barrage, my heart would soar when he'd say, "The Lakers are on fire and nobody's going to stop them tonight!"

I ultimately scheduled my nights, weeks, years, heck, my life around Chick. He was the voice of the Lakers on radio and television from 1961 until a few months before his death from a head injury in 2002 at a reported age of eighty-five, working through a phenomenal string of 3,338 straight games without missing a one. He never held back, he never looked back. It seems like yesterday that I pressed that transistor to my ear under the pillow, hearing Chick's message, the dream, the work ethic, the perfection, the difference, the persona, the life, the world, the universe.

I'd spend hours back then, ten years old on my backyard court, with Chick's voice in my head. Physically I was all alone, but spiritually I was out there playing on Bill Russell's team against the iconic legends: Wilt and Elgin and Jerry and Oscar—with Chick Hearn calling the play-by-play.

The best birthday present that I've ever received came early on, when my parents bought me a portable spotlight. I nailed it to the side of our house and plugged it in. And then I could play at night, too.

Regularly—though not often enough for me—during the transition zone between my dad's day job as a social worker and his night job as an adult educator, my mom would pack up the food and all of us into the family car and drive us down to Balboa Park, where we would meet my dad for a picnic dinner. We loved it. The four children would chase one another all over the park, playing, screaming, running, laughing, dreaming, believing. One day I was running wild—again—and came up out of one of the park's magical canyons, only to stumble onto this huge rectangular stucco building that I had never seen before. What's that over there? I stuck my head in the door and saw dozens of guys playing basketball. I had found San Diego's Municipal Gym—Muni.

Muni Gym was the Taj Mahal for people who loved basketball. Open all the time, three full courts side by side, and players playing endless pickup basketball all day and night. You could just walk right in, anytime, and immediately get in a game and play forever. Pure pickup basketball is what you live for. New players, new teams, new challenges, new inventions, constantly in flux, changing all the time.

It's been lost in today's world. There's so very little pickup basketball left anymore. Everything is so organized, so structured. Too many coaches, too much interference from parents, officials, and scorekeepers. Young players thinking it's about fancy gear and stuff instead of the joy of just walking in and starting to play, figuring it all out along the way. Win—you stay on. Lose—you're off, and out. Then work your way back into the rotation. Or move to a side court and create your own new game. That was Muni. It was perfect. The games of our lives never stopped. We lived there.

My dad didn't share my love of basketball. Sports were not his thing; he liked reading, singing, music, and chess. My dad was not a spectator in the game of life. By the time I was in the seventh grade, about twelve years old, I had a game every day of the week, sometimes two, and on the weekends there would be as many as I could squeeze in, often up to six or seven games each day. I would spend all Friday night plotting them out on a map, like a military campaign. If I rode my bike I'd be lucky to make parts of two or three, but if I just had someone to drive me . . . I can play the first half of this game, the second half of that game, the middle part of the third, the whole fourth, the first half of the fifth, the second half of the sixth, and the whole seventh. So I'd beg my dad, who worked all the time, to give up his Saturdays and Sundays to drive me around to all of them, these endless and meaningless games that I never realized were endless and meaningless until I started driving my own children to their games. And my dad would do it. I had the greatest dad ever. We loved him so.

One Saturday I was sitting in the front seat of the family car, broken-down and old as it was, with a basketball in my hands, rubbing and caressing this most perfect orb, drifting and dreaming about the game, about passing and running and blocking and rebounding. And then I looked over at my dad, fiddling with the radio dial, trying to find his loves—Mozart, Chopin, Beethoven, Tchaikovsky, Mendelssohn, Liszt—anything to make his day tolerable. But something was wrong. My dad was an eternally happy man, but this day I noticed his clenched jaw, the tension in his neck, the angst in his face. I sensed in him that day the sadness of realizing one's life is beginning to slip away, as he was helping me chase my dreams.

I reached over and turned down the radio. "Dad, thanks so much for driving me to these games. I can never tell you how much I love you, and how much I appreciate what you're doing for me. And one day, Dad, I'm going to pay you back for you doing this, for your sacrifice. One day, Dad, I'm going to be in the NBA. And when you're in the NBA, Dad, and you're the best player, which I intend to be, they call you the Most Valuable Player, the MVP. And guess what, Dad. When you're the MVP of the NBA, Dad, they give you a free car. And Dad, when I win that car, I'm going to give it to you, in appreciation for what you're doing for me right now."

My dad looked quizzically back at me as he reached to turn the car radio back up and said, "Well, Billy, that's really nice. Now tell me. What is this NBA you're talking about?"

A dozen years later I was proud and fortunate to be able to present to my dad that NBA MVP car. Only it was a truck, a brand-new Ford pickup with a camper on the back that came when I was named the MVP of the Portland Trail Blazers' 1977 championship team—although we all knew that Maurice Lucas was the real MVP. But they gave it to me, and I was not smart enough to give it straight to Big Luke, nor was I going to turn it down. My dad was so happy, and real proud. Every day, through to the end of his life, my dad would drive all over town in that MVP truck and wave to all his buddies. There is nothing like the pride of a dad. Nothing.

My dad was a great father and a great man, and we had a fantastic home life. We all had dinner together every single night without fail—nobody ever missed, we weren't allowed to. We'd share stories, listen to music, play music—I played baritone horn and a bunch of other horns in the family band—and read books. My dad loved the outdoors, and we went on the greatest family vacations, driving all over the Golden State: the eastern Sierra, Sequoia, Kings Canyon, Yosemite, Lake Tahoe, the volcanoes—Shasta and Lassen, Big Sur, Big Basin, Santa Cruz, Monterey, Santa Barbara, and the northern redwood coast. I would get to sit in the front bench seat of the car, next to my dad, holding the big folding map and navigating our route. We'd spend weeks at a time camping out, hiking, swimming, climbing, running, laughing, reading, playing chess, and staring at the stars. Singing around the campfire became a nightly family ritual: "Oh Susannah" . . . "Clementine" . . . "Tom Dooley" . . . "Travel On" . . . "This Land Is Your Land" . . . "God Save the Queen." It was all just better than perfect.

My dad also took me on special all-day hikes all over east San Diego County's spectacular backcountry. We'd regularly cover twenty-five to thirty miles at a time.

During my time with the Sisters of Perpetual Misery at Blessed Sacrament, the big year was 1960, when I was eight years old. But the date that is seared into my mind is March 20, 1965.

I was perfectly happy living a television-free existence, not that I knew any different, since both my mom and FCC chairman Newton Minow had declared TV a "vast wasteland," with nothing on it worth watching. I had my books, music, newspapers, and Chick Hearn on the radio. But then one day I read in the paper that the 1965 NCAA championship game between UCLA and Michigan was going to be televised live from Portland, Oregon, that night. I had never seen a basketball game on TV, but I asked my neighbor friend Mickey if I could come down to watch it on his set. When the game came on—in dynamic and vibrant black-and-white—I was stunned, staggered, and flabbergasted by the scene.

The Michigan Wolverines were introduced first. They were undefeated, ranked No.1 in the nation, and had the most prominent player
in the country. They were the big, powerful bullies from the Big 10,
led by the iconoclastic forward tandem of Cazzie Russell and Oliver
Darden, backed up by the bruising center Bill Buntin, and coached
tenaciously by Dave Strack.

Then it was UCLA's turn. They were the reigning NCAA champions, but without the previous year's star, Walt Hazzard, who had graduated. I had known of the UCLA team through the newspaper and radio,
but I was dumbfounded to see how tiny, skinny, and scrawny the Bruins actually were—particularly compared to the Michigan behemoths.
Keith Erickson, Kenny Washington, Gail Goodrich—they all looked
like little children straight out of Disneyland. I thought they actually
looked a lot like me! Goodrich was so short and cute that they called
him Stumpy. My first thought was, There is no way these little, skinny,
scrawny UCLA guys have any chance whatsoever against the big brutes
from Michigan. I knew firsthand how these games played out, after
having lost so many battles to my brother Bruce and his ultimate teammate, the pampas grass. I just knew and feared that the Bruins would
end up crying to their moms! I had no idea what Johnny Wooden was
going to do here.

But then the game started, and I sat transfixed in complete amazement as the Bruins proceeded to put on an absolute clinic. They ran
the Wolverines right out of the gym with perfect John Wooden basketball: physical fitness, fundamental skills, teamwork, full-court pressure defense, and a relentless fast-break attack. The Bruins never got
tired, and the five starters stayed in for almost the entire game. UCLA
ran mighty Michigan off the floor, and little Gail Goodrich scored an
NCAA Championship game record 42 points. It was that day, that moment, watching in awe and with incredible and developing respect, that
I said to myself, That's what I want to do with the rest of my life. I want
to go to UCLA. I want to play for Johnny Wooden. I want to play like
that and be a part of an NCAA championship team.

CHAPTER 3

Here Comes Sunshine

I can't come down, it's plain to see
I can't come down, I've been set free
Who you are and what you do don't make no difference to me

In the 1960s, a raw, naïve, and confused reporter asked boxer Sonny Liston what he had done to land time in prison. Sonny's bearishly growling reply: "I found things before people lost them."

I was lucky. The things I was looking for didn't belong to anybody; they couldn't be owned.

In the sixties I found myself—and a lot more. At school I found Rocky and basketball. In books I found Bill Russell, White Fang, the Joads, Israel, Ireland, the Sea of Cortez, and Michelangelo. On the radio I found Chick and Jerry West, Elgin Baylor, Wilt Chamberlain, and Oscar Robertson. Far beyond the Laker games were the rare and special nights when Don Dunphy, ringside, would bring to my bedroom—or the living room, as my dad liked these, too—the vivid blow-by-blow brilliance of Muhammad Ali, taunting and dancing over the latest in a parade of humiliated foes in a winning streak that would run to 30 straight before Joe Frazier ended it on March 8, 1971, when I was a UCLA freshman. In newspapers I found John and Bobby Kennedy, John Lennon, Martin Luther King, Sargent Shriver, John Wooden, the Alberts—Schweitzer and Hoffman—and the self-centered Ronald Reagan and the soulless Richard Nixon.

By the time I was fourteen, my days of boredom were so far behind me. I didn't think things could get any better. But then I found rock 'n' roll. And things were never the same again.

Music had always been magic to me, the way that the sound and rhythm and poetry could captivate people and unite complete strangers in an instant and intimate emotional bond with no conversation necessary. With my deeply embarrassing and limiting speech impediment, that last part was enormously important. When I enjoy music, everybody around me knows it and my pleasure multiplies by theirs and theirs by mine, and the musicians are in on it, too, all of that emotion expanding in endless loops of intensifying euphoria and everybody sharing every bit of it. It makes me happy. It's the same thing that happens on a winning basketball team or on a long, hard climb on my bike.

I grew up in a classical music household, with music playing all the time. My dad taught music, played piano, and sang, and exposed all of us to the masters—Beethoven, Mozart, Tchaikovsky, Rachmaninoff, Bach, Chopin, Liszt, Schubert, Haydn, Schumann—from our earliest days. Tchaikovsky's *1812 Overture* became my first go-to song when I needed to get ready.

My dad insisted and required that each of us take structured music lessons. One of my greatest failures as a dad was that I didn't demand the same from our own children. We all played different instruments and even had a family band—Bruce on trombone, me on the baritone horn, Cathy on flute and clarinet, Andy on sax, and my dad on piano and vocals, although he could play any and all instruments. He could sight-read and play by ear. He could do anything and everything. My dad was awesome!

As certain as I was that Rocky, Chick, Russell, Wooden, Ali, Martin

Luther King, Bobby Kennedy, Shriver, and all my other heroes had somehow targeted me, little Billy, to receive, grow, and thrive from their teachings, I was also sure that the new music I was starting to hear on the radio and records from the Beatles, the Beach Boys, the Rolling Stones, Dylan, Joan Baez, Creedence, and all the rest, was not just music that was meant for me—their songs were actually about me. And not just me, they were about all of us. This would become a critical and essential element in my life, as it still is today.

These days, San Diego is the eighth-largest city in the country, but in the mid-sixties it was still a small town. How were we to know? It was what we had, where we were, who we were. San Diego was home to our country's first dog beach and first clothing-optional beach. Those were some of the primary places where we hung out.

Dogs run free, why not me?

In our inland neighborhoods there were endless miles and miles of open space, hillsides and valleys and rolling fields that were empty—no roads, no houses, no businesses—nothing but dirt, rock, brush, and limitless blue sky. On Friday nights, and all through the weekend, we would gather with our friends and cover entire hillsides with blankets and coolers. Our local bands would set up generators and amps and microphones and we'd have our own festivals, rocking all day and night. I never had such a good time.

One day we were hanging out at Black's Beach, the fantastic stretch of the Pacific just below the cliffs of La Jolla and Torrey Pines. At the end of a long day of swimming, bodysurfing, and celebrating all the joys that nature has to offer, we hiked back up the canyon to where the security of the UC San Diego campus had kept our car safe. Today UCSD is one of the top universities in the world, but in those days it was just getting started, mostly Quonset huts and tents. But it did have its Main Gym, which we knew well. Still buzzing from the beach, in our cutoffs and little else, we saw crowds of cool-looking people gravitating toward the center of campus. They had to have been heading for the Main Gym.

What's going on here?

I walked over to a guy standing at the entrance. "Hey, what's up?"

"There's a concert tonight."

"Really? Who's playing?"

"Some new, young guy from Tijuana. Says his name is Carlos Santana. Come on in!"

We looked at each other, shrugged our shoulders, said, "Here we go!" and walked right in—no tickets, no money, no shirts, no shoes, but plenty of service. We elbowed our way down to the front of the stage. And . . . oh my gosh! The throbbing energy and racing pulse of Carlos's music, with his array of drummers, percussionists, and dancers, live, right there in front of us, was like nothing I had ever heard or felt before. It electrified me. It became me. And I became the music—and I shared it and it shared me with everybody else in the place.

And then the lightning-bolt flash of inspiration seared through my entire being: This is ME!

Now there was so much more to my life. It wasn't just basketball, or a Laker game or an Ali fight on the radio, or a book late at night. I'd recently upgraded to an AM/FM combo radio, which took all of what little money that I ever had. Most important, this capital investment in my infrastructure expanded my mind and my universe. It was on the FM band that I found KPRI, where you could lie back and trip over the entire seventeen-minute version of "In-A-Gadda-Da-Vida," followed by a full side of the new Doors album, from "Break on Through (to the Other Side)" to "Light My Fire," with no commercials to ever bring you down.

Our new best friends became KPRI's DJs. They were our tour guides, teachers, and travel agents. Like the librarians and my bike, they could take us to previously unreachable destinations with the Doors, the Stones ("Satisfaction"), the Byrds ("Eight Miles High"), Jefferson Airplane ("White Rabbit"), Otis Redding ("Tramp"), Velvet Underground ("I'm Waiting for the Man"), Country Joe & the Fish ("I-Feel-Like-I'm-Fixin'-to-Die Rag"), the Beatles ("Strawberry Fields Forever"), the Chambers Brothers ("Time Has Come Today"), Hendrix ("Purple Haze"), Procol Harum ("Whiter Shade of Pale"), Cream ("Sunshine of

Your Love"), the Moody Blues ("Nights in White Satin"), Dylan ("Like a Rolling Stone"), and the Who ("I Can See for Miles").

We were on our way, and nothing was going to slow us down.

One day we were listening to our new friends at KPRI as they were blowing out the most incredible guitar and rhythm jam. It went on and on, just the way we liked it, for what seemed an eternity, and we couldn't keep our soaring minds and bodies tethered to this earth. When the jam sadly ended, the DJ came back on with the information and the instructions: "Boys and girls, that was a new band from San Francisco. They call themselves the Grateful Dead, and the story goes that when they played a concert up there last weekend, so many people showed up that everybody got in free. Well, boys and girls, the Grateful Dead are supposed to be playing a concert this weekend in Los Angeles, and my guess is that if enough people like you show up, you'll all get in free, too!"

That was all of anything we needed. Let's go! And so many people did that things got perfectly out of control. Or, maybe it was that proper order was restored. Yes, we got in free. And some of us elbowed our way to the front. Being extremely tall, with red hair, freckles, and a speech impediment, I somehow never had trouble getting into anything—or up to the front of the stage. One more time, things were never the same again.

From those moments until now and forever, every concert for me is a gathering of the tribe in celebration, where the drummers and the bass set the beat, the rhythm, and the pace; and the guitars, piano, and singers tell the stories of life and death, success and failure, love and loss, hope and despair. It's what I live for.

I began having a recurring dream where all of it would come together. The music and the basketball were the exact same thing. You have a team with a goal, and a band with a song, and fans cheering because they're happy, but also to make the players perform better, faster, and to take everybody further. During the game, during the song, everybody goes off, each in their own direction, playing their own tune. But then with the greatness of a team, the greatness of a leader, and the willingness to play to a higher calling, they're all able to come back and finish the job together—to win the game and send the people out into the night ecstatic, clamoring for more.

Listening to Jerry and the Dead, or to Dylan, Neil Young, all of them, you always think, Yeah, that's the guy. He knows my life. He knows what I'm thinking. He knows what I'm feeling. He knows where it hurts and what's going on. And he's always right.

The music I was hearing and the basketball I was playing became one. The way it starts and then plays out—guys getting together, gathering around with equipment—they just start playing and figuring things out. Music, basketball, it's all the same.

It all rolls into one.

A wonderful thing about basketball is that on every one of your trips up or down the floor you have an opportunity to make a positive contribution to the outcome of the game. It's the same with music. If you're going to win 88 games in a row, as we did at UCLA, or 142 games in a row, as we did spanning Helix and UCLA, or you're going to be up onstage to bring euphoria to millions of people over the course of fifty years, you have to do basically the same thing. You have to master your own skills, anticipate all the possible movements of the other players, and know how to react to everything, especially when things go wrong or off the tracks.

I had very little experience as a child with things going wrong. I have my parents, Rocky, and Chick to thank for that. And San Diego, too, where everything was beautiful, everything was positive, and everything was going to be just fine. That was the way my world was. I thought that was the way the entire world was, even though I should have known better. I knew that my dad's job as a social worker exposed him every day to terrible sadness in lives that were far from perfect. But he never brought any of that negativity home, and he and my mom were always cheerful and supportive of everything we children did or thought. It never dawned on me that problems in the world were pervasive, permanent, overwhelming, or unsolvable. And with Bill Russell and Muhammad Ali showing us how to win all the time, who or what was to stop us?

Over time I learned that few have the kind of perfect childhood that I did, particularly a lot of my NBA friends, and that even fewer were able to overcome their difficult circumstances with the glorious success and dignity of Bill Russell. The roughest early going that I know of was Spencer Haywood's, as he brilliantly chronicled in his book, *The Rise, the Fall, the Recovery.* Spencer grew up outdoors, without a house, with no roof over his head, between the town dump and the cotton fields where his family slaved for subsistence in Mississippi, along the big river and its delta. When the dump trucks came they ate and found clothes and the stuff of life.

Jerry Garcia carried a real burden of sadness throughout his life. And people never stopped dumping their tragedies on him. One of Jerry's greatest strengths was his ability to take on the sadness of this hard and cruel world and to make it beautiful with that guitar, that soulful, spiritual voice, that honest emotion in the lyrics that he sang and wrote with his band and coconspirators, particularly Robert Hunter and John Barlow.

Take a sad song and make it better.

We were having the time of our lives going to Grateful Dead shows whenever we could. To say nothing of the big weekend rock festivals that were the precursors to Woodstock. It was 1967, the Summer of Love in California, and there was a concert or festival, big or small, in San Diego or Los Angeles or even Tijuana almost every weekend. And not only would I go—always without money, without tickets, just show up—but sometimes I knew the people who were working on the shows. And they would give me a special T-shirt and some cash and say, "Okay, Billy, you're the bouncer today." Only, I wouldn't keep people out. I'd let 'em all in! And let them do whatever they wanted! At the end of the day, I had cash in my pocket, a new T-shirt, and a giant grin on my face.

I was into everything. I loved the totality of it all. Knowing full well the importance of hydration, nutrition, and aeration, our preparations would begin many hours in advance, just like getting ready for a game. Our experiments taught us a lot about how to achieve peak performance on command. We got pretty good at it, and on the days when it didn't work just right, we knew we'd have another chance at perfection tomorrow. We were practicing all the time. And I love practice.

That was my world, as it still is today. We never slowed down. And to me that was always the real beauty of basketball, music, and life in California. Like the sun, it just keeps coming. The only time we'd ever stop was when we just couldn't stay awake any longer. But even after all-night journeys through the universe, I still always got up at the crack of dawn so that I could dive right back in, ever more deeply into another new day. The thought or question of How am I ever going to find something fun to do today? never crossed my mind. We had it all. Basketball, music, books, my bike, the universe. What more was there?

By now, the music was constantly playing, even without the musicians or the stereos. It was in my head. It was in my soul, with a relentless rocking backbeat that empowered me to shift into a higher gear and keep going forever. I could not get enough of basketball, and I now was playing as much as I could, not only at Muni Gym, but also in the gym at Helix, where my heroes and idols played.

Helix was a great school. Big, with thousands of students, terrific teachers, wonderful facilities (although they didn't build the swimming pool until just after we graduated), and plenty of beautiful girls, including the future wives of Pat Riley and Danny Ainge—Christine and Michelle. (I'm pretty confident, and most hopeful, that they didn't get married until the angels were already out of high school.) With remarkable and very cool teachers at Helix, there was always so much to do: Mrs. Drake and Mr. Higby, English. Messrs. Braun and Walker, algebra. Mr. Ramsey, chemistry and physics. Messrs. Boone, Feezer, and Woods, history and civics. Mrs. Duke, calculus. Mr. Freid, geometry. Mr. Ray, photography. Messrs. Vogel and Nash, biology. There were some who were not much fun and kind of weird, but they still got the job done.

Every fall, just before classes for the new year started, my dad would visit Mr. Benton Hart in his principal's office. My dad always wanted to know what teachers I was going to be assigned to. And if he didn't approve, he would convince Mr. Hart to make the appropriate change. They developed a great relationship.

Long before I got to Helix, they already had a storied tradition of winning basketball, with multiple championships under their legendary coach Bob Speidel. The core of the mid-sixties teams that I so idolized from my days in elementary school consisted of Bob, Willie, and Emory in the backcourt, and brothers John and Al up front. All of them had part-time jobs opening up the gym for the free public play that was the norm in those pre-Reagan days—everywhere. Holding keys made them kings. Bob had a younger brother, Dave, who was— and still is—my best friend, for more than fifty-two years now. My friendship with Dave meant everything. Both of us had older brothers, with older friends, and we were always pushing the outer limits. And the fact that his older brother had a key to the Helix gym made everything even better.

When I was just a skinny sophomore at Helix, Dave's brother gave me my own personal key to the Helix gym, and this added a whole new dimension to my world. I now held the key to the kingdom. Every player in town soon knew I had it, and we could now organize a high-level game at a moment's notice. This included the new guys in town, the San Diego Rockets, an expansion NBA franchise that started up in 1967. Oh my gosh! Little Billy, now or soon to be running at Helix with my newest, biggest, famous friends: Elvin Hayes, Rudy Tomjanovich, Calvin Murphy, Don Kojis, John Block, Pat Riley, Jim Barnett, Hambone Williams, Toby Kimball, Rick Adelman. And the coaches! Pete Newell, Alex Hannum, Jack McMahon, giants all. Who knew or cared that the first-year Rockets would finish with the worst record in the league? They were in the NBA! They were our heroes. And we were playing with these guys! And they were our friends, too, and still are! They couldn't have been nicer.

One day I was home reading, dreaming, planning, scheming, when the phone rang. My mom picked it up only to hear a deep and very mature voice demanding on the other end, "Is Billy there?"

My stunned mother was caught completely off guard. "Who is this?"

"Is BILLY there?"

"WHO IS THIS? I'm Billy's mother."

"Ma'am, you just tell Billy that the Big E is looking for him to open the gym tonight."

My mom put her hand over the phone and yelled to me, "Billy, who is this guy Biggie?"

"Mom, please! That's Elvin Hayes!! Now please, Mom. Please give me the phone!"

"I don't know," my mom said. "Who's Elvin Hayes? And what does he want with YOU? He sounds so old, Billy! Is everything all right?"

I was never so embarrassed.

It was during a day of pickup basketball at Helix that summer of '67 when I was having a big day, just on fire, and I was torching some really old guys—they were in their thirties. They did not like this little fourteen-year-old boy with flaming red hair, freckles, and who couldn't talk having his way with them, and much more. So they took me down with the old one-two, high-low. They tore my knee up, then stood over me with happy smiles on their faces.

I knew right away I was in trouble. It hurt a lot, and I couldn't shake it off or out. I knew I couldn't play for a while, but when it wasn't getting better by the fall, I had to have surgery. Now I was scared. It was the first of what has come to be thirty-seven orthopedic surgeries on this body. I was fourteen. It was 1967. The doctor didn't know what to do. After the surgery, he told me to just go home and lie in bed for three months and hope and pray for the best.

Three months later, when I got up out of bed, I realized that I had grown six and a half inches, although I gained only five pounds. My parents were shocked. My coach was overjoyed.

When I got back onto the basketball court, I realized that I could no longer run like Jerry West or Pete Maravich. So I decided that I would now pattern my game after Bill Russell's. I figured out how to make it work, and before practice one day, I explained it all to my Helix coach, Gordon Nash: "Coach, it'll be great. I'll just play half-court. I'll stay at the defensive end, block all the other team's shots and get all the rebounds, and our guys will race up the court and I'll throw them the ball so they can score in transition. And I'll just wait for the game to come back to my end and do it all over again!"

Coach Nash was the perfect successor to Rocky, and once again, things fell into exquisite order for me. When I was a freshman, the program had still been run by Speidel, who'd been around since the fifties. He was a good coach who'd had championship teams, but the old-school style he favored was a methodical, slow, plodding control game that Helix would win, by a score like 42–39, all because of the brilliant strategic endgame choices of the coach. Speidel's players were rightfully proud of their success, and I looked up to those guys and to Speidel. But it wasn't the exciting, dynamic, up-tempo game that I had learned to love from Rocky and Chick, and yearned to play. And it didn't fit any of the music that was in my head. Please, let my people "play" basketball!

I like it fast and explosive, always have—up and down, with an open throttle. One day at the end of our freshman year, Coach Speidel called all the players in for a meeting. Next to him was Gordon Nash, a very cool guy, but who never really said much as Speidel's assistant coach. He was the biology teacher. Speidel stood up and announced, "Boys, I've got some bad news for you, but good news for me. The bad news is I'm leaving Helix . . ."

We had to hold back to keep from cheering. His good news was that he'd taken a job as a coach, or something, at some sort of college, I guess, in Missouri or someplace. Who knew?

"But I want to tell you," Speidel continued, "that Coach Nash will be the new head coach, and I have full confidence that he'll be able to carry on with everything I've been able to establish here at Helix."

Speidel said goodbye, and Coach Nash waited until he left the room and the door was closed. Then he waited another twenty seconds or so. Finally, in a careful, guarded voice, he said, "Guys, we're going to do things a little differently from now on. We're going to run. And we're going to press. And we're going to score as many points as we possibly can every game. And everything is going to be about the fast break. And we're going to win—big—and have tons of fun all the time."

We couldn't believe it. We were so happy. This was like everything Jerry, Bob, and Neil promised. We were saved. We were delivered. We were set free. We could not contain our joy and good fortune. We started cheering and yelling like crazy.

The new way for us at Helix was what we knew from the streets, and it was fantastic. I loved rebounding, blocking shots, and starting the fast break. It became, and remained throughout my career, my favorite part of the game. I was getting the ball or grabbing it off the board or out of the air and firing quick-release outlet passes to my teammates, who were all speedy midsize guys, like I used to be.

Well, not all my teammates were whippets. One was my brother Bruce, now a big, strong, bruising, 6'6" stud who was literally twice my weight. I was still recovering from the surgery through most of our sophomore season, but the next year we really got going. When we got past two early embarrassing and puzzling losses when I was a junior, we soon found a rhythm, style, and groove. The crushing wins and fluid command performances started to come with great regularity.

We were beating teams by 30 or 40 every game, with me averaging good numbers at both ends of the floor, despite getting double- and triple-teamed, which made it ever easier for me to find open teammates for simple baskets. With the increasing success came more of the violence and dirty play that took my knee in '67, and the endless elbows, forearms, and fists were coming from every angle, rearranging my nose, teeth, jaw, ribs, and fingers. It was the new pampas grass bush—with legs.

By now, though, Bruce was my best friend, and he had stopped stealing my food. He became the perfect big brother, and he made it his priority to protect me. Midway through the season, we came up against El Cajon, one of our big rivals, not that they were ever any good—just a bunch of guys who thought they were tough. In our first game with them that season, two brothers who were linebackers on their football team took turns pounding me as we opened up a huge lead. At one point I was finishing a fast break, taking off for a layup when one of the brothers ran under me and brutally cut me down with a cross-body block. As I writhed on the floor and Coach Nash threw his clipboard and screamed at the refs, the El Cajon fans cheered as the guy who assaulted me strutted across the floor, pounding his chest. When the game got going again, we were back on defense when, all of a sudden, the same guy who took me down went down himself, like a sack of bricks, as if he'd been shot by a sniper. I didn't know what happened—nobody did. There was total silence while he lay there, gasping for breath.

Down the road, Bruce came clean. "There was a big crowd under the basket, and as he came through my space, I knew it was one of those perfect moments when I could nail him with a classic shot to the sternum—boom!—and knock every bit of wind right out of him. You get hit like that, you feel like you're going to die, like you want to die. It was perfect. Everybody was looking around, thinking, What the heck happened? Because nobody saw the shot. By the way, Billy never had another problem with El Cajon."

We won that game, by almost 50 points, and never lost again, 49 straight wins, ending up 62-2 over our final two seasons at Helix. I am not, and never was, a stat guy. My goal, my game, my life has been about being on the winning team. In a world gone mad before our eyes over statistics, where you are deemed to have played well if you put up big numbers, my world was defined by UCLA and John Wooden, and the Celtics with Red Auerbach and Bill Russell. If you are on the winning team, you played well. If you're on the losing team, you stunk it up and it's time to get back to work.

In our senior season our average margin of victory was 36 points. We won seven games by 50 or more, and one by 96, after leading by well over 100 in the closing moments. Defense, rebounding, and passing were, and always have been, what I loved most about basketball. I scored when I had to—29 points a game, shooting 79 percent from the field, to go along with my normal 25 rebounds and dozen blocked shots.

—

I was John Wooden's easiest recruit ever. I knew from the time I was twelve I was going to go to UCLA—if they would have me. Coach Wooden didn't know that, nobody else knew it, but I did. I always liked playing up—against bigger and better competition. Playing for Rocky, then Gordon Nash, then John Wooden seemed like the perfect

progression, and dream, for me. Even before shutting out all other future possibilities as I watched that UCLA-Michigan final in 1965, I had
been mesmerized as a twelve-year-old by Coach Wooden's lecture at a
University of San Diego basketball clinic that Rocky had arranged for
me to attend.

By the time I was a junior at Helix I was receiving too many letters
to count, every day from every college in the country. I didn't even
bother to open most of them. The only letter that really mattered to me
was the first one that came. I was still a skinny, scrawny sophomore. It
was from Denny Crum, the assistant at UCLA, the one Wooden put in
charge of finding the next generation of Bruins.

The letter went something like this:

Dear Billy,

*It has come to our attention that you are a good basketball player.
We just want to make sure that you are aware of our interest in you.
We also want you to be aware that UCLA has strict academic stan-
dards and that you need to make sure that you are fully prepared
and qualified when the time comes so that you can be accepted into
UCLA.*

Sincerely, Denny Crum

I was so excited, I showed that letter to my mom and dad, and to
Dave and all the rest of my friends.

While I was still healing during our sophomore season, we had a
very good team, losing in the final game of the California Interscholastic Federation championships to Mount Miguel, our rival from the
next burb over the hill. They went undefeated that season and were
coached by a former UCLA and John Wooden player, Dick Ridgway.
I am still close to several of their guys. Then our junior season began
and we had that really good team, one that kept getting exponentially
better by the day.

One morning in Los Angeles, Denny Crum walked into John

Wooden's office and said, "Coach, I've just come from watching the greatest high school basketball player I've ever seen. His name is Bill Walton. He's from San Diego, he's six ten, and he's got red hair and freckles."

At the time Crum spoke those words, Coach Wooden had under his supervision the greatest college basketball player anybody had ever seen, Kareem Abdul-Jabbar, and UCLA was on its way to winning its third straight national championship under Wooden, and fifth in six years.

As Crum tells the story, Coach Wooden stood up, walked slowly and silently around his desk and across the office, shut the door, and then fixed a cold, hard stare at Crum. "Now, Denny," he said. "Don't make a stupid statement like that. You've recruited other guys who were probably a lot better than Bill Walton. Did you tell me he was a redheaded, freckle-faced boy from San Diego? Well, San Diego has never even had a Division One player that I've ever heard of. Much less one with red hair and freckles. People are going to think you're crazy, Denny."

Crum shrugged. "You know, Coach, Bill's dad is a Berkeley grad, and if we don't get him, we're going to be playing against him. And I want you to know—he's going to be really hard to beat."

Wooden was far from convinced.

Crum urged, "I think you'd better go see him play, Coach."

Wooden eventually gave in to Crum's relentless pressure, and under Coach's orders, Crum called Wooden's wife, Nell, to tell her that Coach wouldn't be home for dinner that night. "Because he's flying down to San Diego to see a young man play high school basketball," Crum told her.

"That's impossible," Nell replied. "John never goes to see a player!"

"Well, he's going to see this one," Crum assured her. "And he won't be home for dinner."

After the short flight south and a drive in a rented car, they arrived at the gym. Trying to slip in quietly, they found seats in a remote corner of the stands. But immediately the crowd started buzzing, then chanting Coach Wooden's name, then lining up for autographs. Down on the court, every guy on our team was thinking, Coach Wooden is here, and he's going to notice ME and I'm going to get a scholarship to UCLA if I have a big game! So right away our regular game plan—based on defense, fast-breaking, high-octane offense, and discipline—went out the window and everybody started jacking up shots whenever they had the ball. We were playing wildly and totally out of control. Coach Nash was livid. He called a time-out and barked, "Now come on, guys! I don't care who is up there in the stands tonight. We are Helix, and we are going to play our game!" So we settled back down and got rolling again, and ended up winning in another typical rout. I had another big game.

Coach Wooden sat there watching me play for the first time, and Crum swears that he barely said a word. "Game ended, we got in our rental car, drove back to the airport, got on the plane, got off in L.A., walked to my car. I drove him back to campus to pick up his car, and all the while he said nothing. Not a thing. As he got out of my car, Wooden said, 'Okay, Denny, that was great. I'll see you tomorrow morning.'

"And then he looked at me for a few seconds, thought a bit, and finally said, 'Well, he is pretty good.'"

After that, I began getting a phone call every Monday night at 6:15—for this, dinner would wait—either from Coach Crum or Wooden, often both. They would tell me about everything going on at UCLA, and not just about the team and their building plans for the future, but about life as well—what was happening in the world and on campus, the debates and issues and politics of the day, since emotions were beginning to heat up in Westwood as they were in colleges and cities across the country. I appreciated that they treated me like an adult, very much like my parents did, always interested in me and what I was doing, reading, and thinking.

One night Coach Wooden came to our house for dinner. We all sat down at the table and my mom brought out an enormous bowl of potatoes. Coach later told me his first thought: Okay, this is a very nice way to start dinner. Then he realized that that bowl of potatoes was just for Bruce. Since Bruce had already committed to play football at UCLA, Coach's next thought was: How are we ever going to feed these guys?

The only way I would not have gone to UCLA was if they didn't want me, and that didn't seem to be the case. But that didn't stop a lot of coaches from trying to change my mind. From the time I was fifteen, the coaches came in relentless waves with their offers and promises.

Billy, come to our school and we'll make you the most famous player in the history of our program. You'll set all the records.

Here are the three C's of college basketball: cash, car keys, and a condo.

Mr. Walton, how about a new job?

Mrs. Walton, how about a shopping spree? How about some new jewelry?

Billy, here's the cheerleader's phone number. She's our closer!

Let your imagination run wild.

The madness about where I would play college basketball continued to swirl. But Coach Wooden closed the deal with his simple but powerful and direct message: "Billy, I know what the other schools are promising you. That's not the way life works. There are no guarantees out there. The only thing I can promise you is that I'll give you a chance—a chance to be a part of something special. But please recognize that to be a part of something special is a privilege—a privilege that you will have to earn every day. Billy, I've seen you play. And you're the kind of spirited and enthusiastic competitor that we like at UCLA. But if you want to be a champion in everything you do, from now on—forever—it's not how good you are. The determining factor is who your teammates are—and how good they are. You are good enough to get it done, but if you want to win everything, all the time, you must make choices in life to play with players like the ones we have at UCLA. Because your ultimate level of achievement, accomplishment, happiness, and success in life is not really based on what you do. It's dependent on how good those other players are. And those other players are what we have at UCLA."

Pretty soon, most of the other coaches knew not to waste their time on me. But one who would not leave me alone was Johnny Dee of Notre Dame. I kept telling him, "Look, I'm going to UCLA. I have no

interest in going to Notre Dame. Why would I want to do that?" And
he'd come right back with, "No, no, Billy. You're a good Irish Catholic
boy. You need to come to Notre Dame." He just would not let it go. He
chased me all over, even after high school when I was on the road with
the U.S. National Team. Finally, I grew so tired and exasperated with
him chasing me around all the time that I called Coach Wooden and
said, "Coach, there's this guy named Johnny Dee—"

Coach cut me off. "Bill, you don't need to say another word."

I never heard from Johnny Dee again.

I wasn't the only easy recruit for Denny Crum and UCLA that year.
There were two other All-Americas in the state of California: Greg Lee
from Reseda and Jamaal Wilkes from Santa Barbara by way of Ventura.
We all knew of each other, but we never met until the three of us went
on a simultaneous recruiting trip to Stanford after our junior seasons,
in the spring of 1969. It was the only official recruiting trip I ever took.
Greg was a 6'5" guard who had grown up around UCLA sports. His
dad, Lonnie, had played on the last pre-Wooden UCLA team, coached
Greg at Reseda, and also managed all the ushers at Pauley Pavilion and
the L.A. Coliseum, so Greg had been at every UCLA sporting event
from his earliest conscious moments. He was a UCLA ball boy, valedic-
torian of every school he ever attended, and a superstar basketball player
in high school—a two-time L.A. City Player of the Year. He spent his
summers as a counselor at Wooden's basketball camps, and it was the
natural progression and order in life that Greg would become UCLA's
next great playmaking guard. He was virtually a son to Coach Wooden.

Jamaal was, in his own way, the same kind of guy as Greg. The
son of a Baptist minister, Jamaal was 6'7" and even skinnier than me.
He was a great student, a terrific leader, polite, sweet, and articulate.
And his game was classically pure. He could run, pass, shoot, dribble,
defend, rebound, think, catch, and slide swiftly into any position with
his impeccable footwork. Many years later, when Coach Wooden was
already long retired, he was asked to reflect on his vision of a perfect
player. Coach said, "I would have the player be a good student, polite,
courteous, a good team player, a good defensive player and rebounder,

a good inside player and outside shooter. Why not just take Jamaal Wilkes and let it go at that."

At Stanford, the three of us endured a weekend of unrelenting hard sell from the Stanford family and their coach, Howie Dallmar. It wasn't until the very end of the trip that we finally found ourselves together and alone—eating strawberries on the veranda of the Stanford Country Club—at last with some private time to talk. Coach Dallmar had excused himself from the table for a moment. Instantly it was clear that Greg, Jamaal, and I were all thinking the same thing: Let's forget about all this nonsense and just make a deal right here and now that we'll all go to UCLA together. Our commitment and the deal were sealed.

When we were seniors, arrangements were made for the three of us to watch each other play. Greg would have a game in L.A., and Jamaal and I would connect at the gym to watch him. "Now that's our guard," we'd say. Another night, Greg and I would go together to Jamaal's game. "Okay, that's going to be our forward." And then our Helix team had a tournament game somewhere in the suburbs east of L.A., Covina, perhaps, and Greg and Jamaal would be there. "This is going to be our center." That night, the first time Greg and Jamaal saw me play, the halftime score was 79–6 in our favor. We had a good team at Helix.

Greg remembers being astonished by what he saw. "We go to see Bill play. He doesn't take a shot the entire game—and ends up with forty-five points. What? Then you realized: He got every rebound, blocked every shot, and every time one of his teammates missed a shot he just tipped it back into the basket. No shots. Forty-five points."

As our winning streak at Helix mounted, we started drawing really big crowds, and we got to play several of our games at the 12,000-seat San Diego Sports Arena, as early-evening preliminaries to the NBA Rockets' games. One of those Rocket games was against the Lakers, with Jerry West, Elgin Baylor, and Wilt Chamberlain. That also meant that Chick was there. We'd get to stay and watch the game after ours was over, but as soon as we finished we had to get off the court as quickly as possible so the pros could start warming up.

As I was walking off the floor with my head down, still so painfully shy and self-conscious in public, I was aware of the Lakers coming onto the court, but I didn't raise my eyes or head. With our game over, so was my opportunity to express myself. Basketball, books, and music set me free, but the social aspects of the rest of my life were still a major, painful, and very difficult challenge for me.

All of a sudden I was stopped dead in my tracks by a gigantic, thick, heavy, black arm.

I looked up—and it was Wilt.

And Wilt looked down with the biggest and warmest grin on his gigantic bearded face and said to me, "That was a great game, Billy."

I was shocked and amazed and awed.

And then from Wilt: "We'll be seeing you up here in the NBA real soon!"

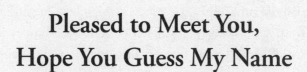

CHAPTER 4

Pleased to Meet You,
Hope You Guess My Name

What's puzzling you, is the nature of my game.

I was just seventeen. Our team at Helix had gone 33-0 in my senior year, running our two-season winning streak to 49 games and winning our second straight California championship. It was early March 1970, and the best seniors from around the country would now go on to play in various all-star games and showcases, the biggest and most famous of which was the Dapper Dan Classic in Pittsburgh.

Jamaal, Greg, and I had already committed to play for UCLA and John Wooden, but we were done for the school year and would have to wait until college started in the fall. This was utterly ridiculous. Everybody else from around the country got to play on the national stage, but not us. We were bound by the rules of the California Interscholastic Federation (CIF). Sadly, the CIF high school rules of the day didn't allow players from our great state to play on any team but their own school's in any event that fell under CIF jurisdiction. That included all the national all-star games. It was the CIF's rule, their game, their world, and what were we to do? I had not yet formulated or incorporated into my life the mantra that it is easier to get forgiveness than permission.

Nonetheless, there was still plenty of great ball to be had. Muni was always there. As were the NBA's Rockets. Epic runs all day and night. We played all the time, every day, at a very high level, against everybody we could find. We also made regular trips across the border to Tijuana, where we would jam all night in every kind of game imaginable. Oh my!

It was great, but I missed playing for something big, up on the grand stage. Then one day a phone call from a distant relative changed everything forever. Fon Johnson was coaching a team down at the Naval Training Center, and he wanted me to play on it. So down I went to check it out. All the guys there were grown men, adults in the Navy. And they could all play. They were fit, tough, rugged, and played with a purpose and passion that reflected the dire straits they were facing: either make the team and get the job done, or get sent to Vietnam.

In 1970, all of us between the ages of eighteen and twenty-six lived under the constant threat of getting drafted and sent to Southeast Asia. Most guys would do anything they could to avoid the draft—stay in college as long as possible, deliberately fail the draft board intelligence test, pay a shrink to declare them insane, claim that they were gay, even move to Canada. When the options ran out and guys had to actually put on a uniform, they would then do everything they could to escape combat deployment. Some got to write for the newspaper; some got to play in the band. The ones who were tall, strong, fast, and talented got to play basketball.

When Coach Fon showed me around that first fateful day at the NTC, the fog lifted, and I was bathed in the glorious sunshine again. NTC was about an hour's bike ride from home each way, but I sometimes got a ride in a car.

And it was all perfect. All of the other players were at least five or six years older than me, recruited for the team mostly out of colleges and inner-city basketball hotbeds from across the land. They were essentially pros, not quite good enough for the NBA, but they were really good, tough—and fit. And now me: 6'10½", maybe 190 pounds, a skinny high school senior coming to check things out, chasing the dream. I was ecstatic, although, I readily admit now, very naïve.

We practiced a lot. And Coach Fon loved the fast break. Up and down we went, endlessly celebrating how great it was to be playing ball. A lot better than Vietnam. And, with rules that allowed dunking, which was prohibited in my high school—and college—years.

But there were also games. It was March. Spring. The end of the basketball season, with a new flowering opportunity—an upcoming tournament, the California AAU Championship—a title that no team from San Diego had ever won before—and the CIF couldn't stop me from playing. Perfect! Running at full speed and never looking back, we tore through team after team all the way to the final round, where the championship would be decided in a best-of-five home-and-home series against a very good squad from downtown L.A. that called them-selves the Live Five, for very appropriate reasons. These games were as exciting and fun as any I have ever played in my life. We packed college gyms in both cities, the refs rarely called anything, and a typical score was something like 150–147. It was fantastic, up and down the floor at the fastest conceivable speed, every trip a fast break. We won the series and the title—and it was only then that I learned there was even more to come. The California winner got to move on to the National AAU championships, to be played in Columbia, South Carolina.

I had never been east of the Grand Canyon, and that was by car on a family summer trip. But I was chasing it down, building my life, and I was not going to let anything or anybody stop me, certainly not my parents, who were very concerned about what little Billy was doing. Not the least of their concerns was that I would have to miss some days at school—TO PLAY BASKETBALL, of all things!

And so I went. South Carolina was a long way from San Diego, in many ways. It was as far as I'd ever gone from everything I'd ever known, and on my first cross-country flight I stared out the window the entire way. When we got off the plane I couldn't believe how different everything was. Not only did I feel far removed from California in miles but also in time. A lot of what I saw, heard, and felt there made it feel like the Civil War never happened, and that the civil rights movement was just an inconvenient truth. Only two years earlier, police officers had opened fire into a group of South Carolina State University students gathering outside a segregated bowling alley, killing three teenagers and injuring twenty-eight more. Most of the students were shot in the back. Despite efforts to bury the incident, wounds from the Orangeburg massacre were still very fresh within the black community when I arrived in the state.

Being in a place so out of touch with the reality of my world was weird. And when we started playing basketball, things got even weirder.

There were eight teams in the national championship tournament, from all the basketball capitals—New York, Illinois, Kansas, North Carolina. A lot of the players were military, and all of them were grown men, much older than me. I was the only teenager, still nominally in high school. But I was there to play, and I was ready.

As we checked into our motel in Columbia, Coach Fon instructed everyone to meet in the lobby at the appropriate time the next day for our ride to the gym for our first game. I was so excited I could barely sleep. I have always enjoyed the preparation for a game as much as anything—figuring out how we were going to get it done, and summoning the emotional commitment that would be required. There is nothing like the way your body finds its rhythm as you build toward getting into the zone for the game.

Hating the waiting, I was the first one down in the lobby the next day, plenty early, more than ready to get going. Then the coach arrived and we waited for the rest of the guys to join us at our appointed meeting time. And we waited. And waited. And waited. Ten, fifteen, maybe an interminable twenty minutes went by, and nobody else showed up. Where were they? We had a game. Let's go!

Finally the coach handed me a room list and said, "Billy, you better go look for them."

So off I went, knocking on doors but finding no one, until finally a door eased open under the pressure of my knock, and I found the whole team packed into a single room, in a haze of smoke, drink, and pungent fumes, enjoying themselves and the company of a handful of beautiful women in various stages of . . . everything.

Here we were, ninety minutes from our first tournament game, and these guys had the mother of all parties well under way. They all looked at me, inviting me in, as I stood there in the doorway, staring in disbelief.

"WE HAVE A GAME—LET'S GO!"

I had never seen anything like this.

I quickly herded the guys up and out of the room, down to the lobby, and into some cabs. We were finally on our way. We got to the gym barely in time to dress and warm up. Then the game started—and we were immediately destroyed.

Our guys were moving in slow motion, totally out of everything. I was flabbergasted. Since I was the only player on our team who could move, and I was otherwise feeling great, I had a big game. But we lost by an incalculably horrible margin and were immediately eliminated from the tournament—an embarrassing one-and-done.

While I was in South Carolina, I had some contact with the University of South Carolina coach, Frank McGuire, who knew about my commitment to UCLA—but that didn't keep him from trying to change my mind. I also somehow found my way up to Duke—there are vague memories of a private jet or something—but I was only interested in playing with Greg and Jamaal, and for Coach Wooden.

I soon went back to San Diego and was figuring out what would come next—besides finishing high school. I wasn't there long when the phone rang—again.

"Billy, my name is Colonel Hal Fischer, and I'm an officer with the United States Army. And Billy, our team just won the championship of that national AAU tournament in South Carolina. I saw that game your team lost, but I liked what I saw of you, Billy. My Army team is heading over to Yugoslavia to play for the world championship, and I just want to tell you, Billy, that I'm hoping you would consider becoming part of our team. It'll be a great three months!"

World championship? Yugoslavia? U.S. Army? Three months? I could hardly believe what I was hearing. Even though I had no interest in the Army, or any of this colonel stuff, it took me only a nanosecond to answer Fischer, "YEAH!!! LET'S GO!!!"

When I told my dad the news, it took him even less time to firmly respond, "No way!"

"Billy, I was in the Army," he said. "I've been over there. That's not for you! You're not going."

My high school principal had pretty much the same reaction: "Absolutely not! You can't leave school for three months! What do you think we're running here?"

But I was going. In fact I was already on my way. I just grabbed my stuff and left.

The Army sent me an airplane ticket, and I flew to New York and found my way to someplace called Fort Hamilton in Brooklyn, where the team was holding tryouts. Coach Fischer hadn't exactly mentioned that I would have to earn a spot on the team. There were twenty-five of us: twenty-four men from their mid-twenties on up who were all U.S. Army soldiers and essentially semipro basketball players, and me, just barely seventeen, and on my own. They quartered us in some dusty, drafty old barracks, with terrible beds that I couldn't squeeze into. Everybody hated the conditions, but at least they fed us—or anyway, something that I thought was food.

Then we gathered for our first training session and meeting with Coach Hal Fischer. OH MY!

His opening remarks went something like this: "Gentlemen, I am the coach. There are twenty-five of you motherf—ers here, and there are only twelve spots on MY team. We are going to have three weeks of tryouts. We are going to play all day, every day. And at the end I'm going to pick twelve guys. Those of you who make the team will fly with me first-class to Europe. For the twelve who make the team, it will be the best trip you've ever had. And for you thirteen f—ers who don't make it, I am a colonel in the U.S. Army. We are at war in Southeast Asia, and I will personally sign your combat orders for Vietnam. Everybody get that? I'm going to find out which of you a—holes really want to be on MY basketball team." He finished by taking a long swig from his hip flask.

Fischer was the scariest and meanest person I ever met—to this day. He would yell and scream and curse constantly. And drink out of that flask. I was stunned.

As a student in the game of life, I always loved math. And while I don't know the exact percentage, it is a most conservative estimate that more than 50 percent of the "words" that came spilling and slurring out of "Coach" Hal Fischer's mouth would never be used by any normal human in front of their parents, children, or on television.

Every other coach I ever had as a young player was a John Wooden disciple. Wooden, like Lenny Wilkens and Jack Ramsay in Portland, Gene Shue, Paul Silas, and Don Chaney with the Clippers, and K. C. Jones and Red Auerbach in Boston, gave their lives to coaching, teaching, and promoting the game in its beautiful, purest sense. They were constantly out in their communities selling the dream of what could be. That sales job affected every community and coach in the area. It's the foundation of how the game was built into what it is today. And that early foundation worked its way down to little Billy, first through Rocky, and then through my fabulous coach at Helix, Gordon Nash.

But Fischer was the antithesis of everything I knew and loved about basketball, and life. Fortunately all the other guys on the team were great to me. After Fischer would yell, scream, and curse in my face, my teammates, particularly Kenny Washington, who had played on UCLA's 1964 and '65 NCAA Championship teams, and Tal Brody, Art Wilmore, and Darnell Hillman, would come over, put an arm around me, and whisper, "Don't worry, Billy. Johnny Wooden is nothing like this maniac."

I ended up making the team—but I was totally unprepared for a three-month overseas trip. Some of the guys took me on the subway into Manhattan to get a passport and some clothes. The next thing I knew, we were on a plane flying across the Atlantic. Our final destination would be Yugoslavia, but on the way we made a series of stops across Germany, France, and Italy, and I'm sure a number of other stops for training and exhibition games against local club and national teams.

The trip was at the same time the best and worst experience of my life. The best part was the travel, playing ball, and being with the guys. We would move every day, from city to city, usually by bus, sometimes by plane or military jet, arriving each time to a grand ceremony, welcomed by dignitaries, bands, news media, and a festive lunch. The worst part was the coach. You could not invent a more miserable human being than Colonel Hal Fischer. He made Bob Knight look like Mother Teresa. Fischer would greet each city's host and ranking officials with a handshake and a snaky smile, and if he was satisfied that his English was not understood, he would curse each person out in some scurrilous way, loudly enough for all of us to hear, purely for his own amusement. He was an arrogant, crude, vulgar, boorish bully of the lowest order.

Practice was fantastic, though. I was having the time of my life playing every day, all day with such terrific players, guys I'm still close with today—Kenny, Darnell, Tal, Art, Mike Silliman, Garfield Smith, Warren Isaac. But the games were a miserable disaster, at least for me. In a new, exciting city every night, in a sold-out arena filled with raucous fans, our team would burst out of the locker room onto the floor, the game would start—and Fischer would never play me. Never. I would just sit there on the bench, game after game. And while he never played me, he certainly never missed an opportunity to yell and curse me out.

We were closing in on the start of the World Championship Tournament, soon to begin in Ljubljana. One particularly beautiful spring day we arrived in a spectacular coastal city on the Adriatic—Zadar. At lunch, Coach Fischer came up to me with his usual deranged look in his bloodshot eyes. I had become numb to his rants by this point, basically just ignoring him, wanting the whole thing now to just be over as quickly as possible. But this time was different. He surprised me with a new kind of sneer mingled in with his daily F-bombs.

"Hey, Billy, this game we're playing tonight . . ."

Yes . . . am I finally going to get to play?

". . . the team we're playing just had all their big men called up to the national team. They don't have any big guys for tonight . . ."

What is he telling me?

". . . Billy, would you mind playing for the other team tonight?"

He wants me to play for the other team?

"Yes!" I begged. "PLEASE!"

I just wanted to play. I'd been sitting on the bench forever.

"Please, just let me play," I said. It didn't even matter anymore who I played for.

I am not sure I was ever more excited before a game, then or since. When we got to the arena that night, I made my way to the host team's locker room. They gave me a uniform that didn't fit, I couldn't understand a word of whatever language my new teammates and coach were speaking, and they didn't speak a word of English. But this was basketball!

The place was packed and the joint was jumping—it always was. This was Team USA, on the move. Events like this didn't happen every day in Zadar. And the huge throng of loyal local fans went even crazier when they saw the tall, skinny, freckle-faced, redheaded American boy go out to jump center for their team.

Zadar has a terrific basketball history. It was home to the legendary Kresimir Cosic, a seven-footer who became an international star and Hall of Famer after playing college ball at Brigham Young. He turned down opportunities to play in the NBA to remain loyal to Yugoslavia and Croatia, but has been named by FIBA, the International Basketball Federation, which sits atop and has jurisdiction over the entire sport, as one of the one hundred greatest basketball players EVER—which covers a lot of ground and time. Cosic had just been called up to the national team when I arrived in town, and with me in his place, the scene was surreal. The crowd grew louder and crazier as "our" team proceeded to give Team USA all it could handle. I was having a huge game, torching the guys I had played with in practice every day for the previous ten weeks.

Now, besides being an evil person, Hal Fischer also knew every dirty trick known to man and devil. Fischer took great pride in coaching his players on how to play dirty—how to hit guys, knee them, trip them, submarine them, kick them in the groin—and get away with it. That was his game. That was his life.

And so, in my role this night as the Zadar team's center and savior, I decided that I would take full advantage of my opportunity to use all of Coach Fischer's tricks against his players—my own real teammates. The crowd took great delight in all my strategic employments of elbows, feet, knees, hips, and hands, and so did the Yugoslavian refs, who I don't think called a single foul against me the entire game.

I was on fire, and we took the vaunted Americans right down to the wire, maybe even into overtime, losing by only a point or two at the final buzzer. To the fans it was as good as the upset of the millennium. They stormed the court, ripped off my jersey, hoisted me onto their shoulders, carried me out of the arena, and ran me up and down the streets chanting, "WAL-ton! WAL-ton! WAL-ton!" When I was finally able to break away and get back to the hotel, the guys were waiting for me. Even they were amazed by what they had just witnessed.

We were back at it again the next day, moving inexorably toward Ljubljana, and unbelievably—staggeringly—nothing had changed for me. I was back in my customary spot on the bench—and there I stayed for the rest of the trip. Hal Fischer never said another word to me. In the world championships, our team ended up disgracefully in fifth place. Yugoslavia, led by Cosic, was the champion, followed by Brazil, the Soviet Union, and Italy.

Years later as we reminisced about what went wrong, we came to the inevitable but unanimous conclusion that if we hadn't had a coach, we would have won the whole thing.

As soon as our last game ended, Fischer astonished us with the news that he was immediately booking our team on another exhibition tour, this time through Greece and Africa. Mutiny ensued. Nobody wanted to spend another minute with this guy—so there was an immediate and unanimous NO! and we all went home. Three months had gone by. I needed to get away from this madman—and so did everyone else.

Back in the United States, at New York's JFK Airport at the baggage claim, with all the guys saying goodbye to each other, Fischer approached me. I just stood there staring blankly at him as this slithering serpent tried his best to be human and say thank you. He offered an extended handshake. I would not take it. He finally stopped mumbling; there was nothing left for him to do or say. I stood tall and held my ground. The only thing that I could and did say in parting was "F— YOU."

To this day I am still the only high school player ever to be a member of the U.S. National Team in a world championship or Olympic tournament.

Back in San Diego, I still had to deal with the small matter of graduating from high school. I was basically walking off the plane and into my final exams, but I aced them. School and basketball were always the easiest parts of my life. At graduation, I was near the top of my class, and now there was nothing standing in the way of me and UCLA—and Coach Wooden.

More than three decades later, I got a phone call from a complete stranger. She kindly said that there was somebody who wanted to talk to me.

It was Hal Fischer. He was in the hospital, and he was dying. Choking back emotion and tears, he gravely said he didn't have much time, and he wanted me to know before he left for good that he was sorry for what went down between us. He said he should have played me in Yugoslavia, and that if he had, we would have won.

I held my tongue, biting it until it bled. I told him that it was okay, that I had gotten over it and moved on.

When the line and everything else went dead, I don't think I believed what I had just said.

CHAPTER 5

You Say You Want a Revolution

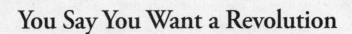

Tin soldiers and Nixon coming, we're finally on our own.
This summer I hear the drumming, four dead in Ohio.

Growing up, I was raised to believe that Americans were different, somehow better, because of what we were all about and what we stood for. That the wars we fight are moral and just, and always in defense of truth, honor, and righteousness. That people who work hard will get ahead, that our workers and our products are the best in the world, and that our economy and taxation systems are structured to ensure that there is never a lack of opportunity and jobs. That we settle our differences through compromise and open and honest elections, never resorting to political trickery, bribery, or assassination. That all of us are equal, and that any discrimination left over from a darker age based on skin color, religion, gender, national origin, sexual orientation, or personal lifestyles and choices would quickly fade away. And that on our team, most everybody has something, because when only a few have it all, we really don't have much of anything.

I was able to see John Fitzgerald Kennedy in a parade that stopped by our school in San Diego in June 1963, and his smiling image, waving to us in our uniforms from his open limo, said all of this about America and more. But almost immediately things started to get sadder and stranger. Exactly six days later the civil rights leader Medgar Evers was murdered in Mississippi. JFK was killed seventeen days after my eleventh birthday. Riots consumed Watts, Detroit, and other urban deserts. The year 1968, with my basketball flourishing, also brought the terrible chaos and carnage of the Orangeburg massacre; the murder of Martin Luther King and the Holy Week Uprising; Bobby Kennedy gunned down; and bloody riots at the Democratic National Convention in Chicago. Ronald Reagan, representing the beginning of the selfish and greedy dismantling of our greatness, was in the California statehouse. Richard Nixon, the prince of darkness, somehow conning too many that he stood for a better tomorrow, won the White House.

In January 1969, while I was dreaming about my UCLA life that would begin after one more school year, violence shocked the Westwood campus. The increasingly assertive Black Panther Party and a rival black nationalist group called Organization Us were locked in a struggle over control of the African American studies program. At a meeting in Campbell Hall, an argument boiled into a gunfight that left two student Panthers, Bunchy Carter and John Huggins, dead.

Everything I had grown up believing was turning upside out and inside down.

By the spring of 1970, I had already run away to join the circus on the European tour with Colonel Hal Fischer and the U.S. Army. While I was having the best and worst experience of my life both at the same time, the world that I would be coming home to was changing drastically—and I didn't even know it. As we rolled along trying to survive the madness of Fischer, there was barely any news available from home, so who knew anything, in our little insular world, about Nixon's decision in late April to launch a massive invasion of Cambodia, vastly expanding the war in Southeast Asia?

On May 4, just a few days from the start of our basketball world championships, who on our tour of madness had any idea that powerful, emotional, desperate protests were breaking out on virtually every college campus in the America that we had left just a few months ago? We were in communist Yugoslavia, itself overwhelmed by its own massive dysfunction. It wasn't until later that I learned that at Kent State University in Ohio, our own National Guardsmen, charged with protecting us, had opened fire on unarmed young demonstrators, killing four of them and wounding nine others, setting off a pervasive nationwide strike by students, effectively shutting down more than 450 colleges and universities. At UCLA, a state of emergency was declared and hundreds of riot-geared, club-wielding "peace officers" arrested more than seventy students. Less than two weeks later, there was another college town police massacre, this time at Jackson State in Mississippi, where two more students were killed and another twelve wounded.

What if you knew her and found her dead on the ground,
How can you run when you know?

The May 6 UCLA *Daily Bruin* editorialized: "The violence on this campus may be just another indication that America's chances of achieving peace, in both external and domestic affairs, have slipped away. [Students are] angry because every day America seems to become more callous, more ruthless, and there is nothing they can do about it."

They said they'd stand behind me when the game got rough
But the joke was on me, there was nobody even there to bluff.
I'm going back to SAN DIEGO and UCLA! I do believe I've had
enough . . .

Nixon creeped and sleazed in with his secret peace plan. Vietnam exploded, then the campuses, then Watergate, and we looked around, thoroughly disgusted. What are you guys DOING? Everything and everyone we thought was right and normal and cool was being shot down, beaten up, and thrown in jail. And we were being told to go to Southeast Asia and kill all the people there. Yeah, right. For what?

Muhammad Ali said, "I ain't got no quarrel with them Vietcong."

Bob Dylan said, "I ain't gonna work on Maggie's farm no more."

Nixon boasted, "When the president does it, it's not illegal."

Dylan finally asked, "Will all the money you've made ever buy back your soul?"

The supercharged mix of emotions ignited the firestorm. The nationwide student strike in the spring of 1970 was another breaking point for a whole generation, inspiring and driving a movement to upend the old rules that impeded honesty and freedom. The calls to action came from Dylan, Joan Baez, John Lennon, the Doors, Crosby, Stills & Nash, Country Joe McDonald, Richie Havens, Jimmy Cliff, Phil Ochs. The world as it could be. The songs did not only express anger; they clamored for peace, freedom, hope, joy, and love.

—

Two days after the Kent State shootings, thousands of Boston-area college students packed the plaza in front of the MIT student center, where the Grateful Dead played a free concert be-in that did its best to turn things to the bright side. They opened the show with a new anthem of the day:

Callin' out around the world, are you ready for a brand-new beat?
Summer's here and the time is right for dancin' in the streets.

I arrived at UCLA in September with my eyes and mind open much wider than ever before. And what I saw, heard, thought, and dreamed left me more excited than ever about the dizzying possibilities ahead.

It doesn't matter what you wear just as long as you are there.

And we were there. I was fired up and ready to go—wherever!

The first issue of the *Daily Bruin* for the new school year offered a campus politics catch-up from the riot-torn ending of 1969–70, covering how Angela Davis, the twenty-six-year-old assistant philosophy professor, had been fired by the UC Board of Regents for being a communist, and cataloging the various UCLA student groups that were gearing up on campus: the YAF, the SDS, the BSA and BSU, WLF, RAC, ARM, MECHA, SMC, and more.

I was more than ready to get started. I was ecstatic about the freedom of getting away from my parents. There was the energy and activity of all the politics, the classes, professors, lectures, and books in the library; great new people to meet including so many beautiful, extremely friendly, and warmhearted coeds. And there were the Grateful Dead and all the other bands to go hear on campus and all around L.A. any night of the week—endless possibilities and opportunities for plenty of high-altitude training.

There'll be music everywhere!

I was going to college, and I was going to be roommates with Greg Lee and play basketball with Greg and Jamaal for John Wooden at UCLA! And UCLA was the center of everything that I wanted to be involved with. It seemed to be in perfect harmony and order: the combination of opportunity to turn back Reagan and Nixon, the ensuing freedom, music, learning, loving—and playing basketball on a team that always won the championship. It was all part of the purpose and passion in our lives. We were fighting for what was right, as students and as Americans. The notion that any of these aspects could have possibly been in conflict was hypocritical. You can't separate them. It's life. It was all one. We live in a political world, and it was wholly fantastic—and we were right.

It all rolls into one, but nothing comes for free.

I was over-the-top stoked when I got to UCLA that first day and checked in at my dorm, Dykstra Hall. "I'm Bill Walton, from San Diego. And I'm here to move in with my new roommate, Greg Lee," I said proudly.

The woman at the desk shuffled some papers and then looked up, dazed and confused. "Oh, no, Mr. Walton. That's not right. You're rooming with Gary Franklin, across the way at Sproul."

I didn't say a word. I was stunned, staggered, flabbergasted. This is not right. What's going on? There must be some mistake.

I left what little stuff I had right there in the lobby and walked out the door, turned right, and went directly down the hill to the athletic department, on the other side of Pauley Pavilion. I went straight to Coach Wooden's office, just walked right in and sat down.

One of the endlessly great things about Coach Wooden was that everything was always about us, never about him. His job was to make us and our team great. His ego was always in check; there were no trappings of power, no formality that excluded anyone. You could always just walk right into his office and say something. Anything. Even on your very first day!

"Hi, Bill, how's everything going?" Big smile.

"Coach, there's a problem here."

"What's the matter, Bill?" Smile fades.

"Coach, Greg Lee is supposed to be my roommate. Not Gary Franklin."

Gary was another freshman player who had been Greg's high school teammate at Reseda. What was Coach thinking? I knew I had told him that Greg and I were going to room together, and as much as Greg was like a son to Wooden, I couldn't understand how Coach could let this transgression of human decency, honor, and kindness go down.

He just sat there, looking at me, quiet as can be, speechless for what seemed an eternity as it all played out in his mind.

And I just sat there looking back.

Finally, I said very slowly, "I came here to room with Greg Lee."

Smile completely gone, chin in hand, index finger crossing his pursed lips, Coach continued deliberating, while considering—everything.

When he finally spoke, it was a simple "Okay."

With that, I was gone. I put the matter out of my mind until years later, when I began to learn many of the things I thought I had already known. Wooden had known Greg since he was a child. He was a superb player and a brilliant student with a razor-sharp mind—a mind that was very much his own. Though a freshman like me, Greg was already in his second UCLA quarter that September, having graduated from high school in February and enrolled at UCLA for the spring quarter in late March. So he was way ahead of us in experiencing all the wonders of life in Westwood. Greg was on campus when the strike and riots unfolded after Kent State and Jackson State. Now along comes young Billy, up from San Diego, and little Billy thinks he's going to room with Greg, only to find out that, no, Mr. Walton, you're rooming with Gary Franklin. Now Billy sits before Wooden, who never fails to think through everything before it happens, and says, I came here to room with Greg Lee. Wooden does a lot of fast calculating—and allows the change.

Trouble ahead, trouble behind
And you know that notion just crossed my mind.

If I had a fallback position, which I really didn't, I guess I could have roomed with Jimmy Connors, who was also in our incoming class. That would have been very cool—for me.

Anyway, I got back to Dykstra as fast as I could, and with help from Moke, a legend on Greg's world-beat-scene from Santa Monica and the beach, I moved in with Greg and we unpacked our things—which took all of five minutes. Moke and I have remained inseparable ever since. Our room was the same one that Kareem and Lucius Allen lived in when they were freshmen in 1966. It had the special extra-long and wide bed that had been brought in for Kareem. Even better, it was the closest UCLA dorm room to Pauley Pavilion and campus, with our own exit and entry stairway right outside the door. One flight down and you were out and on your way, sometimes in Greg's VW Bug, but always ready to go. We had it all.

One late afternoon Greg and I were sitting on our beds, which doubled as couches, figuring it all out: What are we going to do NOW?

Greg spotted an announcement on page two of the *Daily Bruin*: "Hey! Neil Young . . . in Royce Hall . . . tonight!"

I said, "We'd better go NOW, or we'll never get in!"

We raced over and up to Royce Hall as fast as we could, only to find the place deserted. Some football players manning the doors of perception as "the security" said, "You're way early, but sure, come on in." No tickets, no money (the tickets were $2.50 apiece), no problem, and we walked into the empty hall and down to the second row, claiming a couple of prime seats. We weren't bothered at all by the wait, or by anybody laying claim to our seats. We were in church, and there were always plenty of sacraments to be had everywhere—we practiced lots of deep-breathing exercises, inhaling the freshness and all that came with it in the stimulating UCLA night air.

Neil was incredible as always. We were in his show, sucked into the vortex of the magical musical world of his singing and playing of every instrument known to man. I have no idea whether the hall ever filled up behind us; we never turned around. Why would we look back with the world and everything else in front of us? Heck, we were already inside the show!

When I flash back to that night, the set list turned into the story of my life—then and now. "On The Way Home" . . . "Tell Me Why" . . . "Old Man" . . . "Cowgirl in the Sand" . . . "A Man Needs a Maid" . . . "Don't Let It Bring You Down" . . . "Ohio" . . . "See the Sky About to Rain" . . . "Dance, Dance, Dance" . . . "I Am a Child" . . . and so much more than words can tell.

That's how it all started for us at UCLA, and it never slowed down. It was so much better than I could have ever imagined.

I had dreamed about playing basketball at UCLA since I was twelve. Now, here I was, and the reality was better than the dream. The first day of practice, October 15, was also the day after John Wooden's birthday and, by tradition, media day. The harmonic convergence of Coach's birthday with the annual renewal of the sport never escaped us—for ninety-nine years. There was always a cake and lots of smiles and laughter at the beginning. The transition to real practice the next day was seamless. It was all so exhilarating, even though Greg, Jamaal, and the rest of the new guys—not allowed to play with the varsity in those days—would spend the season playing exhibition games for the freshman team while the varsity went out to try to win UCLA's fifth straight NCAA championship—and sixth in seven years. They were led by the incomparable Sidney Wicks, along with Curtis Rowe, Steve Patterson, Henry Bibby, Terry Schofield, and Kenny Booker.

We were ready to roll all day that first time out. Just before the start, always at 3:30 p.m. sharp, Coach Wooden called all the freshmen together and walked us into the locker room. There, he sat down on a stool and began his lecture to us. We sat there like dutiful sponges ready to soak it all up, knowing that he was about to give us the key to heaven on earth, show us the path, guide us to become the next great team in history.

His first words were, "Men, this is how you put your shoes and socks on."

We were stunned. We looked around and at each other. Are you kidding me? We're all high school All-American players, and here is this silly little old man showing us how to put on our socks and shoes!

Meticulously, he demonstrated exactly how we were to apply the socks over our toes and pull them up tight to eliminate the possibility of any wrinkles, which could cause blisters. And then how to open our shoes so that they would slide on easily and not disturb the wrinkle-free socks, and how to then properly lace and tie them snugly and completely. Over the course of time, he showed us how to tuck in our shirts and tie the proper knot on the drawstring of our game shorts, how to shower and properly dry ourselves, especially our hair (which we were always to keep short and neat), how we would practice and prepare for games, and also how we should study for our classes and conduct our lives.

We were rolling our eyes and could barely keep from laughing out loud. When he took off his own shoes and socks for the demo, we were appalled. He had these grotesque varicose veins covering his lower legs, feet, and ankles. He had terrible hammertoes, and disgusting fungus under most of his nails. Gross!

Talk about weird. We wanted to play ball and get running. But it is very safe to say that practice never once started with these words from Coach Wooden: What do you guys want to do today? When we finally were ushered back onto the court, Coach directed the eight new freshmen (six of us scholarship players) into the stands on the north side of the main court in Pauley. And then varsity practice started.

Oh my gosh!

Such precision, flawless execution, incredible pace, nonstop chatter from everybody, and an ever-faster celebration of a team playing with determination, pride, structure, discipline, organization, passion, and purpose. A few minutes in, Coach stopped the train in its tracks and everything became eerily and instantly silent. He turned to us in the stands and crisply delivered a most pointed and succinct message: "From this moment on, you new players are expected to know what to do out here, and when. There will be no further explanation of what and why we are doing these things. Now let's go!"

We thought at the time that a lot of the stuff Coach Wooden was selling—his Pyramid of Success, Seven-Point Creed, Two Sets of Threes, Four Laws of Learning, his maxims, his tools to overcome adversity— were the stupidest things ever. But we never doubted the honesty, righteousness, dedication, preparation, commitment, and excellence that was behind it all. "Your best is good enough," he repeatedly told us. "Don't beat yourself, don't cheat yourself, don't shortchange yourself. That's the worst kind of defeat you'll ever suffer, and you'll never get over it." He was able to distill into one or two sentences the greatest lessons of life. To this very day, whenever I'm going through the routine of preparing to get ready for something big, whether it's business, personal, or physical, I just keep repeating it all to myself. Inevitably, the right rhythm, beat, and pace finds its way to the surface, enabling me to go get it done.

Early on we came to know Dr. Ernie Vandeweghe, one of the NBA's founding fathers, as a player. Ernie and his terrific family lived right across the street from UCLA in a big mansion, high on a hill, overlooking a golf course. Eventually, everything good in my life from this point forward could ultimately be traced to my long friendship with Ernie.

A defining moment in my life as a fan was Bill Russell's last game, the seventh game of the 1969 NBA Finals, Celtics at Lakers. I was a junior in high school. Russell didn't tell anybody it was the end of the line for him. His friend and teammate forever on the Celtics, Sam Jones, had announced before that season started that this was it for him. Russell did not want to detract from Sam's glory and due. He said nothing of his own future. He just played—to win. Every day—and every thing.

The Lakers had never been able to beat the Celtics in six championship finals dating back to 1959. But this time was sure to be different. Until now, Russell had always been the difference. While Elgin and Jerry had their way, it was never enough. Russell was just too good.

That 1968–69 season, the Lakers traded for Wilt, who began an incredible five-year run with the Lakers that carried them to the NBA Finals four times. And Wilt was sure to be the Lakers' difference maker against Russell and the Celtics, who had been on top for so long, but were now aging and slowing. And besides, this was Wilt.

In today's world gone mad with numbers, analytics, and statistics, Wilt would be in another universe.

When Wilt ultimately retired from the NBA in 1973, he held 128 individual statistical records. When he unexpectedly passed away on October 12, 1999, twenty-six years after his last game, he still held 101 individual records. Wilt always told us that if it ever even remotely crossed his mind that somebody might beat some of his records, he would have just doubled his output.

Never forget that when Wilt played they did not even keep statistics for blocked shots, steals, turnovers, defensive or offensive rebounds—all categories that the NBA started tracking the first year after Wilt decided to stop playing. And, with the growing emphasis on numbers and stats in recent years, even more new categories have now been added. Even with that, today Wilt holds 213 individual NBA records! Halfway through his NBA career, Wilt had cumulative averages of more than 39 points and more than 29 rebounds per game.

And now Wilt was the center on the Lakers, providing plenty of optimism that this time things would be different against the Celtics. It's the seventh game of the NBA Finals, a home game for the Lakers at the Fabulous Forum. And L.A. knows they've got it. Elaborate preparations have been made—champagne on ice, balloons in the rafters, the how, when, and where of the celebration and coronation all set and announced before the game. Sam Jones picked off that championship schedule with all of the festivities laid out nice and neat on a sheet of paper and gave it to Russell.

In the Celtics' locker room before the tip-off, Hall of Famer Jack Twyman, the TV commentator, puts a microphone up to Bill Russell— who is also the Celtics' coach. On camera, Twyman asks a simple, single question: "What's going to happen?"

Russell, directly and matter-of-factly: "We're going to win."

Twyman, taken aback by Russell's bold, quiet confidence: "How do you know?"

Russell: "WE'VE DONE THIS BEFORE."

Little Billy was never so proud as the Celtics ran the Lakers out of their own building that day, leaving everybody in L.A. very thirsty.

Bill Russell never lost a Game 7, going 10-0 in the big one at the end.

—

With John Wooden and UCLA, it was all about training for that big one at the end. And along the ride, we had so much fun. Fun with, because of, and at the expense of Coach Wooden. At times, too much fun. But there was nothing as much fun in life as winning. I was, and am, a very committed guy. I have to win. That was true for both of us.

In 1970, I knew our team would win, and not just our basketball team. I was supremely confident that our entire team of forward-thinking individuals on the side of truth, justice, and honesty would win. There was an opponent, and our job was to win the Big Game. Nixon represented the evil direction that the world had taken, with lies, deception, paranoia, duplicity, thuggery, and militarism. At UCLA, the anger was reflected through the rallies, the music, and daily life, but we were winning. We were moving inexorably toward the Promised Land. When we weren't angry, we were euphoric. The concerts were happening, the games were happening, we were living in the Golden State. Paradise found! I loved it—from the opening tip.

The constant and relentless media scrutiny that had begun in high school continued unabated. By this time, everything I did was known to all. I stuck to my earlier decision to take no notice; to live my life my way, and not be defined by someone else.

I try my best to be just like I am
But everybody wants you to be just like them.

As straight and strict as Coach Wooden was, exponentially more so than my parents, he still personified the goodness that we tried to always see in life.

Gary Cunningham was our freshman team coach, but Coach Wooden, while keenly focused on his varsity squad, kept a very close eye on us at all times. At first, Cunningham had chosen a starting lineup of Greg, Jamaal, Vince Carson, Hank Babcock, and me. But Gary Franklin's dad was gravely concerned that his son's future was being decided prematurely. So he went over Cunningham's head and convinced Wooden that Cunningham should rotate the starters so that each of the six scholarship players got equal opportunities. It made no sense to the five of us, but we did learn from Coach Wooden years down the line to never get in the way of a parent's drive to do what they think is best for their child.

Being on the freshman team presented interesting challenges in part because for the first time there was no ultimate championship prize on the horizon, just a string of disconnected and individual games with no meaning, structure, or goal other than to play, win, and have fun. As shy as I've always been, I have also always craved playing on the big stage, as I had at Muni, then at Helix, with the Navy AAU team, and on to the world championship tour—at least the night I got to play for the other team.

We won all our UCLA freshman games. But what I loved most was the practice. Wooden loved practice, too. Surprisingly, he had rules for it. Did he ever! I never played for a coach who wrote so many things down—after clearly thinking them all through.

UCLA BASKETBALL
John Wooden, Head Coach
Re: Practice

1. Be dressed, on the floor, and ready for practice on time every day. There is no substitute for industriousness and enthusiasm.
2. Warm up and then work on your weaknesses and shoot some free throws when you take the floor and until organized practice begins.
3. Work hard to improve yourself without having to be forced. Be serious. Have fun without clowning. You develop only by doing your best.
4. No cliques, no complaining, no criticizing, no jealousy, no egotism, no envy, no alibis. Earn the respect of all.
5. Never leave the floor without permission.
6. When a coach blows the whistle, all give him your undivided attention and respond immediately without disconcerting in any manner.
7. Move quickly to get in position to start a new drill.
8. Keep a neat practice appearance with shirt tails in, socks pulled up, and hair cut short.
9. Take excellent care of your equipment and keep your locker neat and orderly.
10. Record your weight in and out every day.
11. Do things the way you have been told, and do not have to be told every day. Correct habits are formed only through continued repetition of the perfect model.
12. Be clever, not fancy. Good, clever play brings praise, while fancy play brings ridicule and criticism.

13. When group activity is stopped to correct one individual, all
pay close attention in order that you will not require the same
correction.

14. Condition comes from hard work during practice and proper
mental and moral conduct.

15. Poise, confidence, and self-control comes from being prepared.

We loved the structure, discipline, and organization, even though it
flew in the faces of our lives off the court. Coach Wooden was sixty-one
years old when we started playing for him. Here was this old man dictating to a group of high-achieving, freethinking, totally diverse, and
physically aggressive seventeen-to-twenty-three-year-olds. We wanted
to win, and we wanted to be the best. And we knew that if we let him
have his say, and did things his way, that we would win. We had no
idea—nor were we smart enough yet to know—that our opportunity
to study under him would also turn us into far greater human beings.
Or that later in life we would find ourselves bringing our own children
to Coach's home so he could teach them how to put on their shoes and
socks. Or that it would make us begin writing on our children's lunch
bags Coach's timeless messages and maxims, like "Failing to prepare is
preparing to fail" and "Never mistake activity for achievement."

I was cool with most of what was on Coach Wooden's practice manifesto, although the hair command kind of jumped out at me. I had
always kept my hair short, mostly because nobody ever told me I had
to. I stood out plenty at UCLA in 1970 by being 6'11" with red hair. I
stood out even more so because Coach wanted us to wear our hair as if
we were cops or in the Army.

But I did it. Nothing is more important than being on the team.

Pauley Pavilion was very much like Muni Gym. The open floor
space was large enough to house three full courts, laid out side by side,
each running north and south. Unlike Muni, Pauley also had a center
court, which ran east and west and overlaid the three stacked parallel
courts. Center court was where the varsity practiced and the real games
were played.

The eight members of the freshman team would practice on the westernmost of the three parallel courts, behind a giant blue curtain that separated us from the varsity. Because there wasn't another freshman anywhere near my size, Wooden hired a 6'8" ex-UCLA and NBA bruiser named Jim Nielsen to push me—every day. They said he was a coach, but it seemed to me his job was pretty much to come in and just rough me up. I thought I was done with the pampas grass.

The freshman practices were fun, and Nielsen taught me a lot, mostly about getting up off the floor and how to avoid being undercut. We ran Wooden's high-post offense, the same set offense that the varsity squad used. I have since learned that Wooden's ingenious high-post creation was one of the great inventions in the history of civilization, right up there with the wheel, fire, birth control, and the thermos. But it was not for me. The center in that scheme basically sets screens, hangs around the free-throw line, and swings the ball from side to side so that other guys can shoot.

I was a constant visitor to Coach Wooden's office in the early-morning hours before class started. I'd whine and complain that this was not what I came to UCLA for, and that I wanted to get down low where I could get to work, and handle the ball. Coach would patiently explain that all of that would come next year, on the varsity. This learning experience at the high post would ultimately help me develop the necessary skills for when the opponents would inevitably become bigger and better. I wasn't buying it. And it was here that Coach began a ritual that would be repeated over the next four years with increasing regularity.

"Bill," Coach would say, "that's very nice and admirable that you have these heartfelt and deep-seated convictions. But, you know what, Bill? I'm the coach here, and while we've enjoyed having you here, we're going to miss you."

Each time we arrived at that point, I knew it was time to move on and fall in line, and that I was not going to change his mind—this time.

—

I became a college basketball player at an absolutely perfect time. The game was incredible. We came together at UCLA just after Kareem, Elvin Hayes, Wes Unseld, Spencer Haywood, Artis Gilmore, Bob Lanier, and Sidney Wicks had all taken the front-court action to unprecedented levels. On the perimeter, the incomparable Pete Maravich had just graduated from LSU after breaking the college all-time scoring and points-per-game records. And as I was a freshman at UCLA, a whole new generation of top-scoring perimeter players was finding its form—players like William "Bird" Averitt of Pepperdine and Austin Carr of Notre Dame.

During our extremely competitive and spirited freshman practices, I was regularly called to come across to the other side of the curtain and practice with the really big boys, the four-time defending NCAA champs.

Coach Wooden only had five or six drills that we ran in practice. He had invented, designed, and perfected all of them. We ran them day after day after day—to perfection, and ever faster—the fourth Law of Learning being repetition (after demonstration, imitation, and correction). Wooden was a teacher. He taught you how to think, how to learn, how to dream, and how to compete. And he would be up and down the sideline every day, dressed like he was ready to play, constantly driving us, egging everybody on. Among our drills were his shooting games, the winning team being the first to make fifteen shots from specific spots. To make those fifteen shots quickly, it was best to make sure that they were of the high-percentage variety of game-quality shots, by getting the ball to the next shooter as quickly as possible. "You expect to win a fifteen-basket shooting game by having to take more than seventeen shots?!" Wooden would bark. "That is not realistic!"

Coach Wooden loved the trash-talking nature of athletic competition. He and Larry Bird were the most sophisticated and effective trash talkers I've ever come across. Wooden taunted us constantly, but always in a positive manner, with perfect elocution, and never any vulgarities or even colloquialisms. The nastiest it ever got for Coach was, "Goodness gracious sakes alive!" although we did hear him utter the word *crap*—once. We were seniors and totally out of control by then. Coach was basically through with us as well, fed up because by then we knew every one of his speeches. When he'd start one, we would mouth his words right back at him, showing off, teasing him. We were also faster than he was—ever so meticulous and detail-oriented, all the more so as he got older, by now sixty-five. So while we waited for him to catch up with us on his own speech, we would throw in endless Bob Dylan lines—maybe something like "Never understood why it ain't no good / You shouldn't let other people get your kicks for you"—and this would get him very flustered. Once as we were going down this road, he stopped dead in his tracks, midsentence, and looked across at us laughing and joking and thinking we were so brilliant. He fumed, "If I ever hear any more of this Bob DYE-lan crap out of you guys, I just don't know what I'm going to do!"

We fell over laughing.

His team's preparation was so perfect and proven that, to Coach Wooden, whoever the next opponent was never mattered. The other team was just in the way, necessary for the game, but certainly not worthy of particular consideration. Coach Wooden barely ever mentioned the name of the school we were playing, much less singled out an opposing player by name. In my four years at UCLA he did it twice. We lost both games. Thanks a lot, Coach.

The first time, we were still freshmen, so we weren't even going to play in the real game. It was Austin Carr and Notre Dame, the week the varsity was to play them in South Bend. The second time was David Thompson and North Carolina State, whom we played in the 1974 Final Four—on what turned out to be one of the bleakest days in the history of the known world.

Coach Wooden invented many of the drills that are used by everybody in basketball today. He was part of a great cadre of basketball thinkers from California in the 1950s and '60s that included Pete Newell, Bill Sharman, Tex Winter, and Alex Hannum, all of them in the Hall of Fame, all of them brilliant teachers. All of them instrumental in figuring out this team-basketball strategic movement, developing a brand of basketball that was so much fun to play and watch.

While all the drills were building blocks toward head-to-head competition, there was always an edge to every one of them. The best, and last, of all the drills was Wooden's Three-on-Two Conditioner—the greatest drill in the history of basketball, if not all of sport. Twelve guys constantly running, playing in a continuous fast-break world, encompassing every aspect of the transition game: offense, defense, shooting, rebounding, blocking, dribbling, passing, footwork, spacing, timing, strategy, everything. The ball never stops moving and neither do you. Just perfect. It's exhausting, takes everything that you have, it's the most fun, and you get in fantastic shape doing it, because you're going for everything, all out, the entire time, for a full ten minutes—after which you have nothing left, until you take a breath and are then ready for what's next. We lived for that drill. It was always the high point of the day.

Our practices and drills at UCLA were the most demanding, most challenging, and toughest basketball I have ever played. During the run, there were never any chairs to sit down on. There were never any towels to dry off with. There was never any talking allowed except for the constant chatter necessary to play ball to. And there was never anything to drink. The entire time. Coach Wooden would have prepared the entire practice for hours beforehand—longer than the practice ended up lasting—and drawn up the progression on a three-by-five index card he glanced at throughout the practice. The whole thing was a symphony, with a masterful conductor, although we didn't adequately appreciate it at the time. It was all we knew.

The games—nothing more than memorized exhibitions of brilliance—were easy. In the games there were fouls, time-outs, and halftime. You got a chance to take a breath, towel off, get a drink—or at least a small cup of salt water. Also, in the real games the other teams simply were just not that good. Our second string was better than pretty much any other team we played.

I often played on both sides of the curtain, and one day I was called over for the Three-on-Two Conditioner with the big boys. We cranked things up immediately, and I was absolutely on fire. I was blocking every shot, grabbing every rebound, making every shot I took, tipping in all my teammates' misses (dunking was not allowed during my entire time in college or high school games), and celebrating the greatness of life and basketball.

Sidney, who was the undisputed star of the reigning NCAA championship team and the reigning College Player of the Year, was starting to get mad because I was blocking shot after shot after shot of his. The madder he got, the better I played, loving every minute of it, and inciting Coach Wooden, who was having a high time as well. Every time I sent one of Sidney's shots back, Coach Wooden would hoot and holler and taunt Sidney. "You're letting this skinny, scrawny little redheaded seventeen-year-old freshman from San Diego block your shots?! You're Sidney Wicks! You're the College Player of the Year! How can this be?"

Finally Sidney had had enough of this. In an explosive and wild rage he came down the lane one more time, and one more time he took off attacking the rim, flying with the ball cocked and ready, well behind his fire-breathing, smoke-belching head. I coiled, leaped, and extended as high as I could, and my left hand met Sidney's right, high above the basket. Then he pulled back the ball even farther, all the way back, and swung out his left arm like a boom and just threw me out of the way, using that arm to catapult himself ever higher into the stratosphere. Then he unloaded his right arm with an explosive slam that darn near brought the whole basket down, stanchion and all.

Had there been the customary 12,000-plus fans in the stands, the place would have come apart with the shock wave that rocked Pauley. As it was, every one of us froze and either gasped or screamed. No one was ever allowed to dunk in John Wooden's practice—EVER (rule no. 12 above). Coach Wooden completely lost it. "Sidney, what are you DOING?! Don't you EVER again violate the rules of basketball, sportsmanship, and human decency by doing something like that! Ever again! EVER!"

We held our breath awaiting what was next, but Sidney was already on his way, completely ignoring Coach as he pranced around the court with both arms flung in the air in victorious and thunderous celebration. It was one of the greatest moments ever. Coach was smart enough to make nothing more of Sidney's throw and smackdown, and quickly got on to what was next.

—

Great coaches and teams are always expert at getting to what is next, and that was the epitome of John Wooden and UCLA. What was soon to come was the varsity game at Notre Dame on January 23, 1971. Our guys were 14-0 for the season, 19-0 since the last loss, a late-season game against USC back in March of '70. Two weeks later they won UCLA's fourth straight NCAA title, over Jacksonville, when Sidney completely overwhelmed Artis Gilmore, sending big Artis home at every turn. Now Coach Wooden was uncharacteristically concerned about Notre Dame. I practiced all that week with the varsity, and we were shocked, stunned, and completely caught off guard to hear Coach Wooden repeatedly talk about Austin Carr. Carr was a great player, a 6'4" guard who had scored 61 points in one NCAA tournament game, and was now averaging almost 35 per game. Wooden was so obsessed with Carr that he gave Larry Hollyfield, a 6'7" sophomore backup swing man on our team, the special assignment of playing the role of Carr in our practices all that week.

For Larry, this opportunity was a little like the one I got when I played for the other team against Team USA in Yugoslavia a year earlier. Larry, even more than the rest of us, was not used to sitting on anybody's bench. He was a year ahead of Greg, Jamaal, and me, but he was a UCLA rookie who had played the previous season in junior college. When Larry committed to play at UCLA as a sophomore, he was the most famous and decorated player to join the program since Kareem, even more so than Sidney. Larry was from Compton, and one of the greatest winners ever. Through his junior and senior seasons at Compton High, his year at Compton Community College, and the first half of the 1970–71 UCLA season leading up to the Notre Dame game, Larry's teams had a record of 109-0. By the time he graduated in 1973, his teams' composite record would be 183-1.

Sadly, the "1" came at the end of the week in which Larry played the role of Austin Carr. And played him to perfection. All week long, on instructions from Wooden to shoot early and often—which Larry didn't need any encouragement to do—Larry kept killing our guys, just destroying Sidney, Curtis, and Steve. Nobody could stop him from making shot after shot, from outside or on slashing drives to the hoop, or crashing the boards and tipping in rebounds. Larry was looking like the greatest player ever, taking it right to our guys, who were on their own way to establishing themselves as one of the greatest college teams in history.

As Larry continued his dominance all week long in practice, the tension was mounting. The varsity left for South Bend; we stayed home and watched the game on TV on Saturday afternoon in the dorm.

What we saw looked like Austin Carr playing the role of Larry Hollyfield playing the role of Austin Carr against our guys in practice all week. Exactly as Larry had torched our main guys from all over the court in practice, Carr hit everything he threw at the basket, scoring 46 points, including 15 of Notre Dame's last 17 on the way to an 89–82 upset.

And Larry never even got to play. One might have thought that after the week Larry had in practice, Coach Wooden would actually put him into the game to try to make a difference, seeing as how Larry was probably the one guy in the building who knew what Carr was going to do before he did it. But Larry did not even get in until the final few minutes, when it was already way too late.

Coach Wooden was totally devoted to his starting five, and everybody else was just there to serve. He played his best players the entire game, or at least until it was out of reach. Conditioning was never an issue. We were UCLA. And very proud of it all. Coach was just not into substituting, the same way he never liked calling time-outs. The only UCLA player that I can recall being consistently productive off the bench for Coach Wooden was Kenny Washington, who defined competitive greatness, and always came with his best when it was needed most. The last game Coach ever taught at UCLA, the 1975 NCAA championship game, four players played the entire game, and one guy got sixteen minutes off the bench.

Even though Larry had been brilliant all week impersonating Austin Carr in practice, Larry was a sub and not a starter. "Coach finally called me up to the head of the bench," Larry remembered many years later. "I go 'all right,' so I'm finally going in. I'm real happy, excited as can be. When I got up to Wooden, he says to me, 'Go get Austin.' I said, 'Coach, Austin's got thirty-eight. What do you mean go get him? Don't you think it's a little too late for that? The guy's already on fire!'"

Back in Dykstra, watching this debacle through to the end, Greg, Jamaal, and I turned to each other as the surreal sadness turned all too real, and personal. We muttered to each other, "We will never let this happen again."

UCLA didn't lose another game for three years.

CHAPTER 6

My Lightning, Too . . .
The Music Never Stops

They're a band beyond description, like Jehovah's favorite choir
People joining hand in hand, while the music played the band
Lord they're setting us on fire.

Me and some of my friends, we were going to save the world.

My whole life has been about the dream of being part of a special team. The irony in our world was that the better the team became, the harder it was to keep it a team. The outside powers that were so determined to make it about me could not have been further from the reality of my life.

Why the focus on and promotion of the individual, which minimizes and trivializes the many invaluable contributions that make the team what it is? Whose idea was that?

I spent the summer between my first and second years at UCLA mostly back in San Diego. There's better bike riding, beaches, mountains, deserts, air, and water there. And still plenty of everything else.

Plus I needed some money; our $128 monthly scholarship checks only came during the school year. I got a summer job at the lumber yard, cutting and stacking the wood, filling the swelling purchase orders as the inexorable buildup of the Southland continued unabated. Emory from Helix was one of my bosses. He's still there today. There were lots of UCLA guys there at the top as well.

Back at school in early October, I was beyond the dorms, so I rented a room on Gayley Avenue, across the street from campus. It was in a disbanded frat house, dissolved due to lack of interest at the time. I think the rent was $20 a month, maybe $25. It took a sizable chunk out of my monthly scholarship check. I ate wherever and whenever I could. I was always hungry when I was at UCLA, although never for very long.

The basketball was perfect. Coach Wooden was excited with the newness of the squad. The other teams were licking their chops, sure it was now their turn, what with the departure of Wicks, Rowe, and Patterson to graduation. Wooden was constantly barraged: What are you going to do now, Coach? You no longer have the dominant player (Wicks) or front line. Now all you have is a bunch of skinny, scrawny new guys with no experience. And by the way, Coach—who are those new guys?

One of Wooden's greatest strengths—and it's impossible to rank, rate, or compare them—was his ability as a coach, teacher, leader, and/ or friend to breathe life and confidence into people, players, and situations. He was always outwardly calm under the greatest of pressures, a trait that really helped us. Coach had no problem giving the same answer to the exhaustingly repetitive questions, and the response went something like this: "I like our team and players, and we'll take our chances. I like our chemistry, personnel, and talent. And I will always take talent over experience."

One day early on in the six weeks or so of buildup to the games, Coach uncharacteristically stopped the run and gathered us around. He rarely addressed us in a static environment. So when he started speaking here, his words took on added importance. Coach started talking about who we are, UCLA, what we do, and why. He explained that our game was the fast break, the relentless attack that created endless and exciting opportunities for all—UCLA basketball. Fundamentals, physical fitness, the team game, the full-court press—all leading to commanding and seemingly endless victories.

Coach went on to say, "In the open court, on the run, anybody can shoot. In the fast break, which is our game, no one will ever say a contrary word to you or anybody about assertively taking the ball, shooting a jump shot, taking it to the basket, making your play." But then he turned cautionary, and went on. "If it's a setup situation, though, and the other team is back and dug in defensively, if Walton and Wilkes don't get the ball every time, the rest of you guys are coming out. Now let's get back to it."

——

John Wooden was all about preparation, with purpose, for performance. We were ready, now on the eve of our first game, now as the varsity squad. We had a good team, and it was our time.

In those days, long gone now, players would stay in the locker room until just twenty minutes before the tip, when everybody would go out together for a group warm-up. While we waited anxiously in the sanctuary of our locker room before getting it all going that first time, we were doing our stretches and push-ups, playing pepper with the ball, and slap-fighting each other, getting ready to get down to it.

Coach came in and gathered us around. We sat there dutifully, one more time. Now he was dressed impeccably: suit and tie, clean and crisp as can be. No more caged tiger in his basketball gear from the practices. Now he was the seeming church deacon whom countless millions came to know later in Coach's more public life, after his retirement from UCLA. In the four years that we played for Coach Wooden, his pregame preparation never varied. We never watched film, he never used the blackboard, we never ran a play—didn't have any. And in the games, we never called time-out. Only rarely, and mistakenly, did he mention the other team by name. It was all about us, all the time, and what we were going to do, in our memorized exhibition of brilliance.

So calm, so poised, so controlled, but always with the rolled-up program in his hand, he would look out at us and say, "Men, I've done my job. The rest is up to you. When that game starts out there, please, don't ever look over at me on the sideline. There is nothing more that I can do to help you from this point forward. Now let's get it going, up and down." And then it was time.

The only perceptible variance from this repetitive preparation came on opening night of each year—although this night we were clueless, because it was our first time around. What did or could we know?

On opening night, as Coach was getting it all going, he started talking about the big picture of it all, the importance of getting off to a good, quick start if we were to have a wholly successful season. But as he was talking, he became uncharacteristically distracted. He kept looking off to the side of the room. Finally, he stopped his message and strode boldly over to the wall. He bent down and came up with a penny pinched in his fingers. Holding it up, Coach happily proclaimed, "Look at this, guys. Somebody has dropped and lost a penny. This is a good omen for us. This now-found penny represents good luck, and means that we have a chance at success."

He then leaned over and slid that lucky penny into the slot on the top of one of his penny loafer shoes. And carried it there all season long.

We thought he was nuts.

We started strong. That first night was a blowout, a 56-point take-down of The Citadel, the then 130-year-old Military College of South Carolina. Maybe it was the lucky penny—who knows? I like to think that any bonus luck was from the Grateful Dead and the New Riders of the Purple Sage, since they had just rolled into and through Pauley and had christened our season and locker room with a fantastic concert just a few weeks before.

We won our first eight games by a total of 355 points. At 15-0, our average winning score was 102–64. We beat Notre Dame by 58, and Texas A&M by 64. Teams were trying to beat us at our game—running. It wasn't working. And we were really enjoying it all.

Reporters and the media were never allowed in our locker room the entire time I was at UCLA. Coach thankfully controlled everything. I wanted no part of any publicity. I couldn't talk, was completely unwilling to ever share any cogent or rational thought at all, which might jeopardize our chance of winning, and I never liked or accepted the focus and attention on individuals in a team game. The postgame media routine in those days was for Coach to select one or two experienced players who he thought were representative of the team effort to go outside into the hallway by the water fountain and answer reporters' questions about the game.

After the opening Citadel game, Coach proudly selected his prize new star, the team's sharpest intellect, Greg Lee, to address the media. It did not go well, although nobody knew it until the next day. The newspaper game accounts had Greg, asked to evaluate the evening's opponent, comparing The Citadel to an average junior college team. Coach was beside himself, couldn't believe that his handpicked pupil and virtual son for all these years would ever let him down, much less on the night of his first-ever UCLA game. Wooden was so mad. We had never seen this. He was furious that Greg, or any one of us, would ever belittle the opposition—much less in public.

In his own defense, Greg told us how the whole thing actually went down before his published words were stripped of context. The reporter's statement, not question, was something like, "Come on, Greg. Those guys out there tonight were not any better than the teams you used to beat regularly and easily in high school!" To which Greg, in noble and reasoned defense of the helpless foes from South Carolina, replied, "No, that's not right. They were much better than that! More like one of the junior college teams we played last year as freshmen."

Regardless, Coach did not see Greg's verbal contribution as a positive.

In all other ways, the team was coming along, and what a team it was. Greg and Henry Bibby at the guards, Jamaal Wilkes and Larry Farmer up front with me. Offensively we would have structure and motion that generally got us into a 1-3-1 attack, with Greg out front, Henry on the left wing, Jamaal at the high post, and Larry on the right wing; I got to work down low—just as I had wanted, and as Wooden had promised I would when he made me learn to play the high post as a freshman.

As is always the case with a team, sacrifice was a critical element to our success. Greg rarely shot, becoming the key to our success as the perfect setup guy. Henry, as our lone playing senior, captain, and first-team All-America, was either wide open and scored a ton, or was tightly guarded and threw it to me for big numbers. There was never much middle ground here. Jamaal got the ball a lot from Greg and Henry, and developed the most effective fake-pass any of us had ever seen.

Larry Farmer never saw many touches at all in the sets. Larry Holly-field played some, and deserved more time, but where and from whom was it going to come? Swen Nater played only when I got into foul trouble (rarely) or in the closing moments when Wooden reluctantly took Jamaal and me out. Whatever playing time Tommy Curtis got—ever—was way too much. And the rest of the guys, plus a couple of redshirt players, made up the preparation squad, responsible for doing whatever it took to get us ready. They were sophomores Vince Carson and Gary Franklin, and the old carryover guys, Andy Hill and Jon Chapman. Andy and Jon, to this day, never forget to rightly remind me that they were among the last of the fourteen UCLA guys to win three straight NCAA Championships.

Coach wanted my older brother, Bruce, to be on the team, too. Bruce was an All-America football player at UCLA and an Academic All-America. Bruce also kept a very active social life. So when Coach Wooden offered Bruce a spot on the basketball team, Bruce politely declined. He was concerned that Coach was just looking for an enforcer, and Bruce was quite confident in Swen Nater's potential. Plus, Bruce realized that it was much easier to meet new friends in the stands at Pauley than from the bench.

The most effective, efficient, and fun part of our game was the pressing defense leading to the fast break, where anybody out front had complete freedom to let it grow, glow, and go. Our full-court zone press, which never let up, led to literally everything for us. It was nominally structured (everything John Wooden had structure) as a 2-2-1. Henry and Larry Farmer up front, waiting for the ball to be put in play, and when the other team got the ball up the first fifteen feet to our free-throw line, they would quickly and assertively double-team the ball. Not to steal, but rather to force a pass. And that's where and when the real action began. The second line of defense was Greg and Jamaal, starting at half-court. It was their quickness and sense of anticipation that made the whole thing work so powerfully. They had total freedom, and were strongly encouraged to go for any and every ball. My job was to cover everything else in the back.

Our fans—the original great fan base in basketball history—had their job as well. As soon as we scored, which was quite often, the ball in our net triggered our press. The fans would immediately start the ten-second countdown that the other team had to beat to get the ball over the half-court line. The ten-nine-eight-seven rolling chant reverberating throughout Pauley would completely disrupt the other team and help us immensely, not to mention the refs, who sometimes lost track of the Count. The crowd was very cool in never keeping a constant beat, rhythm, or cadence in their count—very much like the Grateful Dead. As they got ever closer to zero and the resulting violation, our crowd became the Dead as they would pick up the pace, the speed, and the volume of the Count.

The other teams got so flustered, and their coaches regularly lost it—which only inspired everybody involved to go for more.

The gambles and risks of Greg and Jamaal at midcourt constantly forced the other team into fast-break action. Which all totally fed into my game. I would wait, impatiently, at the other team's foul line, salivating for the opportunity to do something—block, rebound, and outlet—to turn the whole play the other way.

The cycle started and went on endlessly, gloriously, and spectacularly, with regular 15- to 20-point runs, often to start the game. We loved it all.

The opponents often crumbled under the weight and pressure of everything. They began to realize that ultimately they had no chance.

Their pathetic, hopeless recourse was to start sucking the air out of the ball and the game by slowing it down and ruining all our fun.

We were destroying everybody. After beating Notre Dame in December by 58 points, we went back to their place in January to complete the yearly home-and-home series. Digger Phelps ruined the day by forbidding his team from trying to win. Their only goal was to not get beat by 58 points. So they hardly ever shot. They held the ball as long as they could—at one stretch for three and a half minutes without so much as taking a step toward the basket. There was no shot clock in those days. It was boring, frustrating, embarrassing, and no fun at all—all of which pretty much describes Digger.

We were ready to run and play; that's the nature of basketball. But we scored only 57 points in the entire game, which was usually about our total by halftime. And still, we won the game by 25. It felt like a waste of a trip across the country, but at least we had Andy Hill along to show us the finer points of enjoying a high time on the road and in the air as part of an NCAA Championship squad.

Andy was the guy whom Coach Wooden assigned to welcome me to UCLA, when I would just show up, still a high school player from San Diego. He would feed me, find me a place to sleep in the dorms, show me the ropes, and ultimately become my tour guide in our one varsity season together.

He had come to UCLA the same year as Henry Bibby and together they formed a dynamic, high-scoring backcourt on their freshman team. They were looking forward to openings on the varsity backcourt as eventually the starters at the time would be termed out. But for Andy, that starting spot sadly never came. It was a burning source of frustration for him, and over time led to serious friction between him and Wooden—though it never affected his commitment to our team, or our friendship, which has lasted and grown stronger over the last forty-five years.

———

Just before the start of the Pac-8 conference season, which was all-important, since you had to win your conference to get into what was then the twenty-five-team NCAA tournament, I came down with the flu and got very sick. I was down and out, couldn't get up. I couldn't go to class, couldn't go to practice, and there was real concern that I would not be able to make the two-day trip to Oregon for the Beavers and the Ducks.

Coach Cunningham would come by every day to my small, dark, dank room on Gayley to check on me, but I wasn't getting any better. I was living alone and not really able to do much for myself. Finally Henry Bibby, our captain and senior leader, took things into his own hands. He came by one day, unannounced, and just walked right in— nothing was ever locked—and started gathering my stuff. I sat up groggily in bed, and couldn't figure it all out. Eventually, when his arms were full, Henry flatly stated, "Come on, Bill. You're coming with me."

I wearily got up and weakly trudged down the hall and stairs to his waiting car. Henry could park anywhere he wanted. He drove me to his "house," which was unlike any living accommodation we had ever seen for a college student. He took me inside, got me comfortable with everything, and then started calling his Angels to come over and help. For the rest of the week, an endless stream of Henry's Angels came by to nurse me back to health, ultimately providing me with everything that I needed. By the end of a week of them breathing life back into me, I was ready for anything. Like going to Oregon.

We played Oregon State first. The Friday-night game at Corvallis was our worst of the season. I felt awful. Couldn't get anything going. We committed 30 turnovers and allowed the top Beaver, Freddie Boyd, to run wild. We barely won, by only 6 points. It was the only game all season that we didn't win by at least 13, until the NCAA title game. By the next afternoon in Eugene I had my rhythm back, and we won by 25. The next game, we beat the Cougars from Washington State in another convincing rout, and we never looked back.

I was also hitting stride academically by this point. I had changed majors, from engineering to political science, and what a lively romp that was, what with the changing times, Reagan, Nixon, J. Edgar Hoover, Vietnam, Watergate, L.A. mayor Sam Yorty, and all.

All this time, the L.A. Lakers were fabulously supportive of our team. Across the board, they couldn't have been nicer. Wilt was everywhere; Elgin was dazzling; Jerry and I would regularly have breakfast together at the Westwood Drug Store; Chick was our best friend and arbiter of information, history, prognostication, entertainment, and all other known things; the entire Laker staff was always so kind, and the people who ran the Fabulous Forum treated us as if we were on the team as well.

The NBA and the Lakers in the years we were at UCLA were stupendous. There were some teams for the ages that regularly came into town on a mission—Milwaukee with Kareem, Oscar, Lucius Allen, and Bob Dandridge; New York with Willis Reed, Walt Frazier, Bill Bradley, Dave DeBusschere, Dick Barnett, and later Earl Monroe and Jerry Lucas; Boston with Dave Cowens, John Havlicek, Jo Jo White, Don Nelson, Paul Silas, and Don Chaney; Baltimore with Earl Monroe, Gus Johnson, and Wes Unseld; San Francisco with Rick Barry and Nate Thurmond. Every night the battles raged. And the Lakers always won— setting a still-standing league record with 33 in a row from November into January.

At UCLA, Wooden taught us from the beginning how to think like champions, how to act like champions, and ultimately how to become champions. It was the natural order of our lives. So after running the table in the regular season—26-0, the UCLA winning streak now at 41—the NCAA tournament was next.

In the twenty-five-team geographic format of the day, our Western Regional was in Utah, with BYU hosting but not playing, having lost in the at-large round to Long Beach State, even with the great Kresimir Cosic from Yugoslavia. We've always loved Utah for all the right reasons: beautiful people, fabulous geography and geology, incredible spirit and drive of the pioneering, entrepreneurial dreamers and visionaries who built the place. Brigham Young was ever so right when he declared, "This is the place." And what a place they had to play ball there on BYU's campus: the Marriott Center, the most beautiful basketball temple one could dream of, right in the center of everything, with 20,000 blue and gold seats and the most technologically advanced floor (along with Stanford's) I ever played on. It was like playing on a trampoline, with unlimited springboard capabilities.

By this point I was suffering from near-constant pain in both knees, and not only because of the operation I'd had on my left knee five years earlier. All the doctors I was regularly seeing, either through UCLA or now also the Lakers, were basically treating the pain and not its source. It wasn't until years later that the medical consensus would conclude that the real and chronic problems all originated with the congenital structural defects in my feet that limited normal and natural movement, and shock absorption and dissipation up through the legs, knees, hips, pelvis, and spine. But I sure loved playing on those forgiving, springy, launching-pad floors at BYU and Stanford.

We played Weber State in the Regional Semifinals and had no trouble with them, even though the refs gave me nothing but grief. I was limited by fouls in a game that didn't require much to get the job done. We moved on to Long Beach State, coached by Jerry Tarkanian and always seething from being so close to but always in the shadow of UCLA. Tark and his squad were convinced that their time was now. They had barely lost to UCLA and Sidney, Curtis, and Steve in the 1971 Regional Final, a game that Long Beach had but gave away. UCLA was saved that day by rarely used subs Larry Farmer and Larry Hollyfield, now key contributors for us.

In the buildup to Long Beach's rematch showdown with us, Tark kept downplaying everything, trying to keep a tight lid on what was sure to be a very volatile confrontation. He strictly instructed his players to not say a word about UCLA, Coach Wooden, or the game. He wanted his team's victorious performance to speak for itself.

Sure enough, as happened so often to Tark, things broke the wrong way. His starting center, Nate Stephens, big, rangy, and athletic but a little undisciplined, went off to the sportswriters the day before the game. He told them that UCLA was a bunch of frauds, that Walton was protected by the refs, and that Long Beach would beat them without any problem. Tark could not believe it, and there went whatever advantage he thought he had. We came out charged, and played well from the start. But Tark had his team slow the tempo to keep us out of our running game, and he packed his defense in with a terrific zone, collapsing around me. Unfortunately for him, that left Henry wide open to score all game, and we won by 16. All Tark could do was chew on his towel—one more time.

The Final Four was next, back in Los Angeles, at the Sports Arena, which was USC's home court. Our game, against Louisville, would be the second semifinal that Thursday night. As we got ready in our locker room, all pumped up and anxious to take the court, the opening semifinal, between North Carolina and Florida State, dragged into overtime.

Coach Wooden never liked us hanging out too long in a cramped locker room; he wanted us moving. So at the regularly scheduled time, we wound our way out and into the tunnel leading onto the court, and suddenly found ourselves squeezed in, side by side, with the guys from Louisville and their coach—our Denny Crum! On the court, the preliminary game kept dragging on endlessly, forcing us to wait, and wait, and wait. Come on—LET'S GO! Wooden hung back in our locker room. And now, out on the launching pad, it was both teams and their coach, who was really our coach and best friend, Denny, heating up.

So we started teasing Coach Crum, who stayed as serious as he could. He knew. He had put both teams together. We tossed off teasing comments like, "Hey, Coach, what are you doing with THAT team? Why don't you join a REAL team?" Coach Crum was clearly embarrassed. We had our relationship with him, spanning years. And here he was trying to maintain the professed dignity of the head coach, taking his new team to the Final Four in his very first year. We kept urging Denny to come back from the dark side and to get back to where he belonged, with a real and winning squad. Ours.

His Louisville players were shocked, Denny himself aghast, and Coach Wooden oblivious as he waited things out by himself in our locker room.

Florida State ultimately beat North Carolina, allowing us to finally get going. Coach Crum decided to try to run with us. And while it made for a really fun game—for us, at least—Louisville, a limited team built around excellent guards, Henry Bacon and Jim Price, didn't stand much of a chance playing our game. They went down by 19.

The title game on Saturday afternoon was memorable on many fronts. We knew nothing about Florida State, which was normal for us. And they came to play. It turned out that they had lots of everything—size, speed, talent, depth—and they were pretty darn good. By the end of the game we knew their names—Ron King, Reggie Royals, Rowland Garrett, Lawrence McCray, Coach Hugh Durham—and they were better than both we and North Carolina thought.

Coach Wooden's constant emphasis on our game and the irrelevancy of the other team always served us well. Typically we simply overwhelmed our opponents with our press and an assertive defense, which ignited an explosive, unrelenting offensive attack that would go on prolonged and unparalleled scoring runs. This game was different, though; really the first time we were ever challenged by anybody other than our second string in practice.

Florida State controlled the early goings, and we had no rhythm, beat, or pace. As we were coming up the court one time, with the game and the fate of the known world seemingly in the balance, I ran by our bench, where Coach Wooden was sitting stoically, watching the wheels go round. I barked out to him that—Hey! Maybe/Probably/Please!—we should call time-out and regroup. He sat up, startled, caught completely off guard, as if I had totally lost my mind. Then he stood up, moved gently toward me on the court with his rolled-up program firmly in hand, and eyed me with the stern look of a most disappointed teacher. He told me right there and then: "We are UCLA. We do not call time-out. Time-outs are a signal of defeat, and only give the other team a chance to regroup." And then as he started to draw small, looping circles in the air with his rolled-up program, he continued: "Just keep going as you are. Everything will be fine." He smiled and winked at me, and went back and sat down.

Sure enough, things turned our way almost immediately, as Henry Bibby and Jamaal took over and went on unstoppable runs. We won the game by a paltry 5 points.

At UCLA, the winning was so regular, constant, and assumed that it was no longer the standard of success. Over our time there, that measurement of achievement ultimately evolved into our own evaluation of how well we performed.

—

Afterward, Coach allowed the press to ask me a few limited questions—which was not a good idea.

I try my best to always tell the truth. That way I never have to remember any story. And when I answered the requisite questions, none varying much from "How does it feel to win the championship?" by stating that it felt unfulfilling and unsatisfactory, in that we and I did not play well and that we did not exercise the usual control, impact, and level of excellence that we pride ourselves on—I was universally vilified as an ungrateful ogre.

But we won! And already being in L.A., we had a very nice postgame party that I have very little memory of, other than waking up with very sore cheeks from smiling so much.

Now it was back to school for the remainder of the term, which generally ran to mid-June, which was all fine and good, since the real nice weather doesn't come to the coast of California until then, at the earliest. By this time, a year and a half into things at UCLA, I was starting to figure more of it out. And now having a better feel for the rhythm and pace, I understood that the basketball season was played in conjunction with the fall and winter quarters. And that the spring term was ours.

When I went into Coach's office one day and told him that I had come up with the very cool, and serious, idea of expanding my mind and my collegiate experience by spending my spring quarters at Cal, up in Berkeley—one of the greatest places on earth, and a real power spot for all that was going on in our world—after being a student-athlete for him at UCLA in the fall and winter, it caught him off guard, but only momentarily. His near-immediate response: No you're not!

I was most disappointed, but it really was just another in a long list of arguments with Coach that I lost. I'm not sure that I ever won any of them.

—

As we tripped and swirled through another glorious California renewal, springing toward one more endless summer, things were starting to change for me much the way they had after my sophomore season in high school. Except now instead of the college recruiting game, it was more the business of sport, with people constantly showing up trying to convince me how much better off I would be if I left UCLA and became a professional. None of it made any sense to me. I was having the time of my life. What was there to change, and why?

I was also starting to receive all kinds of awards, including being named the NCAA Player of the Year, an honor I was ultimately credited with in each of my three varsity seasons at UCLA. None of this was of interest to me—being part of the team that won the championship was what I wanted. But Coach Wooden kept telling me that I had to go to all these ceremonies. Back and forth we went. I wanted to be a college student, not to be flying around the country for awards banquets full of people I didn't know. He kept coming back at me about my RE-SPONSIBILITY. I said he should go in my place, if someone really needed to go. Finally we reached an agreement: I would go, but only if he came with me to each one. And he would give the required speech that I was incapable of delivering. And through that spring, we stuck to that agreement. On the first plane ride, when I told a most intriguing, accommodating, and encouraging stewardess, "I'll have a beer," Coach Wooden's tongue and arm, from across the aisle, immediately snapped, "No he won't." And so it went.

At the same time, throughout that spring, Coach Wooden would occasionally ask me to come by his office because somebody wanted to talk to me about one deal or another.

I tried not to pay much attention to any of it, as I really had no interest. I had what I wanted. But one particular offer was different. Because word was swirling around that with the 1972 Olympics on the near horizon, people were looking for me to play on the U.S. team. Eventually I ended up in Coach's office on this very subject. And here were these very stiff, weirdly dressed, and overly serious guys, meticulously laying out their plan for me to play in Munich.

I sat there next to them, listening intently. Coach, safely behind the barricade of his large desk, with arms folded across his chest, didn't say a word. When they finished their elaborate presentation, it only took me a moment to say yes, sure, I'll play.

I think I caught them off guard, as there was an awkward and very still silence. Coach Wooden had not had the best experience with the Olympic basketball people since Gail Goodrich was inexplicably left off the 1964 team in Tokyo. And even though UCLA had totally dominated "amateur" basketball from that time forward, Walt Hazzard was the only UCLA player to make the U.S. Olympic team during the Bruins' unprecedented run of success.

In Coach's office, there was a brief moment of hesitation, doubt, and uncertainty after I said yes to the Olympics. So I picked it up myself. I still had the stinging memories of my experience with Hal Fischer and the U.S. National Team burning through my veins. Contrary to everything I knew, loved, and believed in, that had seemed to be all about the coaches, bureaucrats, and business guys, with basketball and the players a distant and unimportant concern.

So I laid it out: "I'll play, yes. But there is no need for me to try out again for this team. I just did that two years ago. And I made the team then. I'm either good enough to make it now, or I'm not. We are the undefeated NCAA champions, and I am the NCAA Player of the Year, and an Academic All-America as well. I will show up, in shape, three weeks before the Olympics start. I will be ready to go. We will train then, but I will not play in those endless exhibitions that we already went through as the lead-in to the world championships in Yugoslavia in 1970. I will play in the Olympics, and when the Games are over, I am right out of there. I have to get back to school. Please, I have important responsibilities, duties, and obligations here."

Coach Wooden remained silent.

The Olympic guys looked at each other, then at me, then at Coach, then back at each other. Then they said no.

I looked around at everybody, said thanks and good luck, and got up and left, never giving it another thought.

One thing they never brought up was the idea of bringing our whole UCLA team and Coach Wooden to Munich to represent America. That would have been good. And then, most assuredly, the United States would have won, instead of going down in inexplicable fashion—the team's first loss in Olympic history—to the Soviets.

CHAPTER 7

Commissars and Pinstripe Bosses Roll the Dice, Whichever Way They Fall—Guess Who Gets to Pay the Price

Don't you let that deal go down!

If I lived my life by what others were thinkin'
The heart inside me would've died.
I was just too stubborn to ever be governed by enforced insanity.

One of life's greatest challenges is the search for the master teachers who can be the guiding force and moral compass in our quest for deliverance. I was so lucky to have so many great leaders converge so harmonically at UCLA during my years there to help me along my path, especially as they stood in such stark contrast to the people who were deciding the fate of the rest of the world during the same time.

There was Charles Young, the chancellor who for almost thirty years guided UCLA to unparalleled heights; J. D. Morgan, generally regarded as the greatest athletic director in the history of intercollegiate athletics—he was there for forty years; Ducky Drake, who came to UCLA as a student in 1923 and stayed—in a myriad of positions, from coach to trainer to friend and confidant—until he died sixty-five years later. And John Wooden, a relative short-timer for twenty-seven years, our basketball coach—I guess you could call him that—but he was really so much more.

While there were, and are, many people who have made UCLA as great as it is, these four guys were at the top for me. And their unique yet different abilities combined to create a positive environment from which young people could chase their dreams and build their lives. There I was, at seventeen years old, in California, at UCLA. It was all good, and getting better.

And yet, on the macro level, Nixon is president, Reagan is governor, and Sam Yorty is mayor of L.A.

While a long life teaches us that there seems to be continuous and endless tragedy in the world, it is impossible to come up with a greater moral and ethical divide in my lifetime than what was done in our name in Vietnam, where the bottom line on the ground seemed to be that we had to destroy the people there in order to save them. And the duplicity and double standards deployed by the war's proponents only made it worse. For while they were always telling us how great and noble was their cause, they weren't willing to go and do the job themselves. And while they led the cheers to go for the kill, they threatened us with the very same fate. "We'll send you off to the war" was the unrelenting sword over all of our heads, and the height of hypocrisy. The buildup of horrors here at home included political and cultural assassinations, civil and racial violence, and the ultimate devolution of our society to the point that the game was not on the level.

One of the critical elements of leadership is the willingness and ability to say no. And that is where we stood, at the crossroads of our lives. Faced with the greed, selfishness, war profiteering, cronyism, incompetence, and the lunacy of where our "leaders" were taking us in Southeast Asia, we had no other choice.

The isolated happy vacuum that some prefer for their lives and college experiences was not what I was looking for. And with its long and proud progressive history of integration and social and political involvement that includes the likes of Ralph Bunche, Jackie Robinson, Don Barksdale, Rafer Johnson, Walt Hazzard, Arthur Ashe, Kenny Washington, Mike Warren, Lucius Allen, Kareem, and Sidney Wicks, UCLA was just fine with, and for, me.

UCLA has always been a place where students stand tall and speak their minds. Just before I came up from San Diego, one of the Bruin basketball players, Bill Seibert, had done just that. His public displeasure with most things Coach Wooden ultimately led to Seibert being banished by the Coach to Tasmania.

But now the peace rallies and the rage against Nixon and the war were a constant part of our lives. Speakers, programs, demonstrations, seminars, sit-ins, be-ins, love-ins, teach-ins, you name it and it was happening at UCLA. And we were at all of them. Yet the powers that be kept reassuring us that everything was fine, there was nothing to see here, and that we should all just keep moving along.

So now we had completed our 1972 undefeated championship basketball season, the Olympic deal had passed me by, and I was finishing up the school year, trying to figure it all out. Then, almost two years to the day after the Kent State and Jackson State massacres, Nixon ordered a new and massive expansion of the Vietnam War—with naval blockades, the mining of harbors, and an enormous aerial bombing rain of terror.

The opposition—us—surged forward to say "NO." Thousands of students came together at Royce Quad, soon making our way down Westwood Boulevard as people spilled out of the surrounding buildings, swelling our ranks. I recognized and knew most of them. We became one. Through the village that was the campus's commercial heart, we made our way to Wilshire and Veteran, with our sights on the 405 freeway. The police drew their line there and held us back. We hung there for a while, sitting down in the intersection but not venturing farther, before heading home for the night.

The next day, May 10, 1972, the *Daily Bruin* ran an editorial that said it all.

"Today is the day to strike," it began. "Today is not the day for 'business as usual.' Today is not the day to go to class. Today is the day to rally, to march, to close down the university. Because today is the day to end the war."

Right. I get that! It went on powerfully from there. So we came back, with more—and for more. Some of the peace marchers worked their way down to the massive federal building at Wilshire and Veteran. Others went building to building on campus, recruiting and encouraging everyone within earshot to join us. Some of us headed to Murphy Hall, the administration building, just off Royce Quad. We spent the night there and fortified our positions with everything that could be moved—tables, chairs, trash cans, and fire hoses. We left early the next morning, figuring it was better to keep moving, and by noon there was a new and huge gathering of people near the top of Janss Steps, roving around looking for the action that seemed imminent.

The LAPD was soon on the scene, and skirmishes began to break out, back and forth across the Quad. At one point, the "peace officers" were moving us forcibly out of the Quad in an easterly direction toward Murphy Hall and the law school, when, on one of the upper floors of Haines Hall, just east of Royce Hall, a student stuck his head out a window and turned a full-on fire hose on the rear guard of the shocked police battalion. We loved it, and the cheers rang loud, proud, and true. The entire corps of armed guards turned and raced into Haines in hot pursuit of the guy with the hose. When they were all inside the building, either climbing the stairs or riding the elevators up for the capture, the guy with the hose threw it out the window and used it as a rappelling rope to shimmy down the exterior wall of Haines, hitting the ground on the run and sprinting over to the safety of our midst, where we engulfed him in a warm, welcoming roar of approval.

The red-faced cops had had enough by this point and soon were busting heads with nightsticks and slapping handcuffs onto anyone they could catch—and that would include me, as well as fifty-one of my very good friends. As I sat there handcuffed on the police bus, waiting for it to fill up and take us to the federal building and then to a jail in the San Fernando Valley, I spotted Chancellor Young, sadly and sorely surveying the carnage of everything that he had built and loved so much. I yelled out the window, "F— you, Chuck!"

I later apologized to the chancellor for that personal attack, making it clear that my apology did not change my way of thinking or what side of the fight I was on.

After a few unpleasant and boring hours in the jailhouse, I was out before nightfall, as UCLA and Chancellor Young sent a team of lawyers to set things right for all of us. And then, somehow, I ended up in a car with Coach Wooden driving me back to campus. I was nineteen, and I'm pretty sure it was the first time I was ever alone in the restrictive confines of a car with the Coach.

Coach was not happy, to say the least. And he was in my face, in a most determined fashion, unlike anything I had ever seen or witnessed before. And he went on and on, about how I had gone TOO FAR THIS TIME. And that I had let EVERYBODY down. Him, his family. My family. UCLA and its family. The NCAA—and its family. And basically anybody he could think of, which pretty much included the history of the world. And their families, too. He was hot.

What was I to say?

I was guilty—of wanting PEACE NOW!

As we got closer and closer to campus, I started arguing back. And I began telling him how this whole deal is wrong, and we have to do everything that we can to stop the military madness . . . RIGHT NOW!

He kept coming back at me, assuring me how wrong I was—on EVERYTHING.

Finally I turned to him in the driver's seat and said, "Look, you can say what you want. But it's my friends and classmates who are coming home in body bags and wheelchairs. And we're not going to take it anymore. We have got to stop this craziness, AND WE'RE GOING TO DO IT NOW!"

Coach was taken aback, and his voice suddenly changed. He started up again, this time in a more somber tone, about how he didn't like the war, either, but that I was going about the whole thing in the wrong way. Because my actions, as a participant in the peace rallies and initiatives, were infringing on the rights of others to continue on with their pursuits and choices in life.

My tone didn't change. "RIGHT . . . like everything is JUST NORMAL and that if we only let it all ride, everything will be fine . . ."

Then he started talking about how to reach goals, and that in this case the best way to get my point across would be by writing letters of disagreement to the people in charge.

"Write letters? Are you kidding me? That's the dumbest thing I've ever heard. What good is that going to do?"

What if you knew her and found her dead on the ground?

"LETTERS? Goodness gracious sakes alive!"

How can you run when you know?

We were pulling up now to my rooming house on Gayley. This was not ending well. There was certainly no resolution or common ground.

There was no mention of Tasmania.

As I thanked him for the ride, I told him that I would see him tomorrow at school. Just as he was pulling away, the lightning-bolt flash of inspiration seared across the smoking crater that is my mind one more time.

LETTERS! YEAH, RIGHT!

So I turned away from the rooming house, cut across and through Dykstra Park and headed up the back way toward Pauley, and made a direct line to the athletic department and Coach Wooden's office. He would certainly not be there, having just dropped me off; assuredly he was on his way home to see his wife, Nell. Imagine what she had to say!

As I made my way to the second floor, the offices were all empty, since it was late in a very difficult UCLA day. But Coach's secretary was still there, closing things down for the night. I asked her sheepishly if she had any stationery, since Coach Wooden had talked to me about writing some letters. She nodded willingly and shuffled through some files before producing some of the finest and cleanest-looking UCLA/ John Wooden/NCAA Championship Basketball stationery you can possibly imagine.

I thanked her profusely, with a big smile, and she said quietly, "I hope everything is okay, Bill."

I assured her that all was well—even more so now.

So I headed back to my room, which was less than half a mile away, and started writing. I scripted a letter to Nixon on Coach's UCLA stationery. I outlined all of Nixon's crimes against humanity, then demanded an immediate end to the war and the return home of all our troops. Then I demanded his immediate resignation as our president, and I thanked him in advance for his cooperation.

And I signed it. And went to bed.

The next day at school, all the guys were there. The same way that they were all at the rallies the day before, and most every other day as well. But they had not been taken down. They were all very concerned. Bill, what did Coach say? What did he do? What's going to happen?

I told them everything was cool, that Coach had been very nice (I lied), and that he told me that instead of going to all these rallies and getting arrested and all, I should instead write letters. And I had written one.

They were all excited, and so I showed them my beautiful letter, on Coach's stationery. They got all fired up, and as they were reading this heartfelt manifesto of freedom and peace, they asked if they could sign it, too. And they did. In big, bold, brave script.

So I went to see Coach. Now he was nice and cordial, having calmed down from yesterday's intense and confrontational car ride home from jail. "Bill, it's good to see you. I hope that you got something positive out of our discussion yesterday."

With a big smile, I told him that I had, and that I had taken his advice and had, indeed, written a letter. And that I hoped he would sign it.

Puzzled, perplexed, he looked up at me and asked to take a look. When he saw that the letter was written on his stationery and addressed to Nixon, he stiffened. And while he held this masterpiece of literature in his worn, gnarled, bent fingers and hands, the blood started to drain, his extremities turning white, and his calm, poised demeanor changed to uncertainty and boiling rage. I could see and feel that he wanted to tear the thing to shreds.

When he finally got to the end, he took a very deep and long breath. He looked up at me with the sad, soft eyes of a father. A father who had been let down; in life, and everything else.

He looked at me and said, very quietly, "Bill, I cannot sign this letter. And you're not going to send this, are you?"

With a big, joyous grin I told him, "Coach, you told me to write letters! And I did. I always do exactly what you tell me!"

Slowly and sadly he handed me back the letter, in perfect condition.

I mailed it that day. And sure enough, Nixon resigned, although not soon enough, as the dead and broken bodies kept piling up.

———

Twenty-two years later, it's the spring of 1994, and I'm with Coach Wooden in Washington, DC, the city of hope, where all good things are possible, and some of them, by then, had actually come true. We were both there to be honored as the newest inductees into the Academic All-America Hall of Fame.

My relationship with Coach spanned forty-three years. It moved through three distinctly different stages: as a recruit in high school; as a player at UCLA; and then as his friend, until his death in 2010. The entire time, I was his student. He loved to teach. And he would often tell me that I would never learn what I didn't want to know.

So we were there at this very nice hotel, right next to the White House. It was over-the-top nice. I called Coach early, since we were both always up before the dawn. "Let's get out of the hotel and go do something fun before the day turns into work," I said.

I hired a big car, and we rolled through the center of town, past all the museums of the Smithsonian and all the great buildings where our civilized society takes care of things. It's so beautiful there.

I asked him what he wanted to do or see, but he didn't want the responsibility of the decision. I reminded him of his childhood friendship with Abe Lincoln, and that there was a place nearby where we could go say hello. He rolled his eyes.

We were now pulling up to the Lincoln Memorial, and despite the early hour there were already dozens of folks there. We got out of the car and made the long, hard climb up the steps, two old guys struggling to get to the top, not sure who was helping who more. When we got up there, it was a surreal moment of perfect weather, a glorious sunrise, with so much of our national cultural history there before us.

Immediately a crowd surrounded Coach, noisily wanting pictures and autographs. He quickly put an index finger to his lips, asking for quiet and respect, then held out both palms just in front of his chest, and whispered that this was sacred ground and not the right place for irreverent behavior.

The crowd settled down but still circled around him, me standing by his side.

Then, without prompting, Coach began softly reciting Lincoln's Gettysburg Address, from memory, even though the words are inscribed on the marble wall on the south side there.

"Four score and seven years ago . . ."

In this temple of so many emotions, not least hang sadness and disbelief over the hate, bigotry, selfishness, and greed that created a world gone mad before history's eyes.

"Now we are engaged in a great Civil War, testing whether that nation, or any nation so conceived and so dedicated, can long endure . . ."

As Coach continued, all the people surrounding him that morning were crying, tears rolling down their cheeks, and Coach soldiered on.

"We here highly resolve that these dead shall not have died in vain—that this nation, under God, shall have a new birth of freedom—and that government of the people, by the people, for the people shall not perish from the earth."

When he finished, a round of applause and cheers started to roll through the massive stone chamber, but Coach immediately shushed the people, and they properly complied.

It was time to go, Coach and I, arm in arm, limping down the steps with the Reflecting Pool, the Washington Monument, the Capitol, and everything else out in front of us. Now at the bottom, Coach took a step right, toward the car. I had my hand on the inside of his left elbow. I stopped him, and he turned his head back toward me. I looked straight into his eyes and his soul, those eyes that had seen and done so much, that soul that had felt it all.

He was puzzled; the car was just a few steps away.

"Hey, Coach," I said softly. "Just over here"—I pointed left—"is the Vietnam Memorial. And I'm wondering, Coach, if you would mind coming over there with me, because there are some people there, Coach, that I need to see."

He looked back at me sadly. Despite its place of honor and tribute, the Vietnam Memorial is as sad and depressing as it gets. He said, "Yes, let's go."

We pivoted and walked back north across the face of the Lincoln Memorial, through the small meadow, past the Three Soldiers statue, and then to the heart-wrenching, gray-and-black gabbro inverted V.

We worked our way down the expanse of stone, everyone there crying, many on crutches or in wheelchairs, flowers and pictures of shattered lives and dreams everywhere. Nobody spoke. But hands stretched out and touched the names—58,282 of them, with more still being added from time to time—on the Wall. The waste, the greed, the thievery, the cruelty, the lies—all so overwhelmingly senseless.

I prayed for my friends.

We stayed as long as we could. The only sounds were the birds, the wind, and the muffled, wet sobs of sadness and loss.

It was time to go. We nodded to each other and started the long, lonely climb up and out, knowing that we would most likely never be here together again.

As we started the climb, out of the darkness and silence, Coach slowly and quietly, in hushed tones, started reciting a poem from memory. It was one of his favorites, "Two Sides of War," by Grantland Rice.

All wars are planned by older men
In council rooms apart,
Who call for greater armament
And map the battle chart.

But out along the shattered field
Where golden dreams turn gray,
How very young the faces were
Where all the dead men lay.

Portly and solemn in their pride,
The elders cast their vote
For this or that, or something else,
That sounds the martial note.

But where their sightless eyes stare out
Beyond life's vanished toys,
I've noticed nearly all the dead
Were hardly more than boys.

We got to the top, and ultimately climbed out. The car took us back to the hotel and then on to the show.

Coach Wooden and I always had our disagreements. I would constantly test the boundaries, pushing back against everything from his haircut policy to his politics. But when it came down to it, we were aiming for the same things—just often from different angles.

For years and years, I tried to turn Coach on to the best of the finest things in life, and he was trying to do the same for me. For me, that always meant trying to pull him with us into the vortex of a Grateful Dead concert. Every time, he would kindly thank me and say that, no, he would not be coming. In return, he regularly offered to take me to an upcoming Lawrence Welk show that he and Nell would be attending. Sadly, I never took up his offer, either. We both missed out.

Today, as the sun has set on so many things, I have come to realize that many of Coach's students and players have fully become the proud, fierce, tenacious, determined warriors that he was trying to mold us into.

I'm not sure that he ever realized what a fine teacher he really was.

CHAPTER 8

New Morning

So happy just to see you smile,
Underneath this sky of blue,
On this new morning, with you.

Standing on a tower
World at my command
You just keep a-turning
While I'm playing in the band.

B ack to school. The freshness. The newness of it all. What
could be better? New classes, friends, teachers, teammates—
everything. And all at UCLA—the most applied-to school
in the country—where today more than 100,000 people per
year try to score one of the relatively few, coveted spots of entry.

Back just in the nick of time for the first day of classes in the fall
of 1972, I changed my major again. Disillusioned with the "science"
of politics, which by now was dropping to ridiculous levels of tragedy
and farce, what with Nixon and Reagan running the show, and inspired

by my summer hitchhiking and backpacking trip through the western United States and Canada, I was chasing the new dream of geography— the where, when, why, and who of it all.

I was also putting into full practice all the things I was learning along the winding road, particularly that it was not so much the subject but rather the teacher that made it all so interesting. And with so much brilliance available in the academic opportunities at UCLA, I was always ready for some high-altitude exploration and experimentation. And I found it all with the excitement and dizzying possibilities offered by the geography, history, music, and art departments.

It was all right there in front of us—another fun season of basketball, with a team that I knew was going to be even better than the one that finished 30-0 in '72, and now riding a 46-game winning streak.

—

The team was slightly different this year. We lost three key guys to graduation, although only one of them had actually played in the games. Henry Bibby moved on to the NBA and the Knicks, where he became the second of just a handful of players in history to win an NCAA Championship and an NBA title in consecutive years. Jon Chapman went on to play productively for a number of solid years in Germany before coming home to become an educator, helping countless youngsters chase their dreams and build their lives. And Andy Hill, completely frustrated with the way it had all played out for him on the UCLA basketball team, started an incredibly electric odyssey that included many tickets to ride, leading eventually to a fabulous business career in the entertainment industry. Sitting on the bench at UCLA, Andy had taken enough of the madness, and this was the beginning of what would turn out to be a twenty-five-year estrangement from Coach Wooden that Andy has chronicled in his own masterpiece of reconciliation, *Be Quick, but Don't Hurry,* a fabled story built around the wonderful parable that forgiveness will set you free.

Larry Hollyfield finally got his chance to start and play regularly, taking Henry's spot on the left wing, joining the holdovers Greg, Jamaal,

Larry Farmer, and me. Swen was already a lot better, and giving me all I could handle every day in practice. Tommy Curtis was still there, though playing way too selfishly, and now inexplicably with more playing time. And we had two newcomers, Dave Meyers and Pete Trgovich, who were very good—particularly Dave, who would eventually become a first team All-America himself. It was not enough to simply say that any one of us ever became a champion—we all did that, together.

The routine of life as a UCLA basketball player was better than perfect on all fronts. Class all day, practice every afternoon, the fun and excitement of being a college student in Los Angeles. And the practices and the team just kept getting better. We understood so much more now. The lessons of life that Coach Wooden kept repetitively driving home were starting to take hold, particularly after a summer off to think about it all. And, most important, we were able to keep playing ever faster, as we began to master some of the fundamentals to the point where Coach would say, "Okay, that's starting to become acceptable. Now let's see you do it again. But FASTER this time."

Every day, we would try with everything we had to get Coach to acknowledge our success and progress on the court. No matter how well we did, about the best we could ever get out of him was maybe a twinkle or a gleam in his eye. If we did something really, really well, he might turn the corner of his lip upward in the slightest of smiles.

Finally opening day came, and we were in the locker room getting ready with our push-ups and horseplay when Coach calmly walked in and gathered us around, just like he had a year earlier. Once again we sat there, enthusiastically and attentively, on our stools as he started his regular pregame speech about how it was now up to us, but then he seemed to lose focus as his eyes scanned the room. All of a sudden, he broke his train of thought and strode directly over to the same side wall of the room and bent over, coming up—beaming, glowing, ecstatic—with a penny between his thumb and index finger. "Men, look at this. Someone has lost a penny. Now this is a good omen for us. This signifies good luck. And hopefully this will mean we'll have another good season."

Then he bent down and slid this lucky penny into the slot in one of his penny loafers. Now those of us who'd seen this before all rolled our eyes. I can't speak for the new guys, who were still enthralled with just being there. But we could only hope that this was at least a different penny, and that he was filling the slot in the opposite shoe this time— who could remember? But we'd won a championship and were on track for another. So who could doubt the value of the lost but now found lucky penny?

We started our season strong and were rolling when, one day in December, Coach shockingly wasn't there. He had suffered a heart attack, and missed a game—his first miss in thirty-eight years of teaching—and a couple of weeks of practice. Coach Wooden was a lot of things, not the least of which was tough. He never said anything about the heart trouble, tried to keep it quiet, never whined, complained, or made excuses. He just came to get the job done—every day.

We didn't really pay too much attention to this developing saga. We were so young, naïve, and supremely confident in our own invincibility. And Coach was so old. Looking back later, we should have noticed the rapid deterioration of his health that was taking place right in front of us.

When we had arrived at UCLA three years earlier, Coach, at sixty-one, was still spry, vibrant, and dynamic, with a real spring and bounce to his step. And he went from this dashing, upright, statuesque force du jour to someone who was now stooped, pale, hesitant, gaunt, and outwardly broken. Over the years, we have all learned ourselves to never discount the effects of stress on one's health. But I can see how I wore him down and out.

But the wins kept piling up and the magical mystery tour kept rolling on, including a really fun trip to New Orleans for a holiday tournament—and much more. But as we headed into the conference season after the holidays, it was clear that things were changing, that the other teams were no longer trying to beat us by playing basketball.

Our game was speed, quickness, pressing defense, the fast break, and explosive offensive runs. The other teams clearly had no chance by playing that way, so they mucked it up, roughed us up, and slowed the pace of the games to a crawl, often holding the ball at midcourt for agonizing minutes at a time without even coming near the basket. After we graduated the NCAA instituted the shot clock to try to keep the games moving. At the time, Coach put in some new half-court defensive traps, a 3-1-1 zone—extended to the half-court line—that literally dared the other team to come to the basket and play. The scores were declining—we only topped 100 points once all season, and our average winning margin dropped by 9 points per game from last year, all the way down to 21.

And the games continued to get a lot rougher as the other teams would try to disrupt our flow. We were not a physically powerful team, with the exception of Swen (who rarely played) and Larry Hollyfield. Our game was speed, and skill.

When Coach made it back from his heart attack, it was time for our yearly trip to the state of Oregon for the start of the always critical conference games. Our game in Eugene got completely out of control. A year earlier, when we were sophomores, the Ducks had hired a new coach, Dick Harter, who had been very successful at Penn in the Ivy League. Determined to challenge UCLA's supremacy, Coach Harter brought to Oregon a rough-and-tumble style that led their fans and media to proudly nickname the team the Kamikaze Kids. It did seem that death was their mission.

The locker rooms at the old McArthur Court were downstairs, and while we would wait patiently for the game to start, the Duck players would gather around outside our locker room, where Coach Harter installed their team's training equipment. Harter liked his Kamikazes to work themselves up into a raging frenzy before a game, and they did so by twisting and flexing on the machines, all the while grunting and growling—right outside our door.

When everybody finally got up to the court for the game, things only got stranger. Now, the Oregon crowd in Eugene is one to behold. Bear in mind that every game we played in, from high school all the way through UCLA, was sold out. Ultimately the same would be true in Portland and Boston. We were used to playing before big, loud, and wild crowds, where anything goes, and usually did. But on the collegiate level, the only road crowd that came close in ferocity to Oregon's was Notre Dame's, and that was at least partly because, until 1972, the Irish student body was savagely all male.

During warm-ups on Mac Court the home fans would go absolutely crazy, to the point that the overhead scoreboard would bounce up and down to their rhythmic roars. Still in the pregame, the Kamikaze Kids would line up across the midcourt line at perfect attention, facing us like statues, staring us down in a show of intended intimidation that was comical, if not so scary, in its weirdness. While we warmed up, and as this madness went on, Swen would walk right up and down the line of these petrified posers, who would not even blink as he nosed up as close as humanly possible without making contact. But they would never even flinch. Although if they ever had to play against Swen— seven feet tall, 275 pounds, and cut from stone—they surely would have. The whole thing was frightfully hilarious. I think Swen tried to kiss a couple of them. It seemed appropriate that they called themselves Kamikazes.

Once the game started and we went about our business—on our way to yet another rout—the inevitable gloom of impending defeat and failure consumed the Ducks and their remarkable crowd. On one play, I got out in front on a transition opportunity and was knocked to the floor and sent sprawling into the front row of fans who, at Mac Court, are literally on the court and in the game—by design. As I tried to scramble back up and rejoin the game—no foul was called—some of the fans held me down so I couldn't get up. As the game continued at the other end, one guy from down the row, maybe a dozen feet away or so, came along the baseline to where I was struggling to get up and back on defense, wound up his leg, and kicked me in the lower back. Then he walked back to his supposed seat, all to the roar of the crowd. They showed the replay several times on TV during the rest of the game. It turned out that the guy worked for the Oregon Athletic Department— at least that day. They fired him shortly thereafter. We won the game handily.

Swen was becoming more and more important to the team in every way as he continued to blossom. With growing confidence, he started to speak up more, and he loved to tell jokes. They were not particularly good jokes, but we all liked Swen, and so every day in practice, as we were transitioning from one drill to another, Swen would stop us with the pronouncement that he had a new joke. We would all look at Coach—he was in charge of everything—and Coach would sheepishly, reluctantly, and begrudgingly acquiesce. And Swen would start and ultimately deliver his clearly well-rehearsed moment onstage. We would laugh politely, some would roll their eyes, and Coach would put his head down, smile a bit in an unseen way, and then mutter something about getting back to it. It became a daily ritual, and we all took pleasure in seeing Swen have so much fun as the center of our world.

In our game that year against Washington State at Bohler Gym in Pullman, Swen was finally in for some minutes at the very end of another rout. Swen was always ready but he rarely got to play, so whenever he did get in, regardless of the situation, he was determined to go for it all. In the closing minutes at WSU, he was lined up on the lane as a potential offensive rebounder for a one-and-one free-throw opportunity by one of our teammates. Swen was matched up with the Cougars' big man, whom he essentially dwarfed. As our guy was shooting his first attempt, Swen and his man started jostling for inside and superior position in case of a miss. With elbows, hips, shoulders, arms, and hands flailing from both of them, the first shot rolled in, earning the shooter a second shot.

Swen and his guy disengaged, and the short, round ref stepped in to break it all up. Swen started talking to the ref about how the other guy was fouling him, committing crimes against humanity and the like. The ref wanted no part of Swen. All he wanted was to get this blowout over with. So he lined everybody back up for the second free throw, and as our guy got ready to shoot, the elbowing, leaning, and contact all started anew. The free throw swished, but the guy from WSU foolishly persisted in antagonizing Swen. As the ball dropped through the net, Swen just unloaded on the poor guy, leveling him and leaving him sprawled facedown on the court, Swen standing over him with a look of angelic innocence on his gentle face. The ref had had enough. He came running in and laid a technical foul on Swen, as everybody rushed in to see what was going down. Swen, realizing that the ref was blaming him for all this, now turned into a raging bull and went after the ref, grabbing and shaking him like a little rag doll, and pointing back at his fallen opponent, who was groggily starting to climb back up onto his knees. Everyone was stunned as Swen continued violently shaking the ref, all the while pointing at the other guy. We thought Swen was going to kill the poor ref, deservedly or not. Coach Wooden was mortified. He actually got up from his seat and started barking at me, "BILL, GET BACK IN THERE! GET SWEN OUT OF THERE! GOODNESS GRACIOUS SAKES ALIVE!"

Swen, what are you doing? You can't beat up the ref!

Eventually, peace was restored, Swen calmed down, and it was all over soon enough.

There was note made of our continued winning ways, particularly as we passed Bill Russell and USF's NCAA record of 60 consecutive victories with another rout of Notre Dame in South Bend. That game was most noteworthy for the time Coach Wooden got up from his seat and walked up the sideline toward Notre Dame's bench. The score was already out of hand, but now the game was getting excessively violent, and some of the Notre Dame players were taking extreme liberties with their home-court advantage and the refs.

Coach had seen enough as he approached the devil himself—their coach, Digger Phelps—and told him, "Look, if you don't call off your guys, and if they don't get back to playing basketball instead of all this ridiculous fouling and trying to hurt our players, then I'm going to put Swen in the game, with instructions to personally restore order."

Coach went back and sat down, and things cooled down to the point where we could finish the whole thing.

Larry Hollyfield—we called him Holly—was also turning out great for us, although his left-handed game was different than Henry Bibby's. Holly was a big-time player who loved the light and loved to shoot.

And could he ever! Holly played on the same, left side of the court as me, so he regularly got the ball from Greg. But much as he didn't like it, Holly was well aware of Coach's direction that when we didn't have a fast break, the ball ALWAYS had to go to Jamaal or me. It was certainly frustrating for Holly. But now our fast break had become less effective because our opponents would regularly concede their offensive board to our defense, choosing instead to retreat quickly en masse to try to minimize their losses. They would invariably pack in their defense to try to slow Jamaal and me down in the paint. It was a strategy that opened up all sorts of opportunity for Holly, especially this season. He loved to score, and he was amazing at it when given the chance.

We continued to roll up victories, and more was made of the record-setting streak that was now ours. We paid no mind to any of it. We had not played anybody yet who was better than we were, and so it was just the natural course of events for us to keep on winning. Which we did.

—

We finished the regular season unchallenged and unbeaten, and now we were on to the NCAA tournament once again, this time with the Western Regionals held at Pauley. Arizona State was our first opponent, and they tried to play their game—a fast, running style that was also our game—on our own court. They didn't have a chance, and we moved on easily to play USF, Bill Russell's school, which had taken care of Long Beach State in the other semifinal. Long Beach still had Tark, but they had lost Ed Ratleff to graduation, and that was an insurmountable loss. USF had some nice players, just not enough of them. Phil Smith was a rising and true star, and Kevin Restani had some solid attributes. But we had a whole team. And we had Coach Wooden.

Sadly, the Dons slowed the game to a snoring crawl, and we scored only 54 points in the entire game. And not because it was a terrific defensive struggle. Although we still won handily, it's a wonder that anybody was even able to stay awake, what with the methodical nature of playing not to win but rather to lose by less.

We were now off to the Final Four in St. Louis, where our first opponent was Indiana, whose young head coach seemed to spend most of his time yelling, cursing, screaming, and drawing attention to himself. The newspapers said his name was Bobby Knight. Coach Wooden never said a word about him, or anything else to do with his—or any other—team. Even with Coach's deep roots in his home state. Even with the decision he made years earlier to pass on an opportunity to play at Indiana, which was much closer to his home in Martinsville, as he headed off to Purdue. Even though the whole thing had to have been extremely personal for him.

Our team stayed in a typically awful motel in St. Louis, right on the expressway, with terrible rooms and food, furniture built for preschool children, and everything else simply miserable. When you go to college at UCLA, it's not like the road trips are exotic jaunts where you get out and see the best the world has to offer. The fun was the team, and the ultimate challenge was to play well and win big on the road.

This was also the first year that the NCAA played its championship game on a Monday night. The Final Four had always been staged with two semifinals on Thursday night and the third-place game and the final on Saturday afternoon. But with the recent success of the NFL's *Monday Night Football*, the wheels were turning and the cash registers churning, and everything was changing—fast. UCLA was by now a huge national draw, having won seven straight NCAA championships, and nine of the last ten. The Monday-night final would be a ratings bonanza for NBC.

Indiana had some nice players and played an entertaining team game with an assertive offensive style, but they clearly didn't have the talent to give us any real trouble. The game saw both teams go on major scoring runs, ours coming first and making it look like we were putting the game away early on, only to have the Hoosiers come back with a faux run at us late. But there was no substance to their charge, other than to wake us up on our way to another run for the roses.

After the game, as we were walking off the court at the majestic and historic Checkerdome, our athletic director, J. D. Morgan, who often sat on the bench next to Coach Wooden during the games—just to make sure everything turned out right—fell into lockstep with me as we made our way to the locker room. He asked me if everything was okay, indicating that things didn't seem right with my contribution and performance that night.

I told J. D. that I was having trouble sleeping at our motel, that my room was right on the expressway and the trucks rolling by kept me up all night, and that I could not fit in my bed, nor could I stand up in my room.

He didn't say anything—at first.

Later, as we were leaving the arena, he came up to me and said that he had a very nice room with a very nice big bed at a very nice hotel in which he was staying in downtown St. Louis, and that he wanted me to take his room so that I could maximize my chances of helping the team do its job. I readily agreed to the switch, and it didn't take me long to gather my few things from the motel and head over to the much nicer place where J. D. was staying. I didn't tell anybody, and I can't say that J. D. did, either. The upgrade was vastly superior, in every way.

So now it's Sunday night, and I'm in my new room and in bed early, what with the big game and everything the next night. As I'm sound asleep, and it's really late, I'm jarred awake by the sounds of somebody at my door, trying to get in. I always lock my hotel room doors as tightly, securely, and as many times as possible. But this attempted intrusion was persistent, and seemingly not going away. Finally it all stops, and I try to go back to sleep, but I'm pretty awake now, and maybe a bit concerned—it's the middle of the night.

A few minutes later the phone rings, and I pick it up.

There's nobody on the other end of the line, and now I'm worried, maybe even scared, but the door is triple-locked—at least.

Five minutes or so later, there's a very loud rap on the door, with the snap command, "ST. LOUIS POLICE. OPEN THE DOOR . . . NOW!"

I climb out of bed, throw on a pair of shorts, and peek out. Indeed, there is a squad of uniformed and armed St. Louis policemen outside the door and down the hall. This is not going well.

There were some other people out in the hall as well. Turns out that when the hotel folks saw J. D. leaving his room to give it to me, they thought he was checking out. So they sold it to somebody else, and the guy was just getting in for the night, very late, and he thought the room was now his.

When I explained what was going on, the police put their guns down. But now I had no room, as the guy was insistent that it was his. What could I say or do? The police and the hotel people asked me to leave. So I quickly gathered up my stuff, and soon found myself standing alone in the hotel lobby at three o'clock in the morning or so. And there are all these NCAA people, coaches, and fans just getting in themselves. And they're all looking at me, standing there all by myself with my things at my feet, and the championship game countdown now under way, and they have the most puzzled and confused look on their faces. What's he doing here? At this hour? All by himself? With all his stuff? Standing in the hotel lobby? There's the game tonight!

Lost, alone, and up against it, I called J. D. He was livid, but remained calm. He told me not to do or say anything, but to go and wait in a corner of the lobby. A scant few minutes later, as the parade of coaches, officials, and fans kept rolling in and looking at me with amazement, some little guy from the hotel came up to me with the most terrified look on his face. He had just spoken to J. D., and I can only imagine how that conversation went. Anyway, the guy said that he was really sorry about what was going down here, but what with the championship game going on, all the hotels were sold out; but they did have one room left that he would let me stay in.

All I wanted was to go to bed. We had a game, it was getting closer and closer, and the Count was on.

So I grab my stuff and follow this guy, who waddles over to some special and isolated elevator. He looks awful, I'm dead tired, and I need to get some sleep. The whole thing is a disaster. He pulls out a special key, and up and away we go.

He soon delivers me to the nicest, and biggest, hotel suite I had ever seen. And playing for UCLA, we saw a lot of very nice things.

I told the guy, who was incredibly apologetic, that this would be fine, that I would be able to make do with this, as my biggest problems were all immediately solved. I had a nice place to sleep, and we now had a better than perfect place for our upcoming championship postgame team party. YEAH! Here we go!

I slept most of the rest of the day and then met the team at the Checkerdome. The guys were relieved; they hadn't seen much of me and didn't know where I was. But they were happy to learn that I had already found the spot for the postgame party.

We played Memphis State that night, who had been able to beat Providence in their Saturday semifinal, a game that turned when the Friars' Marvin Barnes hurt his leg and couldn't continue. Memphis had some real players: Larry Kenon, Larry Finch, Ronnie Robinson, and Bill Laurie. Their coach, Gene Bartow, seemed very dignified and calm, the complete opposite of the madness that we saw on the Indiana sideline during our Saturday game.

The game went back and forth early, very much an up-and-down affair that everybody was enjoying immensely. The Memphis State defensive strategy was one we had not seen before. Coach Bartow had correctly decided that Greg Lee was the key to our team, and his game plan was to shut Greg down. So their defense tried everything they could to deny his passing lanes and vision. They were wholly unsuccessful.

Years later, when Jamaal was on the Lakers and they acquired a certain new player, everybody was all excited about how talented and transformative this young Magic Johnson would be for the NBA. The media kept raving about what a great passer and creative playmaker Magic was—which was, and is, true. All the Laker players were constantly pestered into finding new ways to say how great Magic was, all the time. One day they pressed the always superquiet and reserved Wilkes: "OK, Jamaal, what's it like to play with a guy who can pass the ball the way Magic does? We've never seen anything like it."

Jamaal, in his inimitable and low-key style, simply shrugged and said, "Hey, I played with Greg Lee!" And he walked off.

That was Greg, and he was why our team was so good. He made

it all work, fluidly, selflessly, and effortlessly. When you play against a top passer, the worst thing you can do defensively is try to double-team the ball. That just leaves the scorers wide open. But that's what Memphis State did. They tried to close down Greg, and that just fed to our strengths. And our most basic strength was to take what the defense gave us.

And so the game went on, at a very high level of offensive efficiency for both teams. It was tied at the half, but I had three fouls already, as my guy Kenon, the self-proclaimed Dr. K, was on a roll. As the second half started, I drew my fourth foul, and figured that it was time to stop playing defense entirely, to make sure that I stayed in this really fun championship game.

Greg stayed perfect with his delivery, outsmarting the Memphis defenders every time, and Larry Hollyfield was in a complete passing zone as well, as all the defensive pressure on the perimeter kept allowing Jamaal and me wide-open opportunities wherever we wanted them.

We kept running the same options, and the Tigers stayed—inexplicably—with their strategy. We never let up, and Memphis State ran out of whatever they had. During one of the time-outs midway through the second half, when we were scoring literally every time down the court by doing exactly the same thing every time—either Greg or Holly throwing it in to me for easy baskets—and pulling away on the scoreboard, Greg asked Coach Wooden if we could please do something else for a while. I think Greg was getting bored with how easy it all was. Coach just looked at him quizzically and asked, "Why?" Then he sent us back out for more of the same.

We never looked back or slowed down, ultimately winning by 21 points. When they totaled up what Greg and Holly had been able to do, the record books had been rewritten, with 23 assists between them. Greg had an NCAA Championship game record 14 assists, and Holly had a career-high 9. When Larry Hollyfield gets nine assists in a game, you know it is a historic day. They would have had more, but the refs called me for dunking four times, when all I did was what I always did around the rim. I would simply lay the ball in the basket, always underhanded.

But the refs ruled that my hands were inside the cylinder, and therefore those four baskets were disallowed.

In the postgame comments, with a lot of the focus on my numbers, which were big and record-setting, Coach Wooden was quick to point out to me—as he did up until the day he died—that, "Walton, I used to think that you were a good player . . . until you missed that one shot."

Anyway, we won, and we were on our way to what was next—which for us was the postgame party at my very nice, incredibly spacious hotel room. I had told the cheerleaders. They were already on their way.

As we were getting dressed in the locker room, Coach came up to me and said that there were some people who wanted to see me. He said they were from the American Basketball Association (ABA) and wanted to talk to me about joining their professional league. I wanted no part of any of it. I told him, "Come on, Coach. I love UCLA. I still have a year left here. I love playing for you, and with these guys. I don't want to do this. We just won the championship. I want to be with the guys. Come on, Coach. Please, don't ask me to do this."

But he was adamant and said, "Bill, you owe them the courtesy of a meeting."

Darn it!

Finally, and very reluctantly, I said, "OK. Have them meet me at my hotel room." And I wrote down the name, address, phone, and room number of the suite. I knew them by heart now, as I had already given them to the cheerleaders and the guys on our team. He seemed shocked when he saw that I had not written down anything pertaining to the team's motel. J. D. must not have told him. I certainly hadn't.

So I get up to the room first, and as I'm getting things in order, there's a knock on the door. A few guys, all dressed up in their suits and ties, come into this massive luxury suite, looking around the palace in awe. They're carrying packages, briefcases, and suitcases, apparently on the move. After some brief introductions, they laid out their pitch, explaining that they wanted me to skip my senior year at UCLA and come join the ABA. They said they were prepared to do whatever it took to get the deal done. And that included giving me ownership of my own franchise, which would be located in L.A.; they would get Jerry West to be the coach or general manager, or both; and I could personally select any other players from the ABA to fill out our roster—with the exception of Dr. J, who they said they needed to keep in New York to maintain competitive balance and keep the whole thing interesting. Then they opened up the suitcases, which were filled with cash, and said that all this would be mine, and that there was plenty more of it to be had. Money, they said, was not going to be a problem in getting this deal done.

I looked across at them and shook my head. I thanked them for their kindness, generosity, and vision. Then I asked them to just look around at what I had here. As their eyes roamed the expansive and luxurious hotel suite, with a wave of my hand I said to them, "Look at how great things are for me here at UCLA, and how wonderfully we're treated. How can you guys possibly make my life any better?"

They might have tried to argue, but I made it clear there was no way that they were going to get me to change my mind.

I never gave any of it a first thought.

I played for UCLA and Coach Wooden. And J. D. was always there to make things right. What more could you ask for in life?

If only I could have stayed forever.

As the suits were leaving, taking everything that they had brought in with them, the guys on the team, and the cheerleaders, too, were on their way in. Everybody really liked my room. I can't say how many of them left before dawn, but we did all make the flight home.

—

Back at school, the business guys would not let it go. I wanted to play ball and go to school. With the season over, I had a lot of catching up to do on all fronts. But I could not get away from all the guys who were certain that I was ready to bolt Westwood for the pros—the NBA as well as the ABA. Strangers would wait in Dykstra Park or on Bruin Walk, or sometimes in the classrooms. I don't know how they found me.

I didn't have a phone, and I spent most of my time—when I wasn't in the library or in church—moving around on my bike. But find me they would, and they'd eventually fall in beside me and start it all up. Bill, you won't believe the great deal I've got for you . . . !

Sometimes I said "No" too easily, like the time I vetoed a whole basketball tour and cultural exchange trip to China with the UCLA team. J. D. was setting it all up and held a meeting in his office where he explained what a historic opportunity it was, since China had been closed to most of the world for a very long time. Just two years earlier, a team of Ping-Pong players had been the first Americans to set foot in China since 1949. Nixon went there in 1972. And now it was going to be our turn.

Except midway through the meeting where J. D. was laying it all out, I raised my hand and said I didn't want to go. A lot of people immediately got very disappointed and very mad, but somehow that was it for the trip. Nobody tried very hard to change my mind, and in retrospect I wish Coach, J. D., Ernie Vandeweghe, or somebody had pulled me aside and told me I was crazy. Years later, Coach would just shake his head if the topic ever came up.

I was a twenty-year-old college student fleeing from everyone who was trying to make me into anything other than a twenty-year-old college student. So instead of China that summer, I did what I always did: I got another summer job, quit as soon as I had enough money, then took off on a trip.

Coach Wooden always preached the importance of taking time off from the game during the summer so that the body, mind, spirit, and soul could rejuvenate. The previous summer I had meandered through the West and up into and across Canada. This summer I decided to head up to Canada again—except this time on my bike, all by myself.

I scored some gear from some friends and set out, knowing that it was a long way, and that time was short. I had never done anything like it before, and just three days in, I knew it was not going to work. The things that I love about my bike are the same things I love about playing basketball—speed, maneuverability, quickness, freedom, adventure, lightness afoot, figuring it out, chasing it down and all. But here I was loaded down with so much gear tied to my bike, carrying everything I'd need for my plan to camp out for several months along the winding road.

So at the end of this three-day line, I made some collect calls from the pay phones out there. I was rescued by some friends and switched to a new plan to spend the rest of the summer going to school at Sonoma State College in Northern California. Some of my friends from high school, Jim and Laurie, were already living there full-time, and they had a nice little scene, which seemed ideal for me to slide right into. I could stay with them, go to school from 9 a.m. till noon, then come home for a quick lunch before heading out on my bike until nightfall— every day.

I had an all-around grand time, riding my bike everywhere. One day after school I was riding down the country road to our little house when I began to feel a painful sensation down the front of my right leg. Looking down, I saw this big nasty bee relentlessly pumping his venom into my leg. Thinking nothing of it, and without breaking the power train home, I reached down and flicked the bee off me, which took some force, as it was quite dug in and well attached. The trip from school to Jim and Laurie's place was no more than a few miles, so I was home quickly. I wheeled right into the house, where nothing was going on; we all had different schedules.

But once I stopped riding and caught my breath, I immediately realized that something was wrong—terribly wrong. All of a sudden, my whole body—everywhere—felt like it was on fire. I was pouring out sweat from every pore. My vision was blurring, fogging over. My mouth was foaming, my nose and eyes running. I was losing the ability to breathe, as my throat and tongue were rapidly swelling. And it was all getting worse—fast.

I went frantically from room to room in the house. I found Jim, sound asleep, in his completely darkened room. He was working the night shift at the local Petaluma Creamery—in the butter room—and this was his sleep cycle, the middle of the day. I walked right in and called out, "Jim, something's wrong here. I got stung by a bee. On my bike. On my way home from school. And something is really wrong here."

I turned to leave, scratching everywhere uncontrollably, unable to see or breathe, and boiling over with scalding heat. And then I fell over, passed out, collapsing facedown on the floor, unconscious. I was very fortunate that Jim woke up and got out of bed.

The next thing I knew, I was lying on a stretcher in the back of an ambulance with a doctor pulling a huge hypodermic needle out of my arm. Jim had quickly called somebody; the ambulance had come and was taking me to the hospital, which was way up the road in Santa Rosa. I was still unconscious. The ambulance crew knew I was in real trouble and that I probably wouldn't make it all the way to the hospital. They radioed for help, and were instructed to go straight to the office of a local doctor, who would be waiting on the street for me. As the ambulance screeched to a stop, the doctor threw open the door and stabbed me with the giant needle full of epinephrine and started forcing Benadryl tablets down my throat, hoping to reverse the deadly anaphylactic shock caused by the bee sting. The doctor jumped into the back of the ambulance with me and yelled at the driver to get going to the hospital. We finally made it there, and they gave me all the medicine that I needed. When the doctors were satisfied that I was stable, Jim and Laurie came and took me home.

I was able to get back to things pretty quickly, though I'll never forget what Jim and Laurie did to save my life. And I've never gone anywhere since without my EpiPens and Benadryl.

I soon set myself back into a wonderful summertime rhythm of school and biking, usually close to a hundred miles a day after school got out. I was out there enjoying the ride, rolling on forever, with lots of very serious smiling along the long, hard climbs. I got to explore every corner of Sonoma and Marin Counties, and it provided just the kind of rejuvenation that Coach recommended.

I stayed as long as I could. And then it was time for one final go-round at UCLA, where all we had to do was keep the train on the tracks.

CHAPTER 9

The Great Unraveling

UCLA 1974

When life looks like easy street, there's danger at your door.

Nothing's for certain, it could always go wrong.

S uccess is really hard.
    Duplicating it, replicating it, sustaining it are all the things of which the greatest champions are made.
    It is generally easy to determine what is wrong with something.
    Identifying what makes things right or work is often extremely elusive.

—

As our senior season began, we were ready.

I was in top shape and form, having been on a bike-riding and academic tear for the entire summer. Greg had been playing beach volleyball at a championship and Hall of Fame level and was in fantastic condition, and Jamaal was always ready—for EVERYTHING. We had not lost at anything since we started at UCLA three years before. And things just kept getting better.

The team had a distinctly different makeup to it now, as we had lost two starting wing players, the Larrys—Hollyfield and Farmer—and Swen, who in retrospect turned out to be much more valuable than any of us ever dreamed—all to graduation, or at least to the loss of their eligibility.

Over the previous two seasons, that now made five guys who were critical components, when you count Henry Bibby and Andy Hill, who had all matriculated on to varying professional careers.

But with new talent and maturing returning stars, we were loaded. We had it all.

Dave Meyers would now get to play all the time, which was always a good thing. Andre McCarter and Pete Trgovich were explosive perimeter players, salivating at the chance to finally strut. Freshmen Marques Johnson and Richard Washington were dynamic gems who gave us an entirely new dimension. And Ralph Drollinger took over for Swen.

This was by far our most talented team in the four years that I played for UCLA.

Sadly, we still had Tommy Curtis on the roster. Tommy was the antithesis of everything that I knew and loved about basketball and UCLA. He was a self-centered, overdribbling, statistically oriented, loudmouthed, foul-mouthed fool. He was a shoot-first gunner with an individual agenda that revolved around nonsense. He had none of the values, goals, or ideals that defined who we were as a team, what we stood for, or what we were trying to do. If only he had not redshirted. Who knows how the fate of the known world would have evolved.

—

School, academics, and our social life could not have been better. Ever so close to graduating early, I now took only classes and professors of great interest. The concerts and special events continued unabated, and I was into everything, with rarely a free nanosecond, constantly bouncing from one thing to the next.

One of those things was my introduction through friends to meditation. A bunch of us got very into it, and Coach Wooden was hospitably accommodating in letting us use his office for the quiet time and space that we needed, usually right after practice, on our way to the training table at the Student Union.

When we officially got going with the team, with the usual birthday party for Coach on October 14 and media day, we were all so very excited, dizzy with the possibilities of the pending perfection and the chance to run the table.

Dave Meyers was terrific in all that he did, and I loved his passion, enthusiasm, and challenging intensity. Dave was superfun to play with, and ultimately against, down the road in the NBA, until his back failed him way too early in life. He has since gone on to an extremely productive, albeit quiet, career and life in education, social policy, and missionary work.

Marques Johnson was also destined for greatness. We had known of him forever, as one of Wooden's recruits since he was in the eighth grade. And now we were getting to see firsthand the gleaming talent that Coach Wooden had been beaming about for years.

On the first day of practice, Coach told me that my hair was too long and that I hadn't shaved that day. Despite all of our protestations, he basically threw me out of practice before it even started. He was quick into his "I'm the coach here. And while we've enjoyed having you . . ." routine. I knew I had lost again, and I immediately raced on my bike into Westwood, shaved, and got a haircut—missing the first three minutes of the opening practice.

In the early days of practice, while we were settling into our routine of five days a week on, then the weekend off to rest and regroup, I was out on the court early warming up by myself when I noticed Coach walking with a mission across the court. Now, Coach was always fierce, but on this day he seemed more determined than usual as he made a straight line for Greg, who was also warming up alone, but in the far corner from where I was.

As I went about my business, I could not help but notice their animated conversation, which seemed unusually contentious, more than a simple how are things going, and how are you going to get the ball to Bill and Jamaal today.

That conversation with Greg ended rather abruptly and seemingly not well. Coach then made his way directly to me in the far and opposite corner of Pauley.

When he got to me, he started right in. "Bill, it has come to my attention that you have been smoking marijuana."

Caught completely off guard, and totally surprised, I did everything I could to keep a straight face. In as composed, serious, and sincere a tone and manner as I could muster under the circumstances, I solemnly replied, "Coach, I have no idea what you're talking about."

He took a deep breath and said, "Good."

Then he turned on his heel and went back to getting practice started—right away.

—

A bit later, in our first quiet moment together, I asked Greg what he and Coach had been talking about before practice.

Greg indicated a similar line of questioning as I had experienced.

Whatever Greg's answers to Coach were that day, things were never the same again.

For any of us—none more so than Greg.

If only . . .

Almost immediately our regular lineup, rotation, and style changed.

Greg's selflessness and remarkable ability to deliver the ball flawlessly in the most efficient offense in the history of the sport would no longer be the key ingredient to our unbeatable success.

In his place we found Tommy Curtis.

When you look at all that has gone wrong in basketball today, with little punk guards dribbling incessantly, aimlessly, and without purpose other than to draw attention to themselves and promote some ridiculous individual culture of idiocy, selfishness, and greed, and where the most beautiful game in the world grinds to a halt while nine guys watch and wait for one guy who is dribbling for no reason other than to show off, then you have witnessed the madness and all-consuming disease of conceit that defined Tommy Curtis.

—

And try as we did, with everything that we had, this could not be overcome.

We had Jamaal Wilkes, Dave Meyers, Marques Johnson, Richard Washington, Ralph Drollinger, and me up front. All good players. Jamaal is a Hall of Famer and one of four players in history to have won multiple NCAA and NBA championships. He was also described by Coach Wooden eleven years after he graduated as Coach's vision and version of the perfect player and person. Dave and Marques were both the best NCAA players over the next few years and would be in the Hall of Fame themselves if they had stayed healthy in the NBA and had had better teammates there. And Richard was incredibly talented in his own right. Ralph was 7'2" and could play.

But now with Tommy Curtis, none of us could ever get the ball when and where we needed it, if we could get it at all.

I would be in Coach's office constantly—begging, pleading, trying to explain why Tommy Curtis was not right for our team, our style, our psyche, our game, our life, our fun.

But there was no satisfaction, no getting around it all.

The team became incredibly inconsistent. We were all so used to getting the ball in perfect rhythm, at the instant we were open. And now we found ourselves waiting, waiting, waiting—endlessly, while Curtis kept dribbling for no apparent good reason.

—

We started that year with Arkansas. As we gathered one last time for the opener, Coach was well into his pregame routine, which, like most

everything else by this time, we had committed to memory, if not practice. So when he started in with "I've done my job, the rest is up to you,"
and all the other stuff that we had heard so many times before, we were
just anxious to get going.

As was the now realized custom on opening night, Coach started
down the path leading to his "discovery" of the lost lucky penny.

Now, while I readily admit to being a very slow learner, by this
point, there were some things that I had figured out.

Anticipation is always key in life, so while drifting and dreaming
how this was all going to play out, when the assistant came in to make
sure that everything was in perfect order before bringing the Coach in, I
noticed him wandering over to where Coach usually "found" the lucky
penny.

Seeing him drop the penny and then quickly move toward bringing
the Coach in, I stealthily pounced on the coin while nobody was looking and put it in my pocket, then returned to my stool, dutifully waiting
for the Coach.

So, Coach is now well into his speech, telling us how to have a good
season, it all starts with a strong opening performance. We are all nodding enthusiastically as he heads inexorably toward "finding" the "lost"
penny.

As the speaker, he knows where he's going. As the audience who's
been there before—so do we. As he's building toward his "discovery" he
keeps looking over to where the "lost" penny is supposed to be, but it is
clearly not there, and he knows it.

And he finds himself in the worst of all possible worlds for the
speaker—stuck, with nowhere to go after the big buildup. So he just comes
to a complete stop. Flustered, flummoxed, perplexed. With no way out.

In the incredibly awkward silence that now engulfed our locker
room, I stood up, beaming, grinning. I said, "Come on, guys, let's go!
We're a great team, we don't need luck, and Coach, here's your silly
lucky penny." I reached into my sweatpants and pulled out his good-
luck charm, then tossed it his way as I walked out the door and onto
the court.

That was the year we lost.

Never discount the power of luck.

Ever since, I have been burdened by the Curse of the Stolen Penny.
If only . . .

—

That opener against Arkansas had the lone distinction of being Richard
Washington's first game as a Bruin. A game in which Richard played
only a few mop-up minutes at the very end. Afterward while we were
all standing around waiting to take the bus back to our local team hotel,
the magnificent Bel Air Sands, Richard was heard to say, "Man, I can't
believe that Coach Wooden barely even put me in the game tonight—it
was like I was not part of anything at all. . . . All these thousands of
people in this sold-out arena who came here to see me play my first
game here at Pauley, and the countless more who will tune in tonight
on KTLA Channel Five with Dick Enberg on the tape-delay broadcast
just to watch me play, and that darned Coach Wooden treated me as a
mere afterthought."

Nobody had the heart to tell Richard that UCLA had sold out every
game in Pauley's eight-year history to that point, that the school had
won the previous seven NCAA Championships, and that the team had
won its 76th consecutive game that night.

The next night we played Maryland. Their coach, Lefty Driesell,
was determined to build his Terrapin program there in College Park
into the UCLA of the East. They had a good team, probably the best
that we had come up against in our college careers to this point, with
real players—Len Elmore, Tom McMillan, and a very young John
Lucas.

This was the first outing Greg's apparently wrong answer to Coach
Wooden's early-season queries began to haunt us. With Greg spending
the first minutes of what would turn out to be inordinate and eternal
time on the bench, and Tommy Curtis seemingly taking more shots
by himself than Greg normally took in a month, and Jamaal and me
waiting breathlessly and endlessly for a ball that would never come, we

could not sustain our early dominance and comfortable lead. We did finally win the game, by one, when John Lucas couldn't get it done in the lane on the game's final play.

—

We rolled through the rest of our nonconference schedule in typical fashion—riding our explosive offense, stifling pressing defense, and overwhelming talent to rout the hapless and hopeless opposition.

We opened the conference in early January up in Seattle, where we made mush of the Huskies, winning by 52 and running our winning streak to 84 games.

Then it was off for the always exciting trip to Pullman. They had a very bright, dynamic, and streetwise coach, George Raveling. And now they had a brand-new, state-of-the-art gym with an "innovative" synthetic Tartan floor—hard as a rock, as sticky as if coated in fresh glue, and completely inappropriate for basketball.

It was January 7, 1974, and we were on our way. Then for the first time ever at UCLA, Greg, who had not lost a game as our starting playmaker/ball-handler/leader for the past three years, never even got in the game—without a word of explanation.

And then, during the course of an eminently awful and dreadful slow-down game, I was high above the basket making a play on the ball when a thug from the other team came over from the other side of the court and in a despicable act of violence and dirty play took my legs out from underneath me, flipping me over at the peak of my jump. I landed flat on my back on that Tartan floor and couldn't get up.

I lay there stunned, staggered, and helpless, and soon learned that I had broken two bones in my spine. My teammates tried to help me up, but it was real tough. It was even harder when I tried to keep playing after they finally started the game up again. There was just too much deep, burning pain searing through my entire body. I couldn't continue. The guys helped me to the locker room,

We eventually won the game by 10, but the damage was done.

After the game, the ever-quiet and soft-spoken Coach Wooden said in his postgame news interviews that something had to be done to protect our players from the violent attacks of our opponents.

I spent the next eleven days in the UCLA hospital, the swimming pool, bed, and Ducky's training room, discovering acupuncture and the fine practitioners of every imaginable healing art, as I tried everything in a desperate attempt to get up and get going again.

I missed the next two conference games—couldn't even attend them, much less play. I had a broken back.

Then, with our annual trip to Chicago and Notre Dame right in front of us, I strapped on a corset with vertical steel rods in it for support and flew across the country.

I stayed in the hotel bed for our game at the Chicago Stadium, and then joined the team for the long, late-night, ice-cold bus ride across the frozen tundra to South Bend.

With the awful weather, travel, motels, bus rides, my broken back, and Tommy Curtis, it was all basically miserable. Our schedule those days usually called for us to play late Friday night, then an early Saturday day game. So on that Saturday, January 19, 1974, we played Notre Dame. And I was finally able to play, for the entire game even, and we lost. That day, we broke Wooden's most-oft-repeated admonition: "Do your best; your best is good enough, that's all you and we need. But whatever you do, don't beat yourself, don't cheat or shortchange yourself, because that's the worst kind of defeat you'll ever suffer, and you'll never get over it."

During the pregame warm-ups, one of the Notre Dame fans ran onto the court and up to me. He was dressed as a bumblebee, and he kept trying to sting me, hoping to send me into anaphylactic shock once again.

At halftime, we had a 17-point lead, but Greg didn't play at all in the second half.

We had an 11-point lead and the ball with three minutes to go, in an era that predated the shot clock and the three-point shot. And we gave it all away, losing by one as we went scoreless for the rest of the game, stuttering and stumbling down the stretch, missing six straight shots and turning the ball over four times, while Notre Dame scored the final 12 points of the game, making their last six shots.

I had my chances, but in the end I couldn't get it done, missing some very makeable shots.

It was our first loss since early in my junior year in high school, and it hurt—bad. The last time I'd lost, I walked home afterward. I wanted to do the same now, but Indiana was just too far. Plus I could barely move, what with my back, that corset, the steel rods, and the cold. The whole world now seemed frozen.

—

We got back to UCLA, but things were still not right, as my back continued to plague me and my knees were giving me a lot of trouble as well. My whole body was aching and out of—EVERYTHING!

My practice time became limited and sporadic. Sometimes I could not even get there, as I was constantly trying to relieve the pain, soreness, and stiffness.

But the games, like the sun, river, rain, and tide, kept coming.

Our offense, the key to winning and championships, became erratic, inconsistent, and wildly unpredictable. And for the first time, its failures and limitations were not solely based on the other teams' efforts to slow the game to a crawl.

We sadly and sorrowfully became our own worst enemy. The relentless offensive attack that was the trademark of UCLA and John Wooden basketball became maddeningly, frustratingly, and elusively stagnant.

There were many factors—my injuries, the failure to assertively initiate the attack—but, after forty years of reflecting on it, I've concluded there was nothing as devastating as the continued presence in the lineup of Tommy Curtis.

Tommy's increased role and playing time came at the expense of Greg, who was the real key to our team's offensive flow. And all the things that made Greg so valuable and talented were the things that Tommy completely ignored, or simply considered worthless.

Greg, as a solid position defender, could read and anticipate the defensive play that would start our fast break. Whether it came from a block, steal, deflection, or rebound and outlet, he was on the move, up the court, continuing to build on a play that had already been made.

Tommy, no matter what, always came back to the ball, disrupting the flow and advantage that had already been created.

Greg was always ready to make the next pass ahead, quickly moving things forward.

Tommy seemed interested only in making the play himself, invariably off his own excessive and irritating dribble. And we were never a team that tried to do anything off the dribble, except when Tommy was in and had the ball.

Greg was the master at delivering the ball to a teammate on the move, coming off a screen, on a backdoor cut or lob, or just flashing to an opening.

Tommy was so insistent on dribbling for his own play and shot that we would be on the move, finding key openings, and calling for the ball, only to have to stop, wait, and ultimately lose our advantage as he pounded the ball, back and forth, through his legs, in and out—anywhere and everywhere except where it needed to go.

And Tommy was always talking to the other team, their coaches, the refs, the fans. It was always "In your face," "In your eye," "Your mama," "Too late," "Get back," "Stay down."

It was all so depressing. And every day, I would be in Coach Wooden's office, pleading, explaining, begging for sanity, rationality, reason. But all to no avail. As Greg sat for extended periods and Tommy continued to get more and more of everything, Coach would just sit there with a blank stare as I tried to get him to see what was so painfully obvious to me.

Early on, when we were winning everything by incalculably large margins, the ends of the games often came in the opening minutes.

But after my broken back, everything started to tighten up, and the ends of the games actually came at the end, when Curtis was always at his worst, when he would get even more selfish, more irrational, more obnoxious, more intent on doing everything by himself.

—

Our play hit rock bottom in mid-February, on our annual trip to Oregon and the Willamette Valley. In eighteen hours we lost our rhythm, our confidence, our dignity, our self-respect, and our pride—all the things that made us unbeatable champions since we had arrived at UCLA three and a half years earlier.

We couldn't score, we couldn't play. Greg hardly played at all in either game, and we combined for a total of 108 points in two entire games. Turnovers, uncertainty, hesitancy, and doubt plagued every aspect of our existence. And try as we did, we could not get out of our own way or funk.

As we were leaving the court Friday night in Corvallis, having just lost to the Beavers, the fans stormed the court. One of them ran up to Coach Wooden and, winding up like a cricket pitcher, threw an apple at him as hard as he could from about fifteen feet away, hitting him right in the chest. Coach was sixty-five, and had already suffered at least one heart attack in this latest year.

We gathered around him and carried him down to our locker room, where Ducky loosened Coach's tie and opened his shirt, massaging his reddened and swollen chest as he slumped like the rest of us.

Early the next day, we played even worse, if you can call what we did playing.

When asked to explain things in a postgame interview and comprehend how our great team could possibly play so poorly, with no life, inspiration, fire, enthusiasm, or intensity, Greg quoted Bob Dylan: "When you've got nothing, you've got nothing to lose."

Coach was livid.

—

Back at UCLA during our next practice, Coach stopped practice early on and led us into the locker room for a first of its kind in all my years there "meeting." And as he started to lay out his vision for the rest of our final season, a season that had just seen us lose our only two conference games of our entire time in college, Coach brought out a small portable tape recorder. Not as technologically savvy as some, he fumbled to turn the recorder on and get it working. He told us that while Greg would be returning to the lineup for the rest of the season, Coach would no longer tolerate any of the "Die-Lyn" quotes in the press, and that he would use the tape recorder to ensure that nobody misquoted, misinterpreted, or misunderstood his very carefully chosen words.

It worked. Somewhat. For a while, at least.

The offense came back to life, with more Greg and a lot less Tommy Curtis.

But we still lacked the perfect consistency and flawless execution that had been our standard for years.

We came into the last game of the conference season, against USC, in a rare position for us. Because of our two losses during the Lost Weekend in Oregon three weeks earlier, the USC game was a must-win for us. The rules of the day called for only the conference champion to make the NCAA tournament. So if we lost, we wouldn't even make the tournament that UCLA had won the previous seven years.

We delivered, playing as well as we had in quite some time. Jamaal and Greg were both dynamic defensively, stealing tons of passes and converting in the resultant transition game. I had more rebounds and points at the half than the entire USC team combined. We won by 30.

—

The NCAA Western Regionals were in Tucson, Arizona, that year, and our team hotel was quite a nice desert resort, with all the amenities that young college students on spring break could ever ask for. Although it was more than a break for me, as I had already graduated from UCLA, having gone to school at Sonoma State the previous summer.

We played Dayton in our NCAA opener on Thursday night. We had a big early lead that remained constant through the half. On the opening play of the second half, Dave Meyers slid smoothly backdoor, and Greg laid the ball in his wheelhouse perfectly. The ball went right through Dave's hands and out-of-bounds. By the next dead ball, Coach

Wooden had substituted Greg out of there, and by the time Greg got back in we had lost all our momentum and the Flyers were now red hot, on fire, and basically unstoppable.

One of their front-court players, Mike Sylvester, was in such a zone that none of us could do anything with him. He went for 37 in the game, most of them in the second half. We all had our shot at him—me, Jamaal, Dave, Marques—but with no success.

They took us into overtime, then a second one.

They had two terrific little guards, Don Smith and a very young Johnny Davis—whom I would later play with in Portland. And, like Sylvester, they could not be stopped.

With the score tied in the closing seconds of that second overtime, Dayton came rushing up the floor, pushing a frenetic pace. The ball went to Don Smith on the left side, he made his way close to the basket, and as the buzzer sounded he got off a little floater from about ten feet out, sort of along the baseline.

The ball found the rim and easily swished through, ending it all. Or seemingly so.

In the pandemonium of Dayton winning with that shot, as they were celebrating their upset victory and their fans surged onto the court in wild amazement, one of the refs came running up, waving off the game winner and indicating that Dayton's Coach Donaher had called time-out as his team was racing up the court on the game's final possession.

The Flyers and their fans were outraged, but the ref was right.

And so the game went to its third overtime, and we won by 11.

—

Our next game was significantly less dramatic. And, despite their remarkable and emerging guard, Phil Smith, we beat USF easily in yet another slowdown game.

The next week we were off to the Final Four again, this time in Greensboro, North Carolina. We were to play NC State one more time, after having beaten them handily in St. Louis more than three months ago. We got there and it was miserable—bad motel, bad food, bad weather. I only brought sandals and T-shirts with me, and we woke up to snow on the ground on the day of the game.

We played OK, but we needed more than OK, in a huge game, against a good team, literally on their home court. All the big plays that usually went our way went theirs. We had a number of 14-point leads late in the game, but turnovers, missed free throws, offensive fouls, and Tommy Curtis all cost us down the stretch. I missed a bunch of easily makeable shots—from point-blank range. And then NC State spent large chunks of time holding the ball without even attempting to attack the basket.

The game went to overtime.

They scored first in the extra period. We countered immediately.

Then they held the ball for the last four minutes of the extra period.

We went into a second overtime.

We started strong, but the same nightmarish problems came back to haunt us—none more than the individual agenda of Tommy Curtis. We had a 7-point lead and the ball with just a little bit of time left, but we couldn't or didn't get it done. The decisive plays all went to NC State's David Thompson, who was easily the best collegiate player that we ever faced. David was helped mightily by Tommy Burleson, who outplayed me. And Monte Towe played like a giant. We lost by 3 in the national semifinals.

UCLA's 38-game NCAA tournament win streak—gone. UCLA's string of seven straight NCAA Championships—gone.

March 23, 1974.

Things were never the same again.

If only . . .

They wanted us to play for third place in the consolation game against Kansas a couple of days later. I said I wasn't going to play. I had come to win the championship. I wanted no part of third-place action.

In the miserable gloom and haze of defeat, we spent a lot of time in my dumpy, dingy motel room. Coach Wooden, my dad, and a number of the Marquette players, including Maurice Lucas, who were to play for the title on Monday, were there a lot.

I was disconsolate. It was not as I had dreamed it. I told the guys that I would sit on the bench and cheer them on—as they had done for me for the previous four years.

Coach wouldn't stand for it. I was adamant. And we compromised on a token appearance—as a starter. It was awful.

After the long plane ride back to LAX, I never saw Tommy Curtis again, which is fine with me. And as I got off the UCLA plane in L.A., I turned to Coach Wooden one final time as a player, and through the sadness, loss, anger, and disappointment, I said to him, "I'm sorry, Coach, for ruining it all."

He knew better than to get into it right there. He handed me a note, a new maxim that he had written for me. I opened it up and read: "To Bill Walton, It's the things that you learn after you know it all that count. Coach John Wooden."

—

I have spent the rest of my life trying to cleanse my spirit and soul of the stain that marks me to this day with the Curse of the Stolen Penny. We had it all. Think about how close we came. Think about how good it was. But we lost four of our last seventeen games after going undefeated for so long. We should have won them all. Every time I meet a UCLA alumnus, to this day, I am obliged to apologize for letting them, our school, our team, our coach, our family, and everybody else down.

Coach was ultimately right about one thing here—you never do get over it.

CHAPTER 10

Feel Like a Stranger

THE DAZE BETWEEN

The first days are the hardest days.

Coming back and climbing up from complete failure is really hard. And there are never any guarantees which way it will all go.

One of the great things about basketball being the perfect game is that the many metaphors that define the sport are the ones you need most when everything falls apart. The rebound. The turnaround. Transition. The crossover. Change of pace, change of direction. The fast break. The relentless offensive attack. Time-out. Momentum.

I needed all of this, but I just couldn't seem to find my way home.

Getting off that plane home from Greensboro to UCLA was eye-opening. All of a sudden everything was over. I had graduated already, so there was no reason to be on campus. And I was now so embarrassed about how it all turned out at the end for me at UCLA, all I could do was hang my head in disappointment, shame, and despair.

Still, I had the biggest choices and decisions to date in my young life ahead of me. Where to go and what to do.

And the business of basketball kept calling, as it had for the past few years, as much as I had tried to shut it out.

I was spending time out in the desert, with extended backpacking trips up on Mount San Jacinto, particularly in Tahquitz and Palm Canyons. But push was coming to shove, and it was time to get started again—on to the next dream.

Ernie Vandeweghe, who became everything in my life as both a mentor and a friend, had been telling me for years to take a step back and not rush into anything. He told me to become a Rhodes scholar, to go to England and Europe and continue my education for as long as I wanted. Come back when you're ready, and then dictate what you want to do. He wanted me to pursue a business career that might or might not include basketball.

The NBA was calling, interested to know my thoughts and plans. Basketball-wise, that's what I wanted—the big league, and the big time—but I'd either be headed to Portland or Philadelphia, and I didn't know which, as those were the two teams that would be flipping a coin to decide my future.

The ABA kept showing up in many different shapes, offering everything from franchise ownership to my choice of cities, preferably L.A. One group's entire presentation was a meteorological comparison of the rainy, dreary drizzle in Portland, the frigid misery of Philadelphia, and the beauty of Los Angeles—their ABA dream. It was all news to me. My idea of winter was when the temperature dipped below 70 degrees for a few hours and it got dark earlier than we wanted. And when that happened we either went outside to run up, down, and around to warm up, or we took a Jacuzzi bath, or we simply went to bed, waiting the few hours before it would invariably warm up again. Rain was something that Bob Weir, Phil Lesh, Neil Young, and John Fogerty sang songs about.

Jerry West kept telling me how cool Portland and Oregon were, and that there was a lot of potential and opportunity up there.

Eventually I talked with the NBA. I told them that I had no interest whatsoever in Philadelphia, and that if the 76ers won the coin flip, I would look seriously at the ABA. Or the Rhodes scholarship that was out there.

They flipped the coin, and Portland won.

Sam Gilbert, a good friend and proud, loyal, and enthusiastic supporter of all things UCLA, who had helped other UCLA players with their pro contracts, worked with our mutual friend Ralph Shapiro, a UCLA alum, to get the deal done. We did it before the NBA Draft took place. Everyone kept asking me what I wanted, and I didn't know. The only thing that I cared about after four years with Coach Wooden was that I didn't want anybody telling me anymore when to shave, when to cut my hair, and what clothes to wear.

I was up in Tahquitz Canyon during the draft, having lost all track of everything, and I ran out of supplies. I hiked down and off the mountain and into Palm Springs to re-up at the local market. When I was standing in the checkout line, the clerk said to me, "Hey, Bill, I just heard on the radio that the Blazers drafted you number one. Congratulations." He told me he was from Oregon but now lived in the sunshine of the Imperial and Coachella Valleys. As I headed out and back up the canyon—fully and freshly loaded—he wished me good luck.

When I flew up to Portland to sign the contract that spring, it was a beautiful day in the Great Northwest, and everybody was all excited. I was signing the largest financial deal in the history of all team sports. And Sam and Ralph, the Blazers, the media, the fans, and some "friends" who seemed to think that they were part of the deal were all aglow.

The only thing that I cared about was that Sam and Ralph had indeed been able to write it in there that I was in charge of my own personal grooming—such as it was.

As I sat in the Blazers' offices meeting the staff members—there were eight total front-office employees at the time—I was waiting to go into the conference room to meet the assembled Oregon press corps. As the Blazers ownership group was orchestrating everything and we started to shuffle in, one of them leaned in toward me and whispered in mid-procession that all would be fine, but please don't mention the coach's name (which I didn't know anyway) because they were going to fire him the next day.

And so it began—signing up for something that I was totally unprepared for.

I was ready for Oregon, Portland, and all the things that it had to offer. Phenomenal geography, Native Americans, history and all, with the rivers, valleys, mountains, volcanoes, high deserts, the Columbia River Gorge, a magnificent coast, and so much more that I was soon to discover. A governor, Tom McCall, who was a visionary leader in so many of the areas that I loved and lived for. A city mayor, Neil Goldschmidt, who was very cool and receptive to making everything better. And a population that was totally into the things that turned me on, although in those days, there seemed to be more people in Westwood and at UCLA than were living in the entire state of Oregon.

What I wasn't ready for was the business side of the sport, something that now seemed to take precedence over everything else. Everybody was so nice and trying to help, but I didn't know what I was doing, just getting started, on my own and all, for the very first time.

I was also totally unprepared for the weather, which was unlike anything I had ever seen.

After San Diego, I thought UCLA was cold, damp, wet, and foggy. In Oregon, I was fully convinced that the sun had burned out and life as we knew it was rapidly coming to an end.

The Blazers got me a new car—whatever I wanted. I got a Toyota Land Cruiser, and immediately took the top off. That didn't go well. They were building me my own special house, south of town, on the biggest river and with more fresh water than I had ever seen. It had everything custom-fit for my height and size. It was very nice, but that didn't work out, either—for a variety of reasons. Not the least of which was that it was on Nixon Avenue. What was I thinking?

I was making all sorts of new and interesting friends. It was a whole new world. I read a lot of the history of my new Oregon home, and decided that I wanted to take a summer job as a lumberjack. The Blazers

The Game of Life. *(Family)*

I love parades. *(Roger Jensen/The Oregonian)*

This was supposed to be this book's cover . . . My publisher said NO!!!
(Artwork by Mike DuBois)

BACK FROM THE DEAD

BILL WALTON

This was the next version . . . They said NO again!!! *(Artwork by Mike DuBois)*

BILL WALTON

ONE OF THE 50 GREATEST PLAYERS IN NBA HISTORY

BACK FROM THE DEAD

SEARCHING FOR THE SOUND, SHINING THE LIGHT AND THROWING IT DOWN

And again . . . NO!!! *(Artwork by Mike DuBois, Photo by Jay Blakesberg)*

In the beginning—The Foundation. Rocky and my Dad. *(Family)*

Ernie Vandeweghe—from whom all good things flowed, like an eternally blooming flower . . . He was always the bridge over the deepest chasms. *(Vandeweghe Family)*

The hopes and dreams of young boys who just wanted more from their dad. *(Family)*

There is nothing like the pride of a dad. *(Andrew D. Bernstein/ NBAE/Getty Images)*

Our latest family photo . . . Aspen, Colorado, August 2013 . . . We now have five more grandchildren. *(Family)*

I'm the luckiest guy ever . . . Happy in love and the proud dad of the greatest dog in the history of the world. *(Taylor Hanson)*

Cortez, standing guard, and like Maurice Lucas always ready "to take care of this." *(Taylor Hanson)*

Shining the light, and ringing the chimes of freedom for those in need in Lithuania. *(Sam Morris)*

Trying my best to walk like a giant with these heroic pillars of humanity. *(Family)*

Working together to build the foundation for a better tomorrow. *(Mitchell Layton/NBAE/Getty Images)*

Greg Lee and The Coach . . . if only . . . please reread Chapter 9. *(Associated Students UCLA)*

"No Bill . . . you're not looking for advice . . . you're looking for an accomplice . . . and please, I cannot absolve you with forgiveness for something that I would never initially grant permission for." Please reread Chapter 9. *(Tim Sullivan)*

Duane Roth—the combination of Coach Wooden, Chick Hearn and Maurice Lucas—all in one. *(Philipp Scholz Rittermann)*

David Halberstam . . . A most wonderfully insightful and compassionate friend . . . And quite the personal librarian. *(Arnold Newman/Getty Images)*

"I'll take care of this." *(James Drake/Sports Illustrated/Getty Images)*

Bringing the heat . . . dizzy with possibili-ties. *(Photograph © Bob Minkin)*

How sweet it is when reality is better than your dreams. *(Jesse D. Garrabrant/NBAE/ Getty Images)*

Inspiration . . . Move me brightly. *(Jesse D. Garrabrant/NBAE/Getty Images)*

Team Chase—greatest team ever . . . Riding our bikes, all day, every day. *(Carlos Gutierrez)*

I love my bike . . . I live for the long hard climb . . . My new life as a prop. *(middle: Mike Munk, bottom: Dave Mayer)*

"Nothing left to do but smile, smile, smile" *(Stan Grossfeld/The Boston Globe via Getty Images)*

Thanks Red, Larry and Boston—for giving me my life back. *(Steve Lipofsky/ Corbis Images)*

Larry Bird was so good that the Celtics were able to sell these seats. *(Steve Lipofsky/The LIFE Images Collection/Getty Images)*

K.C. Jones and Robert Parish . . . The epitome of championship greatness—leadership, culture, foundation, sacrifice and discipline. *(Jennifer Pottheiser/NBAE/ Getty Images)*

Family, friends, the team, the locker room—and winning. *(Andrew D. Bernstein/ NBAE/Getty Images)*

The Galapagos, 1979. Figuring out the evolving game of life. *(Family)*

Trying to make sense of it all. Thanks for your patience, Brent. *(Garrett Ellwood/ NBAE/Getty Images)*

Thanks, Chick—for teaching me to love the game of life. *(Catherine Steenkeste/NBAE/Getty Images)*

Celebrating the genius, love and durability of my best friends Ralph and Jo Lawler . . . 2,500 of the worst basketball games and business ever—but definitely the most fun, and intellectually stimulating . . . And finally I got to speak . . . *(Andrew D. Bernstein/NBAE/Getty Images)*

Washington, D.C. 1994. Academic All-America HOF. History. Knowledge. Teaching. "The Other Side of The Game." *(Family)*

Starting the fast break—my favorite part of the game. *(Top: George Long/ Sports Illustrated/Getty Images; Middle/ Bottom: San Diego Union-Tribune)*

The top of The Pyramid . . . Be at your best when your best is needed. *(Hank Delespinasse/Sports Illustrated/Getty Images)*

It's not how high you jump. But rather—where and when. *(Dick Raphael/NBAE/ Getty Images)*

Maurice always had our backs. *(Dick Raphael/NBAE/ Getty Images)*

I went to VIP's but I couldn't get Coach to come to Death Valley on his bike, or on the Grateful Dead Tour. *(Family)*

The bus came by and I got on. *(Family)*

In church on New Year's Eve . . . Ringing the Chimes of Freedom for what's next. *(Family)*

Finding my path forward: Leadership, teammates and the jump rope. *(Roger Jensen)*

What we live for—joy, happiness, accomplishment, winning. *(Ralph Perry)*

The day that I beat Kevin one-on-one in front of the entire Celtic family was the greatest singular moment in my basketball career. *(Bill Brett/The Boston Globe via Getty Images)*

Lenny Wilkens and Spencer Haywood both deserved better—in everything.
(Brian Babineau/NBAE/Getty Images)

Jack Ramsay and Pete Carril . . . Drifting, dreaming, and trying to soak it all in.
(Rocky Widner/NBAE/Getty Images)

A new game, sitting down with a new friend and sweet song. *(Andy Hayt/NBAE/ Getty Images)*

With a lot of help from my friends, I Love It Live. *(Nathaniel S. Butler/NBAE/Getty Images)*

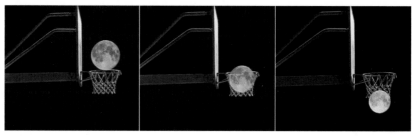

We bid you goodnight, after another perfect day . . . time to get ready for tomorrow. *(Family)*

were aghast, but they did help in every way they could. They tried— man, did they ever try—to make it all work. They helped get a friend and me jobs out in the mountains east of Eugene. We didn't last long. The reality did not meet the dreamy myth, what with the danger, the giant chain saws, cables, trucks, winches, bulldozers, devastation, cutting down the forests and all.

I quit the lumberjack job and headed out on a major backpacking trip in the same central Oregon area, up one of the forks of the McKenzie River, only to be driven out by the giant bloodsucking mosquitoes— which were the size of pterodactyls—everywhere. I quit that trip, too.

I ended up taking a journey of discovery, exploration, and experimentation that began with all the hot springs in the state and ended at the coast, where I met Jeb Barton and bought my first tipi. It was all so stunning, and so different from Southern California. Trees, rivers, wildlife, and no people—WOW!

I connected with Dick Trudell, a Dakota Sioux Indian, who had grown to become a lawyer and master legal expert, ultimately settling in San Francisco. Dick has spent his life trying to right the wrongs that history has forced on us. I've tried to stand in his giant shadow whenever possible. He's still at it, braver, sharper, tougher, and more determined and tenacious than ever. We're still going for it today—together.

Back in Portland, I was reading the local paper and saw that the Grateful Dead were in town that night at the downtown Paramount Theatre, on Broadway—right in the middle of it all.

I hightailed it down there early in the afternoon, stood in line to buy a ticket—general admission, as most of their shows were in those days. Then I used all my quickness, agility, and sharp elbows to get a great seat, dead center and about ten rows deep. It was perfect. It was my first time in this ornate temple. The show was about to begin, and everybody was ramping up their preparation in fevered anticipation for the upcoming ceremony. Most of the focus was on flexibility, hydration, and nutrition.

When the band came out to start the show, they kept glancing out into the crowd with puzzled looks. They kept muttering to themselves during the song breaks, not able to figure out why everybody was sitting down except for this one tall, skinny, redheaded geek. Nobody ever sat down at a Dead show. It was one of the reasons that we went.

Then they changed their way of thinking to—hey, everybody is dancin', but that redheaded guy is standing on his chair and blocking everybody's view. That was untenable. This was the Grateful Dead. Where everybody got a chance to be a part of the deal.

They finally figured out that everything was fine. That everybody was dancing, including me, and that I was just very tall.

Unhappy that those behind me couldn't see, the band sent somebody from the crew out to the audience to tell me that they would prefer that I come and watch from the stage so that everybody else could see.

I wanted no part of that. I had spent the whole day trying to get just where I was. In the perfect spot: dead center, and up close. They pleaded. I turned them down.

What were we all to do? The show was in full swing. I told them that I was staying where I was, but that I would come backstage at halftime. The guy left me two backstage passes, and he and the crowd let me be.

I went backstage at the break, and things have never been the same since.

I had had numerous opportunities to meet the band at many of the shows I had been to before. It's a very friendly place. But I was just too shy. And I couldn't talk. So what was I to do?

But this time I took a chance, and they couldn't have been nicer. As they all still are to this day. What a family. What a team. All of them. Including Ram Rod, who was from Oregon and loved basketball, sports, his home state, and all things Grateful Dead. After seven years of going to the concerts, I was now happily and proudly on their team. And on their team I remain.

Not too much later, the Blazers called me in and told me they wanted their doctor to operate on my knee, the same knee that I tore up in 1967—seven years earlier.

While the knee bothered me, like my feet, and now my spine, it was just part of life at this point. And I had learned to deal with it.

They said the surgery wasn't structural, just a cleanout of all the loose junk that was floating around in there, the stuff that would every now and again cause my knee to lock up so that I wouldn't be able to move it until I was able to physically massage the crud temporarily out of harm's way.

I listened to them and did it, though it was very close to the start of the season. So now I've got this recently operated-on knee, coming on the heels of my broken spine from seven or eight months ago, my chronically sore feet, and a whole new world on every front.

I woke up in the hospital to find our new coach standing over me—Lenny Wilkens—along with his new assistant, Tom Meschery. They had been two of my favorite players as a young NBA fan, and as coaches they were as cool as could be.

—

When I joined the Portland Trail Blazers in the summer of 1974, they were basically still an expansion team, even though they were now starting their fourth year.

They played in a beautiful building, the "Glass Palace," the Memorial Coliseum. It was the same building that had hosted the 1965 Final Four. The same place where the first basketball game that I ever saw on television was played. It held 12,666 people for an NBA game, but the Blazers had never captured the fans' imagination or stirred much loyal interest or passion as they struggled to attract just a bit over half the house to games that they rarely won.

Going into that season, we certainly had some talented players. There were a couple of recent NBA Rookies of the Year in Geoff Petrie and Sidney Wicks; a very nice swing player in John Johnson; a previous No. 1 overall NBA Draft pick in seven-footer LaRue Martin; a proud and fierce semi-tough, semi-big guy, the frustratingly antagonistic Lloyd Neal; a competitive swing man in Larry Steele; and our coach, Lenny Wilkens, who was going to play as well. In retrospect, Tom Meschery should have played, too. But sadly he didn't, except for an occasional romp in practice when we were short of healthy bodies. Those attempts didn't go real well, as Tom and Sidney would eventually get into ugly and brazen fistfights—EVERY TIME. When Tom was an active NBA player, he was the one guy who ever got into it with Wilt. A cerebral genius off the court, Tom loved to fight on it.

But beyond those players, we didn't have what it took to make a complete team. And it was all very disconcerting. For the first time in memory, I was on a team where skills and talent were lacking. Some of the guys couldn't dribble without having to watch the ball. Many had sloppy, careless, or no footwork. A bunch had no left or off hand. Some couldn't catch. Others couldn't shoot, rebound, or pass.

Here I was, at the top, the pinnacle—or so I thought—here in the dream-of-a-lifetime NBA for the very first time, and far too many of the guys couldn't play, couldn't execute the basic fundamentals. What a nightmare! You couldn't make our high school or college team unless you could do everything. That was John Wooden and UCLA basketball, the culture that had been my life.

Lenny and Tom did their best. But they had no power over anything other than the in-game stuff, like substitutions and strategy—such as it was.

I came with high hopes and great intentions and expectations. But I was finding out that the whole thing was a giant step down from what we had at UCLA.

Many different, disruptive, and often devastating cliques developed on the team, and the chemistry was basically awful—if it existed at all. Sidney quickly became my best friend on the team. I would spend a lot of time over at Sidney's apartment in what free time we did have. He was in his third year, and he had a lot of things figured out—none of which he was too happy about. Geoff Petrie was very nice, too. They all were, although Geoff and Sidney did not seem to get along, which seemed quite weird to me.

Geoff and JJ—John Johnson—had nice games, but they were mostly played off their own dribble. And that was not the game that Sidney and I brought from UCLA.

Lloyd's game was a combination of skill and bulk. He was not explosive, but he had good footwork, hands, finesse, and touch. He had two nicknames: "Ice," for all the ice that he constantly used to try to heal his battered body, and "Bottom," a reference to the anatomical part of his body that he used with remarkable effectiveness to knock you completely off balance and out of the way so he could finish a play.

And then there was LaRue, a fine, polished, and well-liked gentleman who was totally miscast in his position as The Franchise. His basic limitation was that he wasn't passionately in love with the game—which is a foundational requisite for ultimate success.

We would all play, and we would all fight and get into everything, little of it good. But we were trying to move forward.

After my knee surgery, I struggled to get back with it on the court. I started playing almost immediately after my knee surgery, continuing an ill-advised and foolish trend of always coming back to the game too soon after serious injury. And my body was just not right in those early practices when we were trying to find any sort of chemistry.

As my hair kept growing, along with what there was of my facial hair and beard, people started to realize that I was serious, and that I was not going to cut my hair. David Crosby was very proud. I became the first player in NBA history to have a ponytail.

And then the business side of the whole deal kept popping up. Everybody wanted a piece of the action. The fast-food companies and the soda-pop people were persistent. A lot of the local companies wanted to do endorsement deals. But that just wasn't my thing. The way I saw it, my deal was to play, to fill the house, and to win the championship—and I would get paid for that.

But this one guy kept persistently coming back, dogged in his tenacity. He had a start-up company, and he had some shoes that he wanted me to wear. I told him that I had a pair of shoes. He told me that he wanted to pay me to wear *his* shoes. I told him I got paid plenty to play basketball, and that I really wasn't interested. He kept after it and kept telling me that I was his guy—Oregon, cool, and all that—and his offers kept getting more and more generous. I was getting embarrassed, because I knew I had already made up my mind. I wasn't going to do it, and there was nothing that was going to change my way of thinking. Finally, he left, never to return.

His name was Phil Knight. His called his start-up company Nike. Who knew? Certainly not me. Phil has gone on to become one of the most important figures in the history of sport. And his Nike dream is the envy of our sporting and business world. Every time I connect with Phil now, to this day, he always shakes his head, echoing Coach Wooden: "Walton, you're the slowest learner I've ever seen."

I joined the NBA at a fabulous time, with lots of great teams, players, coaches, and particularly centers. Every night I would have the opportunity to play against the likes of Kareem, Dave Cowens, Nate Thurmond, Bob McAdoo, Bob Lanier, Elvin Hayes, Wes Unseld, and Clifford Ray. Yes, I was sad to be missing out on the recently retired guys like Russell, Wilt, Willis Reed, and Walt Bellamy. And Artis Gilmore and Moses Malone were in the ABA. But every night there was somebody who was really, really good that I had to beat if we were going to come out on top.

We started the NBA exhibition season in Los Angeles against the Lakers. I got to play that night against Jerry West for the first and only time. He retired pretty much right after the game, suffering from the ravages of time. It was the first time that I had ever played against a guard who had total control of the game. He was as good a little guy as I ever played against. He was incredible even at the very end, hobbled as he was—brilliantly able to dictate every other player's movement on the court just by what he did with his mind, body, spirit, soul, and the ball. It was exhilarating and eye-opening.

We won the game, although I was soon to learn that the only thing more meaningless than the halftime score of an NBA game is the final score of an NBA exhibition game.

Quickly on the move through the NBA exhibition schedule, we landed in Dayton, Ohio, in a made-for-TV extravaganza created by Don Nelson pitting us against the Milwaukee Bucks and Kareem. Kareem was one of my heroes. He was one of the major reasons that I had gone to UCLA. I had worn his No. 33 in high school. He was the standard of excellence that everybody was measured against—and would be for the rest of time.

This was the first time I ever played against him. I had no chance. I was not ready, physically or on any other level. Kareem's Bucks were still very good, although they no longer had Oscar Robertson. They had lost to the Celtics in the NBA Finals the year before in one of the greatest championship series ever played, where the road team won the last five games of the seven that were played, including a Celtic rout of the Bucks in the finale in Milwaukee.

The game for me was a complete disaster, as I could do so very little, and it showed just how far I had to go, both as an individual and in pulling our team—such as it was—together.

Sports Illustrated made the exhibition their cover story that week.

As the games of all kinds kept coming, I kept noticing something very strange that was happening as an everyday occurrence. As soon as the first half ended every night, some of our players, a coach, and some staff members would sprint off the court heading to the locker room. I was used to playing all the time, almost always finishing the half on the court. So what was the rush to get off, and why waste the energy and effort to run full speed to the locker room?

When I would eventually get there myself, imagine my surprise to find the guys in there smoking cigarettes and pounding down carbonated caffeinated soda.

—

The regular season started soon enough, and although we were doing OK as a team and attendance was starting to build, there was no real magic or spark to what we were doing on or off the court.

Lenny and Tom did their best, but as a collective group, we had no tangible, positive chemistry. The ball didn't move much. There were far too many individual agendas. Selfishness and greed were rampant, and there was lack of skill and talent on a flawed roster. The trust and mutual respect that is a must for a team to succeed was nowhere to be found.

And Lenny and Tom could not get the support they asked for and needed from the front office. They kept telling the front-office guys that this whole thing was not working and that team chemistry was the biggest reason.

We kept moving forward, though, ever so slowly, but certainly not in a straight line. And then one day about a month or so into the season, I got to the game and I couldn't run, try as I might. Every time I tried to run, there was this deep burning pain in my foot. And I couldn't figure it out.

I had not fallen or landed wrong on anybody. Nobody had stepped on my foot that I could remember. It just hurt, real bad. And every time I tried to start to run it would hurt more, and more, and more and more—deep inside.

I had lived with foot pain my whole life. My feet ached all the time. That's the way I thought it was for everybody who played ball. But this was different. It felt like somebody was stabbing me in the foot with a sharp, hot knife, and the more I tried to work it all out or to play on it, the worse it got. It felt like somebody was holding a blowtorch to my foot and ankle.

It was late 1974, and things would never be the same again.

At the time, I was playing all right, scoring in the high teens per game, and at the top of the league in rebounding and blocked shots. But now I couldn't play at all, because every time I put my foot down, there was this stabbing, searing pain.

There were no answers or solutions—from anybody. And when I could not return to the court, it all came down. The blame all landed on me. They kept saying there was nothing really wrong with me, and I was just choosing not to play. Or it's my diet—he doesn't eat raw, red meat. It's the vegetable juice that he drinks. It's the music—he likes the Grateful Dead, Dylan, Neil Young, and all the rest. It's his clothes, his hair, his friends, his politics. The criticisms covered every area of my life, with no particular order or reason.

At the same time, two of my friends and housemates, Jack and Mikki Scott, were suspected of being involved with the Patty Hearst kidnapping. Patty had been kidnapped in the Bay Area by the Symbionese Liberation Army (SLA) and held for ransom. When everything went spiraling wildly out of control, Jack and Mikki were, much to my surprise, quietly and secretly recruited to help keep Patty and some of the SLA members safe and alive. But Jack and Mikki had now conveniently disappeared, with me as one of their last points of contact, which brought the FBI calling, convinced I was involved. My phones were tapped, my mail intercepted. I was trailed. Everywhere I went, there were federal agents with guns and binoculars. Everybody I talked to was now subject to the same thing. My family, friends, teammates, and total strangers as well. And all of this got wrapped up in my struggles on the court—or my struggles to simply reach the court.

It was endless, mindless, and senseless. And through it all, my foot still hurt. I could not play, no matter what I did or tried. And I tried *everything*.

I missed a majority of the rest of the season, although I did come back intermittently and try to play. I was only able to play in thirty-five of the eighty-two games my rookie year. And nobody was happy about any of it, least of all me.

In retrospect, I had a stress fracture in my foot, the first of an endless string that would plague me the rest of my basketball career and life.

But that was never suggested. The team doctor, when I pointed to where it hurt real bad, kept telling me that I was looking too close. And in the papers, it was always about me not wanting to play, or not being tough. And that if only I would support Nixon, be for more war, eat a dead cow, cut my hair, quit my friends, smoke some cigarettes, drink some carbonated soda, or something, then everything would be fine.

Many nights, lost, lonely, hurting, and confused, I would call the owners up late and quit on the spot. Then I would spend the night tossing and turning, knowing that that was not right. And I would be up before the dawn, back on the phone with them, explaining that I was not going to let this nonsense and other people's negativity and problems drive me from the game I loved. And that I would be there that day for work, even though I couldn't play, and really had no chance to, for the foreseeable future.

It was awful, and I was stuck. I had gone from the top to the bottom. I went from living on $128 a month for nine months a year at UCLA to being the highest-paid NBA player ever, yet the quality of my life had gone down. I was miserable.

I finished the season with a cast on my foot, though still without any acknowledgment that there was anything wrong. One of the few saving graces were the kind and strong people, including my neighbors Herman and Ruth Frankel, who thankfully and proudly stood behind me when this whole new game got so very rough.

People would recommend and send interesting and inspiring books, which I immersed myself in. Wilt sent me his latest autobiography, *Wilt: Just Like Any Other 7-Foot Black Millionaire Who Lives Next Door.*

I devoured it. I was touched by the stories of struggle by so many, including Wilt, who recounted that as a rookie he was disillusioned and frustrated upon entering the NBA. It was not what he dreamed it would be. And he became determined to do something about it all.

When Wilt played as a rookie in the NBA, he was the NBA's MVP (the first of only two to ever do that) and its Rookie of the Year, and he averaged more than 39 points per game, and 29 rebounds per game.

Despite all that measured success, Wilt related in his wonderfully insightful book how he felt that he had been pushed around and bullied his rookie season by the thugs and goons who had no interest in playing by the rules. So Wilt committed after that first season to the weight room. And things were never the same again—for anybody.

I committed to do the same, and my search led me to Sam Loprinzi's gym on the southeast side of town. I developed a new passion, weight lifting, a sport that I could participate in even though I couldn't run or play ball.

Sam Loprinzi was a legend. His entire family were pillars of the Portland community, and I fell in love with the gym. Sam was my first weight-lifting coach, and like Rocky, he changed my world forever. He opened the place up six days a week at 9:00 a.m. I was there right as he unlocked the door, and I stayed as long as I could still stand. I made lots of new friends at Loprinzi's gym, who were all working through their own challenges. One of my regular training partners was Jesse "the Body" Ventura, as Loprinzi's was a magnetic hotbed of all sorts of activity for the many pro wrestlers who made Portland home.

I have remained passionately in love with the weight room ever since those very early days. And it was there that I recovered and geared up for the coming season.

—

That off-season, Lenny and Tom were able to secure two great new players in the draft: Lionel Hollins, from Arizona State, and Bob Gross, from Long Beach State.

They were both very nice and interesting guys, who were blessed with fabulous athletic talent. They were great from the outset, although Lenny caught endless grief and fierce resistance from nearly every angle for trying to play Lionel, who apparently didn't have the right skin color, and Bobby, who didn't seem to fit somebody else's prototypical vision. It was all unwarranted nonsense. I come from a culture of meritocracy. Bobby and Lionel had everything anyone ever needed. Lenny was sharp enough to know it first. He was willing to give them the time and chance they needed.

We opened the 1975 regular season in Seattle. The Sonics were coached by Bill Russell, and the Blazer-Sonic rivalry was always fierce, with violent fights a regular occurrence. Seattle always had top talent, Fred Brown, Spencer Haywood, John Brisker, and much more. In one of the games we played up there, Brisker got thrown out for fighting only to come charging back out of an exit tunnel ten minutes later to come after our guy who'd been fighting him. Our guy was at the free-throw line, totally oblivious, as Brisker raced out to the court and took a running leap at him, fists flailing away.

As we faced Seattle at the start of the season, I was having a very strong game. And at the end of three quarters, we're in complete control and I have very big numbers already. As the fourth quarter begins, I notice out of the corner of my eye that Coach Russell has summoned a hack from deep on the Sonic bench. On his way to the scorer's table to report in, John Hummer stops momentarily at Russell's side for some quick instruction. As soon as Hummer gets in the game, he comes right by me, and with the play happening on the far side of the court, Hummer stops and sucker-punches me in the face, and then runs off.

Livid, I take off after the thug and chase this goon all over the court, all while the game is still going on. I finally catch him and start pummeling him. When order is finally restored, I get ejected from the game. And as I am being escorted out of the joint by the police and security, I stop to look back in disbelief. To my everlasting dismay, Bill Russell, my hero, is standing there, with that bent stoop of his, stroking his beard, cackling his irrepressible laugh, and sporting a winning twinkle in his eye.

Seattle came all the way back from the depths and beat us that night, and there was nothing I could do about it from the bowels of the locker room.

We got off to a bad start again, dropping our first four games, and I went down with a bad sprained ankle in that time, the first of another frustrating chain of injuries. Lenny was doing all he could to manage a talented but chemistry- and personality-flawed roster that was not of his making. It was often hard to figure out who was in charge and what the plan was in Oregon. I was beginning to learn two of life's greatest business and corporate lessons—that if it's not their idea, it's not a good idea; and that it's their team, company, or deal, and they're going to do whatever they want with it.

On the day of our fourth game and fourth loss, one I missed due to my ankle, my life changed forever for the better as our first child, Adam, was born in a golden beam of light—a light that has never dimmed. It was October 31, 1975, Halloween. And it was, and is, simply awesome—although I can't say that it's ever easy being my child.

When I returned to the court, the team started to do better. Playing at home one night against Seattle and their center, Tom Burleson, the dealing got very rough—again. Driving the lane hard, my nose ended up on the side of my face, courtesy of Burleson's nasty elbow. I had to go to the locker room, covered in blood. As I was lying on the training table they stuck a big, hard, metal rod up my nose and moved the broken thing back to the center of my face. They then packed my nose with gauze to stem the bleeding.

I went back out there, but not too much later, going for the ball, Burleson put my nose on the other side of my face. I'm not sure any fouls were ever called. But I was back on the table, with the rod and the gauze. And when they finally got it all back in place, with the blood flow slowed to a trickle, they asked me if could go back out and play.

As I tried to feel my face, which felt like it had just been stolen right off my head, I staggered to the door and was headed back out there just as everybody was coming in themselves, this one mercifully over for the night.

Not too much longer down the road, on a dark, cold, wet night in Chicago, I was again high in the air going for the ball when I was undercut—AGAIN. Coming down head-first, I put my left hand out to break my fall from above. I broke my wrist. They said it was bad, and that the bone, the navicular, was a tough one to break because of the limited nature of the blood supply there, so healing was no sure thing.

They put a big cast on my wrist—up to my elbow. I continued to play, even though I could not use my immobilized and plastered left hand at all, except as a club or stump. In the very next game, playing one-handed, I made a play for the ball with my one good hand. By the time I looked down, as the play ended, my middle and fourth fingers were completely dislocated and dangling loosely on the back of my hand down by the wrist.

The trainer and doctor rushed me to the locker room, where they were unable to pull the fingers back into place. I was dripping wet with sweat, and they couldn't get a grip. It was all very painful. Finally they stood over me while I lay writhing in pain on the training table. They took a roll of athletic tape and wrapped it around the smashed fingers, leaving the tape attached to the rest of the roll, which they then wrapped around their own hands and wrists for stability and traction.

After making sure that the tape was secure on both ends, they leaned backward, slowly, agonizingly pulling my fingers back into place, with a big loud clunk when everything all fell into line.

They taped some splints on both the front and back of my fingers and hands. And they asked me if I could go back out there and play. I looked down at my hands in my lap. Both of them broken and casted, splinted, and useless. I looked up at them—dazed, lost, and confused. There was nothing I could do. I could not use either hand—for anything.

This took more than a while to overcome, though nothing yet had been able to keep me from the weight room at Loprinzi's, as they crafted special splints to allow me to keep pushing and pulling the steel without moving my wrists or hands.

When I did finally get back into it all, we started to play—very well. We developed a nice rotation. Sidney, Ice, John Johnson, newly acquired Steve Hawes and Bobby Gross up front with me. Geoff, Lionel, Lenny and Larry Steele in the backcourt. Lenny's dream was starting to come true. We were winning. The fans were ecstatic. They could see it. We could feel it. It was happening. And we were on our way—all the way to the Promised Land. Nothing was going to stop us.

We were peaking, and there were no limits. The Memorial Coliseum was packed now every night, the dynamic and vibe electric.

And then one night during a game, as we were riding a very nice winning streak, the side of my lower right leg, just above my ankle, started to hurt like nothing I had ever felt before. I went in and had my ankle retaped. It still hurt. As I complained and pointed to the spot of the persistent pain, the doctor kept telling me that I was looking too close.

During one of several trips to the locker room, he injected my leg and ankle with massive amounts of painkilling and numbing medicine. I did what I could, all the way to the end.

When it was over, I limped out into the cold, wet, dark night and went to the hospital. X-rays revealed a major break in my lower fibula. The painkillers had allowed me temporarily to play through another stress fracture that was now badly and grossly splintered. And my season was over.

I spent the next two months in a big leg cast. Like my first season, I was only able to participate in thirty-five games—not many of them complete or in full health.

When the season ended, they fired Lenny and Tom. It was awful and wrong. These two had done everything they could to make it work. They kept telling the management that the roster was flawed and that with the bad team chemistry the whole thing was never going to work.

The Blazers' management kept repeating their story line. The problem was me. Walton could not get healthy. And that as soon as I did, everything would be just fine.

Lenny disagreed. And it cost him.

When I got the news, I was sad. Lenny had taught me so much. He always showed so much class, intelligence, perspective, and dignity. He showed me how to play against guys who were far more gifted and physically superior. But in the end, I could do nothing for him. I had let him down.

When I got the news, I went out on a long bike ride to try to clear my head and cleanse my soul.

I rode to Lenny's house, to try to say I was sorry and that I wished there was something I could do to help. We sat all afternoon in his beautiful backyard. It was very hard, and I had no idea what to say.

Lenny Wilkens deserved better—from me, from the Blazers, and from the people in Oregon. He was doing more than me or anyone else on the team. Yet he's the one who went down.

CHAPTER 11

Help on the Way

ON A JET TO THE PROMISED LAND

Some rise, some fall, some climb—to get to Terrapin.
I can't get enough. Is it the end, or the beginning.

We'll rise up to glory.

I was there.

After firing Lenny, the Blazers came to me, saying that they needed to operate on my broken wrist. When I asked why now and not when the injury had happened months before during the season, all I got in return was a blank stare.

The Blazers hired Jack Ramsay as the new coach. I had met Jack that spring when he was still coaching Buffalo. He had a radio show as part of his Buffalo Braves deal, and I was a pregame guest. We did an intriguing spot, and I came away very impressed.

When Dr. Jack (with a PhD in education) got to Portland, his first order of business was to go around to all the guys on the team and get a sense of what we had. He came to see me first. We sat in the front main room, my arm still in a most cumbersome cast, and talked about everything. I told him of my concerns, frustrations, and disappointment, that this was not what I had hoped for in joining the NBA.

As he was leaving our house, I begged him to coach us, and to not assume that any of us knew anything about basketball. When that got back to Coach Wooden and Lenny Wilkens, they were more than a bit taken aback.

When Jack was finished with his round of meetings he went straight to the Blazers offices and told the management team the same story that Lenny had been telling them for two years—that there was no way this was ever going to work. That argument got Lenny Wilkens fired. The same line of thinking got Jack Ramsay the NBA championship.

The Blazers listened to Jack, in a way that they never did to Lenny. And Jack began what he was brilliant at—creating the vision and makeup of the team.

—

In the spring of 1976, with the season winding down for both the NBA and the ABA, and with Boston going on to beat Phoenix (who had shocked Rick Barry, Jamaal Wilkes, and the defending champ Warriors in the Western Conference Finals) for the NBA title, the struggling-for-survival ABA found itself in a state of serious contraction.

Late in what were to be the last gasping moments of the final regular season for the ABA, the league was collapsing seemingly by the breath, going from ten teams to seven in the blink of an eye—during the season. Desperately trying to hang on and salvage what was left, the ABA was only a skeleton by now. But all the players had to go somewhere. And many of the really good ones ended up on the Kentucky Colonels, then coached by a young firebrand, Hubie Brown.

Today we know Hubie as the league's elder statesman and a calm voice of reason, sanity, and measured poise and discipline. Things were different forty years ago—on literally every front. It was a different culture then. The players on opposing teams—there was very little player movement from team to team—didn't like each other. And there was next to zero fraternizing with coaches on the other teams. Are you kidding? We were trying to win. Everything.

And so the Kentucky Colonels, with an immensely talented All-Star, Hall of Fame roster that included the likes of Dan Issel, Artis Gilmore, Louie Dampier, Maurice Lucas, Marvin Barnes, Steve Jones, and many more, had a real chance. But Hubie in those days thought it was a beneficial coaching tool to yell, scream, and curse at his own players.

So in one game, Hubie is going berserk, and directing all his wrath and fury in the huddle toward Maurice Lucas.

Now Maurice, who was never anybody's fool, would have none of this. So while Hubie was berating him, Maurice finally had enough and walked out of the huddle down to the end of the team's bench. There he sat, all by himself, arms calmly folded across his massive chest and staring impassively straight ahead, all the while seething inside.

Hubie, incensed at this insubordination and sensing an opportunity to drive his point and style home, now followed Maurice down to the end of the line of chairs. Standing over the seated Lucas, Hubie was now thrusting his pointed finger into the face and chest of Maurice and angrily chastising him for everything, including walking out of the team's huddle and not allowing the coach to continue "the lecture."

Maurice just sat there, stoically statuesque, staring unblinkingly, and unflinchingly ahead. And eventually Hubie, finally realizing that he wasn't getting through and that his time-out was running out, hurried back to the rest of his team and got back to explaining the game plan and the next play.

When Hubie resumed coaching in the huddle, Maurice slowly rose from his chair and stalked over. With Hubie on his knee and having already moved on, Maurice—now in the huddle himself, and towering over the coach—reached down and grabbed Hubie by the shirt, coat, and neck. He jacked Hubie up off the ground, pulling him into Maurice's face. And this time it was Maurice doing the talking. He looked directly into Hubie's soul, right through his now-bulging eyes. And

Maurice calmly and clearly said to the coach, "If you ever publicly embarrass me like that again, I'm going to kill you on the spot."

Maurice then threw Hubie down and walked out of the place.

—

The season was soon over for everybody—Hubie's Colonels fell in the ABA semifinals—and then in late June, the fate of professional basketball was decided in the Cape Cod Room at Dunfey's Resort in Hyannis, Massachusetts. Here the ABA and NBA owners quietly gathered, and NBA commissioner Larry O'Brien ran the proceedings. In all of forty-four minutes, the ABA was disbanded and gone for good, with the exception of the gifting to the Silna brothers in St. Louis of a percentage of the future NBA television money in perpetuity. In this brilliant negotiation, Daniel and Ozzie turned out to be the biggest winners in the whole deal. Only four teams remained—Denver, San Antonio, New York, and Indiana—joining the NBA with a $3.2 million entry fee per team, payment due in full by mid-September. Suddenly there were all these really good but orphaned players from the abandoned ABA squads. They were all without teams, but clearly capable of playing in the NBA. So they had a dispersal draft.

Chicago had the No. 1 pick. And Artis Gilmore was the easy and obvious choice.

Atlanta had the No. 2 pick. And Maurice Lucas was equally as easy and obvious. Except that by now, Hubie Brown had been hired to coach the Hawks.

Jack Ramsay was aware of the Maurice-Hubie history. So the call was made. The Blazers offered Geoff Petrie, a top-flight and highly marketable talent (Princeton pedigree, NBA Rookie of the Year and all) to Atlanta, along with Steve Hawes, a serviceable role player for an emerging team, for the dispersal draft rights to Maurice Lucas.

Atlanta and Hubie accepted immediately.

The deal went down. Geoff unfortunately went down right out of the gate, tearing up his knee and never playing again. Steve Hawes went on to have a decent complementary role-playing career. And in a most remarkable simple twist of fate, Maurice went on to become the greatest Trail Blazer ever.

The Blazers also had their own pick in the ABA dispersal draft. And with the fifth pick we took Moses Malone, who was the same age as Maurice and me, but who had chosen a different route to the Promised Land, bypassing college altogether.

Back in Portland, Jack kept remaking the team. Jack wanted speed and quickness at every position. Sidney and John Johnson were traded. LaRue was released. Steve Jones and others were not asked back. Steve, to his everlasting credit, never looked back, as tough as it always is at the end of the line, particularly in your hometown. Steve went on to a stellar thirty-plus-year career as a top broadcaster for literally every major media company that ever existed.

In the NBA Draft, we were able to get Wally Walker from Virginia with the sixth overall pick, and Johnny Davis from Dayton (and the NCAA triple overtime game in Tucson with UCLA from three years before) in the second round.

Dave Twardzik came from the ABA, and Herm Gilliam came down from the Sonics in Seattle.

Corky Calhoun was next aboard, and then Robin Jones showed up as well.

At the end of the postproduction mixing there were only five guys left from the year before: Lionel, Bobby Gross, Larry Steele, Lloyd Neal, and me.

I spent most of the summer in Oregon on our farm, at Loprinzi's gym, on tour with the Grateful Dead, and once again having to move—at least within our cozy northwest Portland neighborhood.

After my wrist surgery, I was pretty limited physically—screwed, actually, what with most of my left arm and hand heavily casted, and with a screw pinning the fractured bone together. But early on I could go to Loprinzi's and work the rest of me. Then I could eventually get my bike up on the rollers for some much-needed indoor spinning. I also practiced regularly and played endless pickup games all over town with the Portland Timbers professional soccer team. And pretty soon, once I got my hand and wrist back from the cast and surgery, I was riding my bike everywhere.

—

As summer rolled on—and the Oregon summer is often as nice as it gets—Maurice Lucas got to town. He was early, and said he wanted to get together ASAP and get started. We met at Jake's, a very nice seafood restaurant not too far from our house. I walked over. He brought Herm Gilliam with him. We had the best time. It was my first real time with Luke since my UCLA hotel room in Greensboro, North Carolina, from our jointly failed Final Four three and a half years earlier. It was everything I could have ever hoped for—on every level.

As we said goodbye out on the street after we finished it all up, we were shaking hands with good wishes all around, when Maurice squeezed my one good hand real hard. He pulled me in tight, wouldn't let me go, as he looked deep into my soul, right through my eyes, and said, "Hey, this is going to be great. And we're going to win the NBA championship—this year."

I looked back at him like he was crazy. What could he possibly be thinking?

The Blazers were still an expansion franchise, had never won more than 38 games in an entire season (out of 82), and had never even made the playoffs. And Maurice had not lived through the maddening frustration and heartbreaking disappointment of my first two seasons in Portland.

Maurice and Herm could both feel my unease, discomfort, and doubt. That only made Luke squeeze my hand harder. I thought he was going to break that one, too.

And with even greater tenacity, he looked at me with that fierce scowl that we would all soon come to know—and love. And he repeated, but even slower and with more conviction this time, "We're going to win the NBA championship . . . this year!"

I never doubted anything Maurice Lucas ever said for the rest of his life.

—

As we began to ramp things up for the start of the new season, Jack Ramsay was relentless in his preparation, innovation, and attention to detail, including his insistence that on day one, we would all have to run a timed mile in under six minutes, and jump rope for two uninterrupted minutes without missing a beat. We rolled our eyes.

We thought it was all ludicrous. We were young, vibrant, and had everything going our way. Fitness and endurance were not my problems—stress fractures and broken bones were. I had simply had too many of them over the previous couple of years.

Anyway, we all made it, with the exception of Lloyd Neal, who couldn't get the running part done in time. There was a fine involved— five dollars for every second over six minutes for the mile.

Lionel had started going to Loprinzi's with me. Like me, he got totally into it. Bobby Gross was as fine and gifted a natural athlete as there ever was. Nothing was ever a problem for either one of these twenty-two-year-olds.

—

From the beginning, the team had remarkably positive chemistry, all because of Maurice, who as the ringmaster of the circus loved the responsibility of bringing it all together. And with two horrendously bad stutterers in Moses Malone and me, Big Luke had a field day in the pre- and post-practice locker room. He would tease and taunt Moses and me unmercifully, to the point of tears, we would all be laughing so much. And there was nothing that either of us could say or do—no matter how hard we tried. We simply could not talk or respond to whatever Maurice said or did. Maurice was a combination of Eddie Murphy and Jamie Foxx. It was hilariously funny. There is nothing like being on a team. And I've never known anyone better at pulling the team together than Maurice Lucas.

Maurice was also very into the business aspects of professional basketball. In those early days of the shoe company battles for supremacy,

Maurice was playing all sides of the game. At one point he had three different shoe deals—all at the same time. Nike, Puma, and adidas.

Maurice would send the ball boy who took care of our locker room out into the arena before the game to find out which one of the company reps was there that night. And then Maurice would dress accordingly.

We opened the preseason schedule at home against the Lakers, who had completely rebuilt their team when they were able to trade with Milwaukee for Kareem. Los Angeles went on to surround their towering pillar of greatness with Lucius Allen, Don Chaney, Kermit Washington, Cazzie Russell, and now Coach Jerry West. It was truly a raucous and momentous affair, right from the opening tip. I loved to play against Kareem and the Lakers, and now for the first time, I was finally healthy—in a relative sense—and I had Maurice Lucas as my teammate.

In the closing moments, the ball and everything else on the line—the game, our dreams, and chances—was rolling toward the out-of-bounds corner on the way to the Blazers locker room. With the clock ticking down, Maurice fought his way through countless players from both sides. After shaking everybody off and now with the ball firmly in hand and in complete control but with scant time to close the deal, Maurice drove the ball straight to the rim along the right baseline. The mighty Kareem came over to deny Maurice. They both rose higher than humanly possible, and Kareem had all visible angles covered perfectly. But somehow Maurice was able to contort his body around Kareem, glide under the basket, and surface on the far side while still ascending. Big Luke threw down the most incredible reverse slam dunk right in Kareem's face for the game winner at the buzzer. Maurice flung both arms and clenched fists in the air in the classic Muhammad Ali victory pose. And things were never the same again.

That night a tradition started in Portland. Whenever Big Luke was decimating yet another helpless foe, the Blazermaniacs would roar LUUUUUUUUUUUUKE, LUUUUUUUUUUUUUKE, LUUU-UUUUUUUKE!

—

As we rolled through the exhibition tour, some very powerful themes started to develop. We had an exceptional team. Maurice Lucas was phenomenal. And Moses was a raw but unpolished gem, who, shockingly, couldn't seem to ever get into the game.

Maurice was beloved in Portland from the moment he got to town. The road was a different story. I had always been the villain for the road team and crowd, from the very beginning of my playing days. The other team and its fans knew that they had to get to me in some way. But now for the first time, the wrath and vicious invective on the road were directed squarely at Maurice.

I asked him about it early on, and he brushed me off with the casual remark that the last time he had been through this town, he had beaten up the other team's star.

The booing of Maurice Lucas became an everyday occurrence at our away games. But he was a kind, gentle, and warmhearted soul. As it continued unabated wherever we went, I stayed on him about it.

"So, you punched out Artis?" Yes, was his quiet reply.

"So, you punched out Dr. J?" Yes. He seemed to be getting irritated.

"So, you punched out—?" But before I could get out any more names, Maurice turned on me quickly and scowled: "Look, I punched them all out, every one of them—a lot of the coaches, too—and that's all you need to know."

I never pursued this line of questioning with him again.

He wasn't the least bit concerned about the away crowd's reactions. It drove him, I think, to unprecedented heights. He really loved punching people in the face—but only when he had to.

—

Moses, on the other hand, was having a very difficult time, and despite the fact that he was a magnificent player and a great teammate, he ended up being traded away right before the season. When Dr. Jack and the front office gave us the news, we were all saddened and stunned. When they went on to tell us and the world that the reason for the trade was that on the whole, Robin Jones was a better player than Moses Malone, we stood there staring, our jaws slack and mouths wide open in utter disbelief. It sure seemed to me to be an economic move for the Blazers, looking to cut labor costs. Moses had been destroying us in practice. And while Robin was a solid player and a good dude, Moses went on to be a three-time NBA MVP, the lead player on a truly great NBA Championship team, and one of the 50 Greatest Players in NBA History. In retrospect, the Blazers should have traded me.

In spite of the Blazers giving Moses away—for a draft pick, no less—the team was very, very good right from the outset, although we couldn't initially win on the road. Lionel and Dave Twardzik were the starting guards, and Herm Gilliam and Larry Steele backed them up.

Dave was as unique as could be, a six-foot center from his early days who gravitated to ostensibly play guard as he moved up the ladder. He had uncanny anticipation, great hands and vision, a remarkable gift of pace with an extremely creative change of it, and a change of direction, too, that no opponent could ever figure out. He loved backdoor cuts.

Dave and I would spend countless enjoyable hours in the paint, practicing, he on his offense with his imaginative flip shots, me on my defense, trying to send it all back.

I'm the biggest believer in the world in the importance of getting off to a good start and being at your best in the biggest moments and games. And how great it was that Maurice Lucas seconded that emotion. The grander the stage, the brighter the lights, the greater the pressure, Maurice always rose to the occasion. And he didn't like to wait for it to come to him.

As a center, I was always responsible for the center jump—a most critical part of the game of life. But Maurice took personal responsibility for those crucial opening moments as well. Often in the biggest of games, or really whenever he felt the need, he would take his customary position on the offensive edge of the center circle, more than ready to explode and give us that initial possession.

The other team was always aware of Maurice's importance to our team and would try to deny him possession of the ball and his space—generally by pinching in on both sides of his perfectly legal and well-established position.

As the ball was put in the air to start the game, and as all eyes in the building were rising to watch its ascent, Maurice, at the perfect time, would take a big step to his right and elbow the other guy right in the neck. Then he would solidly plant his right leg and come back to his left with a powerful right cross to the other guy's face.

As they all staggered back under the onslaught, Maurice would proudly announce, "We've come to play. And we hope that you have, too!"

It was wonderful to be Maurice Lucas's teammate.

—

We started to come into our own as the season progressed, and from the beginning our fans sensed something special was happening. They all loved Luke; Jack Ramsay's personality and style clicked immediately; Lionel's skin color no longer seemed to be such an issue now that people realized how good he really was; and the team game and spirit that we lived and played resonated with our fans' own daily challenges.

The Blazermaniacs and the people in Oregon have always treated me better than I deserve. But now that I was relatively healthy and able to play some, they went over the top. I lived in as hip and urban an environment as Portland had to offer in those days, on Northwest Kearney and Twenty-Third Streets. And the fans and neighbors would always come by the house bearing inspirational gifts that they would leave on the front porch—food, fruit, brownies, flowers, Grateful Dead stuff, and music. Every day when I came and went there was more. I would ride my bike everywhere, and the people would stop and cheer. I would try to ride my bike to and from the games. With my pregame ritual set, they quickly figured out my route and time of departure. They would line the streets and yell and scream for our beloved team.

Eventually they packed the Memorial Coliseum every night, 12,666 strong. That included the standing-room-only slots that they painted and sold as tickets around the midlevel ring that separated the upper and lower bowls. It was embarrassing for me when I couldn't get tickets for my friends in the Grateful Dead: they would too often end up standing for the entire game in their little designated slot. But come they did, one and all.

The games were so popular and really became cultural events, with all the Blazermaniacs bringing their handmade signs of support, noisemakers, and party favors, which they would regularly share with us.

The team didn't have much of a local television package then, so they started to show all the home games on a big, closed-circuit screen at the Paramount Theatre—the same joint where I originally met the Grateful Dead. While we never were actually in the Paramount during the show (we were the live show across the river), the tales from the golden road through the Paramount became legend. I'm not quite sure how many rules and regulations were ever actually enforced at the Paramount, but I do know that everybody who went had a real good time.

The Blazers fan base, which really started that year, became one of the greatest economic forces in sports business history. Ultimately, our terrific fans bought every ticket for every game for eighteen consecutive years, still an NBA record, and an all-sports record for years, until baseball's Boston Red Sox recently broke the consecutive-games—but not the years—record.

As things were settling into a nice rhythm with this completely new and totally invigorating basketball team, things were changing in the rest of our lives as well. The presidential election of 1976 brought a fresh respite of sanity, intelligence, common sense, and human decency, which had eluded us during the weird, crazed days of the Nixon cabal. When Jimmy Carter was thankfully and finally voted in, we soon got a phone call from some people with his transition team. They told us that they were going to change the direction, focus, and methods of the Patty Hearst–SLA case, and that they were going to stop the FBI from following us around all the time, stop listening to all our phone calls, stop reading all our mail before we did, and basically let us get back to living our lives, free and easy. We were most grateful, although the trust that is always necessary to make things really work was a long time coming in its restoration.

—

We made the playoffs that year for the first time in the now seven-year history of the expansion franchise. We would have done better and finished with the best record in the league as well, but I had missed seventeen games that season, and the team faltered during the stretch. In retrospect, they were two more foot and ankle injuries—twelve games out with a bulbously inflamed Achilles tendon, five with a severely sprained ankle—that could be traced to the congenital lack of mobility in my lowest extremities. In the MVP voting, done in those days by the players, I finished second, runner-up to Kareem.

Our first-round matchup and first-ever NBA playoff experience was with the Chicago Bulls, a team that had played very poorly at the start of the season but came alive down the stretch with an epic run that had them playing the best ball of any team in the league that spring.

They had a lot going for them—tons of talent, an incredible fan base, and a powerful home-court advantage. But what they really had was a raging bull in Artis Gilmore, who was not nearly the best player— that was Kareem. But Artis was as tough and difficult to play against as any man alive. He was 7'2". And who could ever tell how much he weighed? What scale could measure this true giant of a man?

What really made Artis so tough, though, was that he had no com- prehension that there were rules, and not just for basketball—rules like three seconds, double dribble, traveling, and offensive fouls—but for human decency as well.

And right as we were getting ready for our first NBA playoffs, the referees went on strike for better pay and working conditions. It made a lot of sense to me from a labor, social, economic, and political perspec- tive, but as I looked out at Artis on that court without our trained and reliable refs, I was more than a bit concerned.

So here we were at center stage, about to start our first, monumen- tal, best-of-three NBA playoff series against Artis and the Bulls, and a critical component of the whole show—competent refs—was nowhere to be found.

We had the home-court advantage and first chance in our building. And with Game 1 with the Bulls raging on, everybody is in early foul trouble. And while these substitute refs are trying to keep the show going, it's really not working.

Maurice Lucas was helped immensely during his career by the fact that he played during an era that had only two refs per game, and very limited use of television instant replay.

In those days there were physical fights and confrontations in every game. And Maurice was always in the middle of it all. He loved it. He knew others didn't. And he was always willing to do what other people couldn't or wouldn't do. It was the way things were. And after business was settled, and everybody calmed down—we got back to playing the game.

Maurice usually got a technical foul in every game he played, particularly if the refs were paying attention. The reasons covered the entire spectrum—punching somebody, elbowing another, kneeing or hip-checking some hapless soul in the groin, head-slaps with the back of his hand, throwing the ball at someone, pulling an opponent's pants down. You name it, he did it. And we all loved him for it. Because once Maurice became your teammate, none of us ever had to worry about anything—ever again.

It's now early in the second half of our first NBA playoff game with the Bulls, and it is as intense a scene as I've ever been a part of; things could easily go either way. Maurice was as smart a player, guy, and competitor as I've ever known. He always knew the score—in the games of our lives. He and everybody else knew that he had already gotten a technical foul in the first half. So when he committed another crime against human decency early in the third quarter, we were caught off guard. Everybody knew that we had to have Maurice if we were going to win anything. That's the way teams are. He was indispensable.

And so the ball is dead, we're all standing there waiting on the ref, who's ready to make the call on Maurice's latest transgression, and with this second technical, Maurice would be automatically ejected—and with him gone, what were we to do?

The 12,666 Blazermaniacs stood hushed. As we all hovered at mid-court, and with the entire crowd standing but stunned, and everything in the balance, Maurice was about fifteen feet away from the ref, who was standing there poised with the whistle in his mouth, ready to make the call. The other nine players in the game at the time were all right there, between Maurice and the ref, almost like a gauntlet, but really this was between two powerfully opposing forces. As the ref is inhaling to blow the whistle, Maurice quickly takes three long strides straight at the poor unsuspecting guy, reaches out, and grabs the whistle out of the guy's hand and mouth. Now the whistle is also tethered to the guy's neck with the string lanyard that they use. Maurice yanks on the whistle, breaks the lanyard, and is now standing toe-to-toe with the staggered ref, who has no idea what to do.

Maurice, towering over the guy, looks down at him, looks at all of us standing right there, and growls, "Ref, if you blow this whistle and call another technical foul on me and eject me from this game, I'm going to kill you on the spot."

The trembling ref took a step back. He looked around at everything—all of us, the fans, the coaches. He took it all in, including the deepest breath that I've ever seen taken.

Finally, after a seeming eternity, he spoke. "Mr. Lucas," he said, "if you would please just give me my whistle back, we can get on with this great game."

Maurice gave the guy his whistle back, and we went on to win the game. Barely.

———

The show moved to Chicago for Game 2. It was the single wildest game that I was ever involved in. Chicago Stadium was huge, probably twice the size of what we had in Portland. The Bulls had a publicly listed ca-pacity of about 23,000 for basketball. But the upper levels and balconies of the Stadium were just open benches, with no backs to them. And like Artis's true size and weight, how could you ever tell how many people were actually in there?

When the game was finally over, Brian McIntyre, then the young PR guy for the Bulls, released attendance figures somewhere in the neighborhood north of 29,000 fans for the game. Brian was quickly called into the boss's office, where he was immediately told that the Chicago fire marshal was a very good friend of the Bulls' management, and they wanted to keep that relationship positive. And so from this point forward, no matter the actual size of the crowd, Brian was never to report the attendance as more than the 23,000 capacity.

It didn't matter what they said—it seemed as if the entire city of Chicago was inside the building. To help things along for the home team there, there was at least one hard-liquor shot bar outside every hallway leading into the seating bowl. And during every time-out and dead-ball stoppage of play, the fans would race out the nearest doorway, slap down their dollars, and start pounding away.

The game was back and forth, up and down, and every which way. There were something like thirty-nine lead changes and thirty-two ties. At one point when we were surging, one of their assistant coaches came running onto the floor and started choking Herm Gilliam with his entire arm around Herm's neck. Maurice raced over and leveled the coach and pulled Herm back into the game of our lives. Ultimately, we lost, 107–104, setting up the final showdown in Portland.

—

Before the decisive Game 3, Jack Ramsay came to me with some bizarre suggestions on things to try against Artis, who was just really tough for me. They included some defensive fronting while face-guarding Artis, which seemed ludicrous in our discussions but worked very well when I actually tried it.

Regardless, I still fouled out late in the game, joining Maurice and Dave Twardzik, who had both already fouled out. It was not a good spot to be in, but our great fans stayed with us when all seemed lost. And fortunately we had Lionel, who always played his best against the Bulls. He made countless huge plays down the stretch.

While the game was still very much up for grabs, Lionel got into the lane with his own dribble still alive. When Artis lumbered over to shut him down, Lionel flipped the ball over to Robin Jones, who had replaced me. Robin, who did not have the quickest release on his shot, coiled, then unwound, elevated, and let it go from about eighteen feet out in front by the right free-throw-line elbow. Big Artis recovered from shutting off Lionel and was now right there, back on Robin. As the ball left Robin's fingertips, it did not look to have any chance of success. And as Artis soared and extended to try to send it back, he was able to get just a couple of fingertips on the ball after it had cleanly left Robin's hands. Artis's efforts were just enough to deflect the course of Robin's jumper, and seemingly the course of history as well. Maurice, Dave, and I were all standing right there next to Dr. Jack on the sideline, unable to do anything but watch as our hopes and dreams were apparently crushed by Artis.

But that shot by Robin, scraped by Artis, was redirected just enough to bank off the backboard and into the basket.

Chicago responded, and we called time-out. Dr. Jack was none too pleased with Lionel, telling him in the huddle, "We ran the play for you to shoot, not for you to pass to Robin."

We ran the pick and roll again, only this time Lionel was wide open—Artis was afraid to leave Robin—and he sealed the win with a jumper.

We were on our way, and never looked back.

—

Off to Denver, for the Nuggets, who had the talented David Thompson, Dan Issel, Bobby Jones, Bobby Wilkerson, and Coach Larry Brown. Having spent a life with plenty of high-altitude training, the effects of the mile-high elevation never really played out for me. But the players, talent, and coach sure did.

David was better than ever, as his skill level had skyrocketed under

Larry Brown. Dan Issel was always a problem for me, with his excellent footwork, outstanding perimeter shot, tough position defense, and excellent transition game. Plus he was always able to get to the free-throw line against me. The Bobbys—Jones and Wilkerson—were the kind of well-rounded, interesting team guys whose squads just won the games as they went quietly about their business.

Denver had the home-court advantage, and the first game of this best-of-seven series went right down to the closing play.

We were down one, but with plenty of time left for a well-executed play. In our huddle, Jack Ramsay drew up a masterful plan that involved at least four of us, with a combination of a ball swing to the weak side, a down-screen, a cross-screen, and an open-up post opportunity that would schematically create a wide-open jumper on the right side with an option to dump it down low for a power play inside.

Bobby Gross was our outstanding in-bounds feeder. He dutifully got it in to Maurice on the left wing, who totally disregarded everything Jack had just told us. Luke snatched the ball away from the defensive pressure and pivoted inside, swinging the ball in front of him like a truncheon, flinging his defender aside like a rag doll, and then started working his way toward the rim with his own solo dribble. Halfway there, with the clock now against him, to say nothing of the entire state of Colorado collapsing defensively around him, Luke pulled up and delivered a classically perfect jumper, which easily found its way home as the clock ticked down, ensuring our victory, and ultimately the series. As good as Denver was, they had no chance at our place.

Jack was livid at Luke for breaking the play. In the euphoria of the winner's locker room, Jack kept coming back to the fact that Luke didn't run the play. Finally, Luke simply said, "Come on, Jack. We won the game. It's all good. Things will be OK."

We all loved Luke, and he was such a big-game and moment-of-truth performer. It was all good. Over the years, Jack never failed to bring it up, shaking his head and muttering how Luke didn't run the play.

The Nuggets took the next game. They were good, and had a top coach and fans who thought they had a chance. They had the advantage in Denver, but we were unstoppable at home and took the next two games to go up 3–1.

The Nuggets won Game 5 in Denver. It was the first time in sixteen days that we had the real refs, but even so we could not escape the end-less whistles, and I fouled out. Even worse, we lost Dave Twardzik to a severe ankle sprain. This development completely changed the dynam-ics of what lay ahead. What were we to do without Dave? He was great off the ball at both ends of the court, had terrific hands, and was tough as nails. It hurt to lose him.

On the plane ride home, with Dave now on crutches, Coach Ram-say came by my seat and laid his eyebrows on me—the indication that he had something very serious he wanted to talk about.

Dr. Jack is a very earnest and analytical guy, and an extremely smart and deep thinker—and he has these very thick eyebrows, which would furrow back and over his bald head. And when he put the "'brows" on you, it was about to all come down.

He said that with Dave's ankle injury, which was now discovered to be much worse than it initially appeared, Jack wanted me to know that he was planning on putting Larry Steele in Dave's place as our other starting guard with Lionel. As I sat there, crammed into my tiny airplane seat, Jack explained that a lot of his thinking was driven by the desire to keep Herm Gilliam in his natural rotation off the bench, in that Herm was really the only guy on our team who could provide instant statistical production without any help from anybody. Larry would give us conti-nuity, stability, a bigger defensive presence, and outstanding perimeter shooting, which was more critical than ever, what with our opponents being completely unable to come to grips with Maurice down low.

I looked back at Jack while he laid out the whole vision and dream in his always methodical and meticulous way. When he was finally fin-ished, I said something to the effect of, "That's the worst idea I think I've ever heard."

I went on to explain that our game, our real strength as a team, was speed and quickness. And we had a guy who had been sitting there on the bench all season, never getting any play, never saying a word. He was the quietest teammate that I ever had. But he was also the quickest and fastest guy I had ever seen, and if we were going to remain true to ourselves, our style, and our vision of what our team was about, then how about giving our twenty-year-old rookie, Johnny Davis, a chance?

Coach Ramsay muttered something about experience, stability, seniority, and that he was the Coach here, and then he walked back to his seat.

When we gathered that night for the game, No. 6 and hopefully the series clincher, Jack told us for the first time that Johnny Davis was going to start in Dave's absence.

The rest is history, as Johnny went out and in his first real NBA action—the guy had never played in any meaningful action up until that night—absolutely lit the joint up. Twenty-five points, seven assists, four steals, and thirty-nine minutes later, things would never be the same again.

Not only did the Denver Nuggets now know who Johnny Davis was—so did the rest of the world.

Johnny never looked back. Nor did we. His joining our active squad was very much like the night Mickey Hart joined the Grateful Dead. History was made, and the future had a new script. We became incomparable, unstoppable, and beyond description.

—

For us, it was now on to Los Angeles, Kareem, and the Lakers. They had the home court, they had the best player and the league's MVP, but they had struggled with Golden State, going the distance to finally win at home at the Forum in seven games.

We were fresh and ready, and we now had an entirely new dimension to our team in Johnny Davis. Dave Twardzik was not going to be able to make it back anytime soon. But with Johnny's speed, quickness, and explosiveness, there didn't seem to be anything that we couldn't do on the court.

The Lakers had some injury problems. Their guards Lucius Allen and Don Chaney (both heroes of mine as I was growing up) were hobbled with foot and knee problems. Kermit Washington wasn't able to play at all. That left only Don Ford from Santa Barbara to wrestle with Maurice Lucas.

But they still had Kareem, who seemingly never got hurt. At his fiftieth birthday party years later, a grouchy Kareem showed up in a walking ankle boot and using a cane for stability. I asked him what could possibly have happened; he had not played in the NBA since he was forty-two. He was mad as can be, saying that he had to have some carving work done recently on his little toe, and that it wasn't pleasant; it was really slowing him down. I asked him how many surgeries that was for him now. He seemed surprised, then told me it was his first.

We ran Kareem's Lakers out of their gym in the first game, finding a big lead early and never looking back. They couldn't do anything against our team's speed, had real trouble even advancing the ball up the court, and had no answer for Maurice.

Jack Ramsay's strategy for defending Kareem was brilliant. Pressure the advance of the ball full court, make them use the shot clock in setting up, and ultimately shade them to the right side of the floor, forcing Kareem to come across to the ball, and then if he did take his baseline skyhook, their floor balance was at their weakest. My job was to turn Kareem away from the skyhook, and generally Bobby Gross would come as a help defender after Kareem got into his move, going to his right-shoulder and left-hand options.

Real changes came about for our team with the addition of Johnny Davis. Teamed with Lionel, he gave us the fastest backcourt in the history of the game. Offensively, all we had to do was throw the ball up the court and Lionel and Johnny would always get to it first. Defensively, the other team could not get the ball up the court because of Lionel's and Johnny's in-your-face, lockdown tenacity. The Count from our UCLA press came back into play with our great and tireless fans. The injuries to Lucius Allen and Don Chaney only exacerbated the Lakers' problems.

Game 2, still in Los Angeles, was better for them, and not as good for us. Great teams have set rotations, but when a guy is having a big game, you never take him out, running the risk that he might cool off on his own. And that was Lionel that day in L.A. He was on his way to a 40-point day, but late in the third quarter he stumbled into foul trouble and Dr. Jack finally had to take him out. When Lionel went to our bench, he had been the best player in the game to that point, doing everything.

Without him, we were now on the ropes and fading fast. But then Herm Gilliam rotated in and immediately started playing like a man possessed. He stole every pass, picked off every dribble, got every rebound, and made every shot.

We went from being down and out to being in complete control, all because of Herm's brilliance. And it all happened so fast. WHAM! Even though Lionel came back to finish with 31 points and an NBA-record 8 steals, we would not have won that game—and who knows about the series—had it not been for Herm Gilliam that day. And that's what's so wonderfully fun about being on a team in a game like basketball—you don't ever know where that extra boost is going to come from. We loved Herm. He was the oldest guy on our team, with the most experience, and his classically beautiful game was invaluable.

After winning the first two games in this best-of-seven series in L.A., we knew we had it. We were heading back to Portland, and nothing was going to stop us.

As our run for the roses that spring was becoming obvious to all, the Blazermaniacs took it to a whole new level. Not only were they overfilling the Coliseum and the Paramount Theatre every night, but they started to come to the airport to send us off and then to meet us on our return.

Bill Schonely, our beloved TV and radio man, and really the heart and soul of the entire franchise, would announce on the air what our travel schedule would be. And sure enough, huge and ever-growing throngs of fans would show up at the airport. The numbers were staggering. Tens of thousands of people would be there to see us. There was no security at the airports in those days. It probably didn't cost anything to park—I can't remember if the airport parking lot was even paved.

And everybody came. Each trip, there were more and more people. It was incredible. We had real trouble even getting on and off the plane. I have never seen anything like it. And it made us better and bigger than we actually were.

The final two games in Portland against Kareem were fun, and tough, and as always against Kareem, you had to be at your best at every moment. The Lakers ended up playing like great champions, but they just didn't have enough to do anything other than come close. In the closing minutes of the fourth and final game, an exasperated and thoroughly defeated and deflated Prez Ford, ever so tired of the beat-down that had just taken place, finally just wound up and threw the ball at Maurice Lucas. Big Luke just looked sadly and quizzically at Ford, and then the refs. I think the refs threw poor Don out. Who can remember; the game was over and our fans were well into their party. We took both games and moved on.

—

We faced Philadelphia for the championship, although we had to wait a seeming eternity for them to dispatch Houston and our ex-teammate Moses Malone in the Eastern Finals. While you have no control over your opponents, we knew that Philly was eventually going to get there. They were good. Real good. And we were looking forward to it.

Jack Ramsay was from Philadelphia. He had grown up there, went to college there at St. Joe's, met his future wife, Jean, there at a Halloween dance—she mistakenly thought he was wearing a mask. He raised their five children there. He coached at his alma mater, then coached and ran the 76ers himself before moving on to Buffalo and their new franchise.

But even though Jack had all of his important life's connections to our next opponent, like Coach Wooden he never brought it up. Never even mentioned it to us. He was there for us, it was not about him, and he was all business.

Media reports and commentaries had promoted the Philadelphia 76ers all season long as probably the greatest basketball team ever assembled, with the likes of Dr. J, George McGinnis, Doug Collins, Henry Bibby (from our UCLA team), World B. Free, Caldwell Jones, Darryl Dawkins, Steve Mix, Kobe's dad Joe Bryant, Harvey Catchings, and Mike Dunleavy. They had an excellent coach as well, Gene Shue, who had been a terrific college and NBA player.

Gene Shue's specific strategy of having his center Caldwell Jones bring the ball up the court was brilliant for them. So much of our team's success was our guards' defensive ability to deny the advance of the ball. That aspect alone was enough to allow us to beat the Lakers. But Philly's guards were scorers, not setup ball handlers.

In the opening moments of Game 1, while we were setting our full-court defensive pressure with Lionel and Johnny, Philly's guards just trotted down the court, and they left Caldwell, at seven feet tall, and my man, to bring it up. Perplexed and confused, I looked over to Jack for some much-needed advice and direction, and he waved me up to try to pressure Caldwell's dribble.

It was not pretty. Caldwell gave me a few shimmy shakes, I stumbled, and he went right by me. There was no way that I was going to get low defensively and pressure anybody ninety feet from the hoop—heck, even twenty feet from the hoop. I had not been able to do that since I was fourteen, when I first hurt my knee back at Helix.

We had to immediately call off our press for the rest of the series, and one of our greatest advantages was now useless. I had never seen Gene Shue so happy. I was terribly embarrassed, and Philadelphia took Game 1.

There was a four-day gap between the first and second games, but nothing changed on the court, as they pounded us one more time. We could not get anything going at all, and we were demoralized, frustrated, and embarrassed.

In the closing moments of a game that had long been decided, there was a scrum and scramble for a loose ball that Bobby Gross and Darryl Dawkins both came up with. As the refs came in whistling the play dead and calling for a jump ball, neither Bobby nor Darryl would give it up, and Darryl, the biggest, baddest dude on the court, finally ended up whipping the ball around and slamming Bobby to the hardwood floor. As everyone on the court rushed in to restore order, Bobby popped up and started barking at Darryl, calling him an idiot, jabbing his finger at him, and explaining that it was behavior like this that had earned Darryl the nickname of "Double Dummy Dawkins."

Darryl wanted no part of this, so he quickly clenched his fists and wound up to deliver a vicious right cross to Bobby's little head. I'm not sure if Darryl even knew who Bobby was, or that Bobby was one of the greatest athletes on earth. And so at the same moment Darryl winds up to deliver a knockout punch, his teammate Doug Collins is rushing in to calm things down, and Bobby easily dodges Darryl's swing, only to have the punch land smack in Collins's jaw, busting open his lip and loosening some teeth.

As we're all standing there, not quite sure what to do, Maurice Lucas suddenly realizes that it's time for him to "take care of this." He comes in hard, right at Darryl, and WHAM! Big Luke just unloads on the side of Darryl's head with a punch packing the heat, power, and velocity of a giant meteor crashing to earth.

All heck breaks loose, and now Luke and Dawkins are going at it. The two titans are now toe-to-toe, fists clenched and raised, and Darryl is closing in on Luke. It's tense as can be, because most surprising to Darryl, and everyone else but us, Luke is not backing down, and is actually calling him in, as if to say, "Come on, let's go, big boy."

Fans, including Darryl's brothers, all dressed in patent leather suits with matching hats, are now surging onto the court, all rushing to get to Maurice, who continues to hold his ground against all comers.

When everybody finally realized that Maurice was very serious, they quickly dropped their fists and looked sheepishly around for the refs to come in and stop this whole bit of nonsense immediately.

The refs were able to restore order and banish Darryl to the locker room, where he took out his frustrations on the toilets, stalls, and lockers. Imagine how strong Darryl was that he was able to pull and yank toilet fixtures and bathroom stalls off the floor and walls with his bare hands. Meanwhile, we were down by an incalculable margin on the court and quietly finished the game as quickly as we could and limped shamefully out of there.

In the wild aftermath, there was a lot of talk, all of it from Philadelphia. "This series is over!" Dr. J proclaimed. "We know their plays better than they do." Dawkins was still incensed that he had not gotten to Maurice, although it must be pointed out that Maurice was there for him and not going anywhere.

On our end, Jack Ramsay had his finest moment when he solemnly gathered our dejected, dispirited, disheartened, discouraged squad together and told us, "We'll be fine. Our problems are our own. Guys, we have not played our game in this series. And once we get to playing our game, everything will turn out just fine. Please don't listen to, believe, or respond to the junk that we're hearing from the other side. It's all nonsense. We're going home, where we don't lose; our fans will be ready, and the schedule picks up to where we will now have regularly spaced games, no more of this only two games in over two weeks. We're going to find our rhythm, pace, and fast-break game, and it will all be good. Now let's pick ourselves up and get going."

When we got back to Portland, the incredible outpouring of love and support from our fans did whatever Jack didn't accomplish with his prophetic words. At the Portland airport, there seemed to be at least twice as many people as could fit in our arena. They were everywhere. There were so many people there as fans that the airport was not functional. They were yelling, screaming, singing, dancing, partying, waving signs, all fired up as can be, and we had just lost both games. They wanted Philadelphia. They wanted Dr. J. And they really wanted Darryl Dawkins.

Our house and neighborhood in northwest Portland was like a Grateful Dead tour stop; everybody just kept coming, camping in the streets, offering to help put the show on. My older brother, Bruce, recently an offensive lineman with the NFL's Dallas Cowboys, had watched the debacle at the end of Game 2 with many of his teammates. A bunch of really big, tough, and mean-looking guys from Dallas had then flown to Portland to make sure that everything would be OK. I had never seen so many guys who had so many scars on their faces, hands, arms—just everywhere; and all of them with no necks, their muscles bulging straight from the lateral edge of their shoulders all the way to their ears.

They demanded seats directly behind Philly's bench.

It was hard to even get to the first game in Portland, there were so many people in the streets.

What would Darryl Dawkins do?

The noise in our place was deafening, and the game wasn't even close to starting yet.

When the moment came to introduce the players for the game, we couldn't hear anything, and no one knew when it was their turn to run out onto the court.

When they got to our team's turn, the Blazermaniacs turned it up even louder. It was all white noise. It was extremely loud. It was perfect.

When they announced Maurice Lucas, the fans brought even more. It was incredibly intense.

But Maurice, instead of trotting out to our free-throw line the way you always do for pregame introductions, broke from our sideline and suddenly sprinted down the length of the court to Philadelphia's bench, where the 76ers had circled their wagons. Maurice broke through their perimeter and went straight to Darryl Dawkins and got right in his face, and gently put his hand out with a welcome offer to shake.

Nobody could believe what was going down.

Maurice had told no one. I'm not sure if he even knew what he was doing. I never asked him.

The only thing I know is that it worked. Perfectly. Darryl, and the 76ers, melted on the spot. And they never recovered.

Maurice had a way about him of making everything and everyone else irrelevant. He was the master of defining the terms of the conflict.

In Game 3 we were back to being the Blazers that Jack Ramsay had dreamed of: the fast break, the ball movement, the speed and quickness advantage, the skill level, and the fantastic pace of getting up and down the floor and just running the other team out of there.

Everything that Jack had told us would happen after our dismal performance in the games in Philadelphia came true.

And our fans kept pushing and driving us for more. And we just kept going.

And while we had so much going for us, with Jack Ramsay, Maurice Lucas, Lionel, and Johnny in the backcourt, and our incredible fans who would not let us quit or get tired, the ultimate success would not have come without Bobby Gross, who by the end had outplayed the incomparable Dr. J.

Now, Dr. J had the numbers. He had the highlight plays. He had the incredible throwdowns, mostly in my face.

But you name it, and Bobby Gross did it. He ran, back-cut, passed, rebounded, deflected passes, moved without the ball, spaced the floor, defended, fought through screens, selflessly sacrificed for the good of the team, scored in every way imaginable, anticipated the future, and showed us the way there.

By the end, Bobby had set an NBA Finals record for field goal percentage in a series—a record that still stands today.

And his job was never easy. Through that year's playoff run, the guys he was individually matched up against—in succession—were Chicago's Scott May, Denver's David Thompson, L.A.'s Cazzie Russell, and finally Dr. J. All legends. All champions. But we had Bobby Gross. And he outplayed every one of them.

—

Games 3 and 4 of the Finals were over early. We were back to our game, in our town, in our gym, and there was nothing anybody could do to slow us down.

Game 5 was what you live for as a player and team. Back in Philadelphia, they thought it would be a different story. But Bob Gross didn't let up—he was brilliant. We controlled the game from the outset, although they made a faux run late to make the score seem more respectable than it really was.

As a player, in a big game on the road, you want the other team's fans to boo, hiss, and be angry. When they turn that ire on their own team, you've done your job. Through much of the second half, the Philadelphia fans alternated between yelling and booing at their own players, sitting on their hands in stunned silence, crying in their beer, and eventually walking out early.

We still needed one more game. We knew this was ours, but we still had to bring it, and our fans were not going to leave anything to chance.

The scene upon our arrival back in Portland was over the top, even by the standards that our fans had been setting on a game-by-game basis. The entire state of Oregon had come together to be a part of this.

The final Sunday day game started early, just the way we liked it.

Get up. Eat. Get going. Let's play.

And play we did. We had comfortable leads for big parts of the game. And we were fortunate to have just gotten a still-hobbled Dave Twardzik back from his severely sprained ankle from the Denver series. He gave us a spark, but Philadelphia also came to play. For the first time in the series, really, both teams played well at the same time. They closed the gap and had the chance to tie it up on the game's final possession. But our defense shut them down. And when Johnny Davis grabbed a long ball and ran away with his dribble in the closing seconds, nobody was ever going to catch him.

The clock ticked down, and the championship was ours. We became the youngest team in the history of the NBA to win the championship. Maurice and I were twenty-four. Lionel and Bobby were twenty-two. Johnny was twenty.

It was perfect.

As the buzzer sounded, the Blazermaniacs stormed the court. I stripped off my jersey and threw it into the oncoming crowd. The party was just getting started.

———

In the four decades since that moment, I have regularly come into contact with people who approach me with a look of pride, awe, and affection. And their quiet, simple words are always eerily the same. "I was there," they whisper. And that's all that need be said to solidify the bond of something that was truly special—for all of us.

The celebration started on the court but quickly moved to the locker room, and I'm not sure if or when it ever ended. We forgot about time.

I have a wonderful picture in our house, and in my mind, of the moment when NBA commissioner Larry O'Brien presented the championship trophy to our team in a euphoric lovefest. As most of the guys reached out and up to touch our title trophy ball, I instead reached out and placed my hand on Jack Ramsay's head. I knew where the real prize and enduring treasure was.

I didn't want it to ever end. I stayed in the locker room, still in my game shorts, for hours. When I finally did leave the joint, the scene outside was much like being on tour with the Grateful Dead. People everywhere.

I somehow ended up that night at Lionel's downtown penthouse palace, and the next morning there was a parade in our honor. I arrived on my bike, but it quickly disappeared into the crowd. It was the most glorious summer day in Oregon, and everybody was just so happy and having a real good time, and there was nobody there to say no—to anything.

When I finally got up on the stage, after a parade route where our fans were passing everything back and forth, I was simply overwhelmed with the emotional outpouring. When the mayor, Neil Goldschmidt, handed me the microphone, the only thing that I could say was, "Thank you—for a real good time. And will the guy who took my bike down at the start of this whole thing please bring it back, because at some point I'm going to have to get home."

I then turned and poured the championship beer that someone had passed me all over the mayor's head.

He was a big fan of the team, and we were close friends. He acted like it was OK. I can only hope.

But that was the kind of day and deal it was. It was all OK. We were the champions.

—

If you go deep in the NBA playoffs, on top of the regular and exhibition seasons, you're basically playing more than 110 games in that year. That breaks down to having a game nearly every three days, all year round, except it's squeezed much tighter than that, what with a few months off in the summer.

We were so ready to get going again. And when Coach Ramsay decided to have training camp down the road and valley from Portland at Willamette College in Salem, we couldn't wait to get started. It meant more time together, just us. Just the guys. Just the way we liked it.

Jack had us do the timed six-minute mile again this year. I finished second behind Lionel, in probably about four and a half minutes. Startling to Jack, I stopped one stride short of the finish line and waited for everybody else to come across. When a clearly confused and befuddled Jack Ramsay called out the free-time limit, I finally took my last stride across the line, exactly one second late. I then reached down in my sock and pulled out a five-dollar bill that I had stashed there. Handing it to him, I mumbled to Jack something along the lines of us being ready, and it was time to play ball.

Once we actually got onto the court, we picked up right where we had left off three and a half months earlier—just this side of perfection. We were a much better team already, not because of any personnel changes, although Tom Owens for Robin Jones was an upgrade, but rather because we were finally beginning to really grasp the nuances, options, and continuity of Jack Ramsay's offense, and how it always led to something else if the first attempt did not play out.

And while everyone was still riding the euphoric tsunami from the previous spring, most everybody came back in even better physical shape than we were in when we had finished off Philadelphia in June. We were all young, and right from the start of the season we were back in the groove—red-hot and rolling.

We had many great rivals, including the Lakers, Philadelphia, Chicago, Seattle, Golden State, Phoenix, San Antonio, Denver, Detroit, you name them. When you're the champions, they all bring it every night—but so did we.

Like an avalanche, our team just kept rolling, getting bigger by the breath. We were on a record-setting pace through the fall, on the move toward a second championship, in a season when we consistently played near-perfect ball and set the record for the longest home-court winning streak in the history of the NBA, and I would ultimately be voted MVP.

And when it seemed as if things couldn't get any better, on January 14, 1978, the clouds over Portland parted and our second son, Nathan, was born like an unfolding flower, glistening in the morning dew—a flower that has continued an eternal bloom, and shows no signs of ever wilting.

Thirty years after our run, Jack Ramsay was asked to put the team into historical perspective. He succinctly replied: "I like our team. And we'll take our chances. Anytime. Anywhere. Against anybody."

Then, in late February, when Philadelphia rolled back into Portland on their "We Owe You One" tour, in a game that was essentially decided with the opening tip, I was running back down the court on defense and suddenly, unexpectedly, inexplicably felt a deep burning pain in my foot.

And things were never the same again. Ever.

CHAPTER 12

Shadowboxing the Apocalypse, and Wandering the Land—as the rain kept falling from a heavy sky.

THE DAZE BETWEEN: PART II

Such a long, long time to be gone, and a short time to be there.

In the rough-and-tumble world, it is staggering how fragile everything really is.

From the top to the bottom is really not ever very far.

And being unable to play—again—because of the deep burning pain in my foot quickly took me back to a place I'd never wanted to see again.

All the problems from my first two years resurfaced:

"He's soft! Come on, get tough!"

"Be a man, eat a steak."

"There's nothing wrong with him. It's all in his head. He just doesn't want to play."

I had tried with everything I had to move beyond that lonely isolation, where it was just me, all alone, in the great unknown, and there was nothing that I could do about it.

Experience has now taught me how remarkable the human body and spirit are. I have learned firsthand that when you do finally recover from trauma in your life, you do not remember how bad it was and how much it really hurt. If you did, you would never be able or willing to get going again.

So there I was, stuck, one more time, with no reference points from the past to remind me of yesterday's mistakes and follies.

The Blazers and the doctors couldn't figure it out—again. I pointed to where it hurt and tried my best to describe the pain. But every time, they would simply say that I was looking too close and that there was nothing wrong, that I should just go out and play. And that in playing I was not going to make it any worse.

I couldn't, though, and every time I tried, I did make it worse.

And the team, and everything that we had built over the previous twenty months, was falling apart.

There were other serious injuries to my teammates, most notably to Bobby Gross and Lloyd Neal. Ice had injured his knee, and the main weight-bearing bone in Bobby's leg had split in half after he had taken a painkilling injection in order to play. He said he couldn't feel anything when it happened. He just heard a very loud and unusual pop, and knew something was wrong.

I have also learned—the hard way—to never rank, rate, or compare injuries. Each one is unique, but the one that is affecting you is always the worst and the hardest.

The Blazers and the doctors told me that the pain in my foot was a mental thing—it was all in my mind.

They took me to a hypnotist, who had me lie on a table as he swung a watch in front of my eyes.

"Your feet are feeling better," he would chant, over and over. "Your feet are feeling better. Now go out there and win us another championship!"

I looked at him like he was nuts, and I told him that my feet were killing me.

Then the Blazers and the doctors told me that my problems were in my soul. So they took me to a faith healer.

The faith healer and I went outside early one morning before dawn. We waded into the cool green waters of the Willamette River as it meandered through town. We stood knee-deep on the sandy bottom. The sun was just coming up over the Cascades to the east. It was spectacularly beautiful. When the sun was just high enough in the crystal-clear morning sky to be perched right on top of Mount Hood, perfectly balanced and surreal in its position of harmonic convergence, the faith healer reached over and grabbed my wrist and thrust both of our hands together, toward the heavens, chanting, "You're healed, you're healed, your feet are feeling great. Now go out there and win us another championship!"

I looked at him like he was nuts. And I told him that my feet were killing me.

There was never any discussion about the fact or possibility that there was something wrong with my foot. That this was a very real problem. And that maybe I wouldn't, couldn't, or shouldn't be able to play.

The problem was: I couldn't play. And as the playoffs approached, the team was struggling to win.

—

I was not able to play any of the remaining twenty-two games of the regular season. We still finished with the best record in the league, and I won the NBA's MVP Award, voted by the players. But now with each ensuing day, a growing, devolving, spiraling sense of desperation enveloped my world, life, and team.

I kept trying, but every time I did, I only made things worse.

Everything in my life was falling apart. This was my team, my guys, my town, my friends, and my family. And I needed to do something to help.

We started the playoffs against Seattle, now coached by Lenny Wilkens. They had healthy players, and we didn't. We had home court, but they had good feet and Dennis Johnson—who was on his way to establishing himself as the best guard in the NBA.

I spent everything I had trying to be able to play in Game 1. I was able to get on the court but I couldn't get anything done. I could barely move, let alone play, and we went down without a fight.

In the locker room before Game 2, all the guys were looking to me. I had no answers. This was my life, this was what I lived for, this was my time and team. And every time I said my foot hurt, the persistent response from those who were supposed to know was always, "You're fine. You're just looking too close. Go ahead, you can't make it any worse."

In the solitude of the locker room, through the doubt, uncertainty, and halting hesitation, and with everybody looking to me for some sort of easy answer, I turned longingly to the doctor, who said he had an idea.

He pulled out a very long needle, with a huge syringe of xylocaine on the back end of it. He plunged in and injected the pain-numbing medicine directly into the base of my leg, just above the ankle. And for the first time in nearly two months, the pain was gone.

I went out and tried to play. And I could, a bit, but not for long, and not nearly well enough. After a short while, I could not really use any part of my foot or ankle, not that I could feel it. So I just went and sat on the bench as our team crumbled. I couldn't get it done. We won the game but ended up losing big-time in the long run.

They took me to the hospital after the game. Our team doctor told me I was fine and that I'd most likely be ready to go again by the next game.

Later, I'm told, the hospital called the doctor up and said that their radiologists had read the X-rays and that there were terrible problems here, and if the doctor did not bring me right back in, they were going to go and get me themselves.

The navicular bone in my foot had split in half.

—

I lost my trust, confidence, self-respect, and belief that things would turn out right. Our team lost the series in six games.

I was in a cast—seemingly forever. Non-weight-bearing, and on crutches.

I could not believe, or accept, what I had done. Or what I had allowed to be done to me.

—

As I sat disconsolately in my house, seething and alone, I knew I had to get out of this place and space quickly.

Some friends, including parts of the Rolling Stones family, had control of a remote hot spring in southeastern Arizona, near Eden, and they all suggested it would be a good, safe spot. Warm, dry, and sunny weather. Inexhaustible supplies of hot mineral water. No people. Real privacy. And a chance to try to heal everything from my severely broken foot to my spirit, soul, mind, and psyche.

The place was called Healing Waters. It was out there. On the edge. In another time's forgotten space, Geronimo and his teammates used to retreat there, in between his raging battles. They were all trying to hold on against the oncoming and invading tide.

I had all the space and solitude I needed. It was wide-open desert out there, and there were hot-water pools all over the place, including one that was the size of a football field. I would slide into the healing waters, propping my wounded, cast-bound leg high and dry up on the side of the pool. I would stay in the water for hours—sometimes all night, under the magic spell of the remote desert night sky.

—

When I got back to Portland that summer, it was not a pretty scene. The Blazers and the doctors kept telling me I was fine, but after months of solitary reflection while hobbling and hopping around on my crutches, I knew that I was not. There were meetings with the team and doctors.

They kept asking me to make some kind of public statement of support, about how everything was cool, and that any and all problems were of my own making. I also knew by then that this was nonsense.

They never said they were sorry—for failing to diagnose the problems with my feet, for blaming me, for shooting my foot up with painkillers only to have it break apart, for failing even to read the X-rays properly. They never acknowledged they were wrong, or said they'd try to make things right.

I was not ready for anything that they were up to, as I was still living with all the pain on every level.

Trust, confidence, and loyalty are critical elements to the success of any team. And by now I was feeling none of it. I felt betrayed and that they just didn't care about what happened to me. I told them all that I had reached the point of no return, that it was time for me to go. I still had a year left on my original contract with the team, but I asked them to end it.

And I left, never to return to what had been, just a short six months ago, the most perfect thing ever in my life.

That fall, I got as far away as possible. Crutches, cast, and all, I went to Egypt with the Grateful Dead on the trip of a lifetime. There were three all-night concerts at the base of the Sphinx and pyramids. I was able to play with their team. There was a private viewing of the inner chambers of the Great Pyramid, sunrise services in Bedouin tents in the desert sands, and the world's greatest charter flight ever. And much, much more.

After that, we went back to California—not Portland. We took a house on the water on Balboa Island, in Newport, just south of Long Beach. The Blazers wanted me to come back and play, but I couldn't yet walk, let alone run, let alone play. I worked with the doctors of the NFL's Los Angeles Rams, who did everything they could to speed along my recovery. While there, Ernie Vandeweghe reconnected me with Dr. Tony Daly, who had rescued me from the Russian mauling six years earlier. It was wonderful to finally have doctors who actually cared about what happened to me. I stayed with Dr. Daly for the rest of his life. He would go on to perform more than two dozen orthopedic surgeries on my feet and ankles over the next couple of decades.

This was just when Adam and Nathan were starting to grow into fine young boys. And when I could finally stand on my own and start to move under my own power once again, we would spend countless hours on the beach and in a little rowboat that we'd use to cruise around the bay.

I spent more time with the Dead, including a four-night New Year's celebration all around California. Then as spring came to Balboa Island, I started to feel better again, on my way one more time, and cleansed of the negativity that had brought me down in Oregon.

I got back on my bike, then running, swimming, pushing steel, and hitting full stride just as the NBA season was ending. I had missed it all.

While in Newport Beach, a friend from Oregon took me over to see Richard Nixon at his former Western White House compound, just down the way in San Clemente. It was not my best moment. I should have taken Joan Baez with me.

Right before the summer, some NBA teams came calling. I took another trip, continuing the cleansing of my mind, spirit, and soul. A young documentary filmmaker named Bob Nixon, not related to Richard, was making a show for ABC's *The American Sportsman* on the endangered Philippine eagle, and he wanted me to be a part of it. I had no idea why he wanted me, but his persistence won me over. I soon found myself in the Philippines, climbing up a 150-foot tree and holding a giant bird with a beak and wingspan bigger than mine. More than a lot went down on this one, including a run-in with a large band of heavily armed separatists while we were all out on the edge. I had never done anything like any of this before—or since. But I'm glad I made it. Our show won an Emmy.

When I got back to California, I had messages waiting from a few NBA teams, including the Blazers. They hadn't changed their tune, so it didn't make any sense for me to change mine. Of everyone I talked to, the Clippers were the most interested and the only team that was serious about moving forward. Plus they had recently moved from Buffalo to my hometown—San Diego.

I signed a big, long-term contract with them about thirteen months after everything fell apart in Portland. And I was back in the game and climbing up the mountain one more time.

The Clippers couldn't have been nicer. We found a dream house, on the north edge of Balboa Park near the San Diego Zoo. It is one of the oldest homes in San Diego. It's a big place, nearly three perfectly flat acres. I bought the place the first day I saw it. Right in the middle of everything, but on a wonderfully quiet, dead-end street, in a terrific neighborhood where people spend their entire lives. It's also just inland enough and off the beach to be mostly out of the fog bank that often envelops San Diego. When San Diego's founding fathers laid out the city in the early days, their vision of Balboa Park and the zoo was true and pure. It is ideal, and we've now been there for thirty-six years. Nothing good could happen in my life to convince me to move on from here. We're still the new ones on the block. The Clippers helped us get the deal done.

Right after I signed on to the team, Tony Daly did some surgery on both my ankles to cut excess bone back, in the never-ending struggle to try to improve the flexibility in my feet and ankles. But I was back at it right away.

The team was fun, dynamic, exciting, and quite talented. I had lots of new teammates, and some old ones as well. The backcourt was World B. Free, Randy Smith, and Brian Taylor. Up front we had Sidney Wicks, Kermit Washington, Swen Nater, and Joe Bryant. Gene Shue was the coach—and he was awesome, always so positive, upbeat, imaginative, and extremely creative. We were very good and excited to all spend the season together.

But first the Clippers and Blazers had to weirdly work out a deal, because at the time the NBA had a byzantine set of rules for free agency, when a player changes teams by his choosing. The teams involved would figure out between themselves a compensation package that would send any combination of valuable assets back to the team of the departing free agent player—Portland in this case. The system was more like a forced trade or sale, and it really limited a player's ability to choose his own workplace and terms of employment. It would slowly reform in the coming years, through the brave efforts of some legendary players, but at the time it was the only game in town. And if the teams involved could somehow not agree on what that compensation package would be, then the NBA commissioner would make the decision himself.

I was in limbo, since neither the Clippers nor Blazers would budge from their claims and demands. So Commissioner Larry O'Brien had to step in and settle the dispute, with his sole decision determining the equity of my life. The Blazers wanted basically the entire franchise in return—if not all of Southern California. The Clippers argued that the extenuating circumstances of my departure had to be considered as mitigating factors, and that this was not a normal transaction regarding money and value but rather one where I had left Portland because of their medical mistreatment of me.

The dispute dragged on endlessly. David Stern, then a young lawyer with the NBA, worked tirelessly but ultimately futilely behind the scenes to try to make everybody happy through conciliation.

In the end, there were no winners, and nobody was happy with the outcome. Larry O'Brien ended up awarding to Portland Kermit Washington, Kevin Kunnert, a ton of money, and some important draft choices.

The Clippers sold Randy Smith to Cleveland to get the money to pay the bill, just as Randy and I had become great friends and teammates. He never really recovered as a player, and what was all going to be so perfect for so many of us was now turning into a nightmare.

—

We had to pick ourselves up and get going, as goes life and the NBA.

We were already into the exhibition season while this was all coming down and the team was transforming. Very quickly we came up against the Lakers, in Anaheim, at the domed convention center there. They had Kareem as well as Norm Nixon, and now Jamaal Wilkes, who had come down as a free agent from his championship days in Golden State, and Magic Johnson, whom they had taken as the No. 1 overall draft pick the previous spring.

They were good, but we routed them as we played beautifully, powerfully, and with great pride, passion, and purpose. World B. Free was incredible. The entire ownership and management team of the Clippers, who were all L.A. guys, were all there, and there was a tangible sense of euphoria. Everybody was ecstatic, and the thought of greatness for this new team permeated everything, from the locker room to the large and swelling crowd waiting outside for autographs to the joyous bus ride home to San Diego late that night.

We had another exhibition the next night, at home in our gym, the San Diego Sports Arena. After a full day of getting ready with my well-established pregame preparation, I went out to warm up. And the deep burning pain in my foot was back. I couldn't run. Or jump. Or play. All over again.

The bone in my foot had rebroken. And one more time, I spent the next forever doing everything possible to get that foot and ankle to stop hurting and start working again. As I went everywhere, seeing every doctor and trying everything imaginable, so many people from all walks of life were willing to do anything they could to help.

A master biochemist from nearby UCSD thought that if I ingested massive amounts of a broad range of trace minerals, everything would be fine. Who knew if it worked: it totally shut down my entire gastrointestinal system, and I was unable to stay on the program long term, as however much I gulped down, nothing would ever come out.

Another guy, a studiously subdued engineer, designed this physical apparatus with all kinds of hinges, springs, and pulleys and lots of metal, leather, and plastic. I was supposed to wear this thing on the outside of my skin, in conjunction with my shoe. The goal was to transfer all of my weight through the metal and other prefabricated material so that the stress of running, jumping, pivoting, and weight-bearing would be totally eliminated by this device. We never got very far with it.

Then I got a handwritten letter from someone who professed that a curse had been placed on my life. And that the only way to break the curse was to go back to the Philippines and make a trip to go see this witch doctor who would be able to remove the curse; then I would be fine. There was a hand-drawn map with directions how to get there. I was to go past the big tree, cross the river, turn at the big pile of rocks, and there he'd be.

I didn't go. But that was about the only thing I didn't try.

Ever since, whenever I've been up against really bad things, somebody will always chime in with, "Well, I guess we could always go to the Philippines and find the witch doctor."

It was agonizingly painful—for everybody, on every level, and no one more so than me. It was my life, my world, my health, my home, everything. And nothing was working.

One difference this time was that people were no longer thinking that I was just making the whole thing up. There was growing concern as I went from doctor to doctor that there were major structural problems with my feet, leading to the continuing breakdowns. The Clippers and my doctors never brought up or out the painkilling needles, though that didn't make thing any easier.

I did whatever I could for the next several months, and in that time I was able to get better. I returned to play in the NBA in January. But just as I was starting to hit my stride, the bone in my foot broke again.

It was a very depressing and debilitating cycle. I would rest, and the bone would heal. I would play, and the bone would break. Rest, heal, play, break. Over and over and over again. It was endless. And awful.

The doctors—and there were countless numbers of them—were now telling me that I had to stop. That they were no longer treating me in my attempts to return to the NBA, but rather to just return to a tolerable level of pain and a functional life.

Then they began to explain the long-term ramifications of the problems with the oft-injured bone, which they felt was in real danger of dying. If that happened, amputation was the next step.

I was in my late twenties.

—

As this negative downward spiral continued without end, there also began an endless series of legal battles. The Clippers sued everybody—including me, the NBA, the insurance companies led by Lloyd's of London, and the Blazers.

I sued the doctor in Portland who had injected me before the game when the bone in my foot split in half. I was legally precluded from including the team in my claim because I was covered by workers' compensation through my team-provided health insurance.

Lloyd's sued the agent who wrote the policy.

The NBA Players Association sued the NBA over the compensation award that had sent so much talent and treasure up to Portland.

All of my time, effort, resources, and spirit were now consumed with doctors and lawyers.

It was not how I had ever envisioned things playing out.

—

In a constant struggle to find a shining star in the maddening, frustrating, and bizarre world of being a Clipper, one summer five of us went on the trip of a lifetime to the Galapagos Islands. Our younger brother, Andy, was the engine that powered our spaceship. He had plenty of help from our friends. That story will get its own book one day.

Another incredibly bright spot occurred the day our third son, Luke, was born: March 28, 1980. With a shining star twinkling in the clear night sky, I named him after the greatest teammate I ever had, an incredible force of life, spirit, and nature who made everyone around him better—Maurice Lucas. On the day Little Luke was born, Big Luke came bearing a gift, a large picture—of himself in full rage, action, and glory. Going for it all, as only he ever could. Maurice signed it, "To Little Luke, to make it in this world—you've got to be tough, Big Luke." It hung over Little Luke's bed from the first day of his life until Little Luke went away to college, eighteen years later.

At the time, I was on crutches and in a cast—and in and out of the hospital, the doctors' offices, the lawyers' offices, and the courthouse. I missed the rest of the NBA season and would miss all of the next two as well.

My foot was not getting better, despite the constant surgeries trying to create more flexibility in my foot and ankle in a never-ending drive to try to enable the stress of impact to be distributed up and through the normal channels of the musculoskeletal system. All to no avail.

Ultimately, there was a big convergence of all the people involved in the various lawsuits. It was held at a hotel conference room somewhere near LAX. Lots of people were there representing all the interested parties—the Clippers, the NBA, the television networks, the insurance companies, the big-time sponsors from both the team and the league, scientists, and lots of lawyers, accountants, and doctors. People had flown in from all over the country.

My X-rays and medical records were spread out everywhere. And all day long everybody was theorizing, prognosticating, deliberating, arguing, presenting, you name it, and it was happening—all, sadly, with no consensus or positive resolution.

Finally, as the day was getting long and disappointing frustration was enveloping the room, the guys who were in charge, sensing that it was all slipping away, said, "OK. Enough. We need to get something conclusive here. So if you're not a doctor, please step to the back, and all the doctors—please come to the front. Let's see what we have here."

I had already seen all the doctors individually before—at their own offices, hospitals, wherever. But now all the top guys were there together, at the same time, on the same problem.

As we went around the room, they all had their last chance with their diagnosis and plan for the future. My future.

It started bad. And then got worse.

"He'll have trouble for the rest of his life."

"He'll walk with a deteriorating limp forever."

"The pain will never go away, and get worse over time."

"He'll never play again."

"The bone is going to die."

"We're going to have to cut his foot off."

"Amputation is a very real possibility."

And then they got to the only one who had yet to speak to the assembled group. Dr. Bill Wagner, from Whittier, California. The oldest guy in the room.

He leaned in as the room quieted, and after a long pause and deep breath, softly said, "I've got an idea."

In a room full of the smartest people, most with very powerful egos, there was a hushed response. "What now, Dr. Wagner?"

He sat up very straight and said, "I've come up with a new operation, procedure, and technique that I think might work."

"What is it?" echoed throughout the doubting room in fatigue and exasperation.

He went on to explain this incredibly complex, five-large-incision, all up, down, over, under, and around my foot and ankle surgical procedure and technique where he would cut, saw, take lots of bone out, realign the joint surfaces, relocate and elongate lots of soft tissue including fascia, tendons, and ligaments, and ultimately get to what he saw as the root cause of my problems—a congenital cartilaginous and boney bar between the calcaneus and navicular bones in my foot and ankle that was preventing the normal movement and dissipation of stress throughout my musculoskeletal system. Dr. Wagner's goal would be an attempt to remove that coalition bar and realign the mechanics of my foot and ankle.

To a man, everybody else in the room said, "That'll never work."

Dr. Wagner quietly and stoically held his ground.

In unison, the skeptics followed up with, "How many of these have you done, Dr. Wagner?"

"Ten" was his instant but thoughtfully cautious reply.

"How many of these ten have worked?" they asked.

"None."

And still, that's the direction I chose—because Dr. Wagner was the only one offering me a chance at anything.

Dr. Wagner had been a rising orthopedic surgeon and a passionate rock climber when he had a horrific fall that almost cost him his life. Large parts of his skin had been sheared off and he'd broken numerous bones, but a team of surgeons had been able to repair everything—everything except his foot and ankle, which ultimately had to be fused together into a large and rigid stump. Dr. Wagner devoted the rest of his life to helping fix people's broken feet, and he'd built a whole medical center around the science and medicine of the foot.

He was so good, people came from all over the world to see him. He was so busy, he only had the time to see the worst of the worst cases. And when it was my turn for surgery in the early spring of 1981, Dr. Wagner looked right into my eyes and soul as hard as he could and said sternly, "Now listen, Walton. I'm not doing this so that you can go out and try to play basketball again. I'm trying to give you some kind of life here, and to hopefully save you from having the whole thing cut off."

———

The Clippers, meanwhile, were going through a dizzying carousel of players, coaches, executives, and staff members. And as things went steeply downhill for me, I dragged the franchise down, too. We couldn't win. We couldn't sell our product—the team. Ticket sales were nonexistent. Sponsors, corporate partners, and media outlets jumped ship as fast as they could.

The biggest crowd reaction in one dismal stretch of games was to an entry in a Halloween costume contest. The costume: a young man hobbling onto the court with a red-haired wig and beard, a headband, crutches, and a cast on his foot. I think the prize was a discounted option on future playoff tickets.

The team didn't have the players, the off-court leadership, or the financial commitment or resources to make it work. And the world of the Clippers grew even weirder when Donald T. Sterling bought the franchise in 1981, two years after I signed on.

If the paychecks did come, they often bounced higher than the basketballs did. The deferred compensation to retired and disabled players that was standard procedure in those days was ignored and became the subject of yet more lawsuits. Coaches were fired. Players and assets were sold, or just let go. Staff members went unpaid and were basically forced to quit. When injuries shortened the roster, ownership refused to add new players, even when the number of able-bodied players was less than the league-required minimum of eight. Injured players were told to suit up and sit on the bench to meet the minimum.

Practices were held at 7:00 a.m. on local military bases because it was cheaper, or maybe even free at that time of day. There was often no access to any locker rooms or showers. They did let us use the restrooms, though. Flights from San Diego to, say, Portland and Seattle always seemed to go through Kansas City, because somebody had some free coupons on Pan Am or TWA.

Players would talk openly about going out of their way to injure a teammate so that they could keep their own job. Fights were a constant occurrence. Players, coaches, staff—everybody was fighting one another.

Late in one season, with yet another new general manager and direction, they instituted a new marketing push and plan—to get to thirty wins on the season. Out of eighty-two games. That was our goal—to get to thirty wins. They wanted us all to wear these cheap white T-shirts everywhere with a blue No. 30 ironed on. The extras were saved and used as team holiday presents the next year. The new guy was very proud and excited. He thought it was genius. Yeah! Thirty wins. Wow! Here we go!

Budgets on everything were slashed to near zero or eliminated entirely. Medical, travel, equipment, laundry, office, and every other kind of bill went unpaid. We had to keep moving, never able to go back anywhere. The team's basic business model was to sue anybody and everybody they owed money to, figuring the payee would ultimately settle for a lesser amount rather than fight the endless nonsense.

The NBA tried to take the team away from Donald Sterling.

The NBA Players Association worked overtime on our team alone.

—

In the off-season, which always came early because of no chance at the playoffs, we tried to do whatever we could to immerse ourselves in something positive.

I'm an early riser, always have been. I love going to bed early so that I can get going tomorrow. I would regularly be at Mission Beach at dawn for a morning walk. It was just ten minutes away, and a straight shot from home. The best foot therapy that I've ever found is the beach. Walk in the soft sand to find the problem. Then up and down in calf-deep cold water to help heal it. On far too many mornings, Marvin Barnes was already there, working the parking lot.

The USA National Cycling Team was based in San Diego for much of this time. Their team hotel was just a couple of blocks away from our home, up the street at the Balboa Park Inn. We would start a group road ride every morning at nine. We would go out for a three-to-four-hour burn all over town, come back, clean up (often in our pool), have lunch, chill for a bit, and then really get after it in the afternoon, often in the velodrome, which is also right in the park, not more than a couple hundred yards right across the canyon from the hotel.

Dick Trudell was always there, fighting the good fight for the cause of indigenous rights.

The Grateful Dead came through town often, and our home became a sanctuary, never more so than the time we were set up like bowling pins by the police, and half our guys ended up in the jailhouse for the night. Jerry would bring his Jerry Garcia Band over to the house, too. One day, after they had played in San Diego the night before and were on their way to the next show, they stopped for lunch on their way out. The band's tour bus came rumbling down through the neighborhood, escorted by a sizable contingent of Hells Angels, all on their very large and loud Harleys. Some of the neighbors were peeking out from behind their curtains, safe in their locked houses. When everybody was inside our place, all the neighborhood children came running over. While we all ate, swam, and enjoyed a most perfect San Diego day, Jerry positioned himself by the pool in the shade of an Australian tree fern and entertained all the youngsters with exciting tales of adventure, exploration, and experimentation. He signed all their musical instruments and patiently posed for countless pictures. Then they were on their way. And when the roar of the departing motorcycles finally faded into the distance, some of the older people finally felt it was safe to come out of their houses. The children all said it was the most fun they ever had.

There were regular trips to Europe to teach basketball. One time we witnessed for the first time a young Arvydas Sabonis, who turned out to be the second-best nineteen-year-old player I've ever seen, after Kareem. We tried to kidnap Sabonis and bring him home to the NBA, but we were unsuccessful.

I connected with Craig Sherman from Montgomery, Alabama—the youngest son and scion of a pedigreed family of memorabilia collectors. He has stayed on as the curator of the Bill Walton Intergalactic Museum ever since.

Still, I felt like I wasn't making any real progress. It was like I was treading water. And if Dr. Wagner was right, if I would never play again, then I needed a new game.

As I was struggling to get through my latest round of injuries, I came to know David Halberstam. He had become a friend of Jack Ramsay after meeting through a mutual friend, Gay Talese, at Gay's pad in New York City. That friendship blossomed, and then when the Blazers blew up over my medical treatment, David took particular interest. I had known of David for years, being an avid fan and devout reader of all his wonderful work, such as *The Best and the Brightest, The Making of a Quagmire, The Unfinished Odyssey of Robert Kennedy, The Powers That Be,* and *One Very Hot Day.* But I had never met him until he came calling in the midst of his research on *The Breaks of the Game,* his book about the Trail Blazers in the midst of my injuries and divorce from the franchise. It's the only book of his I haven't read—though I've tried many times. It's just too close for me, too personal, and too depressing.

My relationship with David quickly changed from interviewee to friend—and teacher, counselor, and moral compass. We would meet up on our travels for dinner, movies, the theater, concerts, ball games, and events, with our children, too, who became close. And every time he would hear that I had been injured again, he would send me a big box of new books to read. He worked in conjunction with my mom and dad as my personal librarian. The only other time in my life that my parents were even remotely impressed with anything that I ever did, other than introduce them to David, was the time we had internationally acclaimed and award-winning political cartoonist Paul Conrad over for dinner.

When David heard about the Bill Walton Orthopedic Health Summit at the LAX hotel and how I was at the end of the line, he really amped it up and started urging me to get on to something else, not wallow in the muck with Donald Sterling and the Clippers.

He strongly recommended law school as my next step, and when he tweaked even the slightest of my interests, he pounced, telling me that if I was going to go—it had to be Stanford. I had no idea. This was a whole new world for me.

He made the first call. And then he started working both sides. I didn't really want to move the children again. And Stanford was very leery at first, with me being part of the unwashed masses, and a public school guy and all, particularly one that had consistently pounded their own basketball team. Stanford didn't like my LSAT scores. I didn't have the courage to tell them that I took it right after my major surgery with Dr. Wagner and that I was eating very powerful painkillers during my test, with my leg in a cast, the stitches still in, and everything propped up on a cushioned stool.

David brokered a meeting on campus with Jack Friedenthal, the guy in charge of these things at Stanford Law School. Friedenthal was not convinced, but I was by now. And I became relentless in my dogged pursuit. They all recommended that I retake the LSAT, and supplement that with a Kaplan test course and the Evelyn Wood speed-reading program. I did it all, including staying in constant communication with this new Dr. Jack.

I aced the LSAT the second time, and emboldened with my vastly improved score, I just started showing up at the school and Friedenthal's office insisting that this was what I was going to do with the rest of my life. I eventually wore him down, and they let me in.

It ended up being fantastic. We bought a house on Louise Street in Menlo Park, right on the north edge of campus, at the end of a dead-end street. The children were in their own excellent schools, and I was a student exclusively, for the first time in my life since the third grade.

It was a fabulous routine. Up early to get the children off to school, I'd then ride my bike to class, ride home for lunch, ride back to school for more class and library time, ride home for dinner with the boys, ride back to the law library until midnight, then head home and quickly to bed, in order to start it all up the next day.

On many nights the Jerry Garcia Band would play at the Keystone down in Palo Alto, just a ten-minute bike ride from the law library. He would start the show at 11:00 p.m. I could leave the books, stacks, and my cubicle at 10:45, jump on my bike, and be there in place by the first backbeat on the snare drum, and the night was ours. John Belushi and Hunter S. Thompson were regulars on the tour at the time. They often led the ceremonial prayers.

When Jerry wasn't playing in Palo Alto, he was onstage up in San Francisco's North Beach or over in Berkeley, always with the 11:00 p.m. sharp starting time. All the clubs were owned by the same guy—and it worked out perfectly. The rule was always the same: home before daylight, since school started early at Stanford.

The full Grateful Dead began playing at Stanford's Frost Amphitheater while I was there. A majority of my classmates all went as welcomed guests. We were warmly greeted at the back gate by Ram Rod and Big Steve, with the encouraging words, "Have a good time."

With major academic responsibilities at Stanford and being a dad to three young and growing boys, the days were always very full. On October 31, 1982, we were having Adam's sixth birthday party at the house. All the neighborhood children and Adam's and Nathan's friends from school were there. And on that day, our youngest child, Chris, was born—during and at the party. It was a spectacularly beautiful sunny day. And when the other parents came to pick up their children, we could hear the departing youngsters telling their parents that it was the coolest birthday party they had ever been to. And that Adam got a new baby brother as his best present. And mine, too.

The boys loved playing games of street football, in large part because the NFL's San Francisco 49ers practiced right there at Stanford. This coincided perfectly during their rise to glory, with the unbeatable squad of Bill Walsh, Joe Montana, Ronnie Lott, Dwight Clark, John Taylor, Fred Dean, and all the rest. We would see them all the time on campus, we would watch their games on Sundays, and our children were all getting very much into it, so much so that they kept wanting me to go out and play football with them. But I couldn't stand very well because of my foot problems, and I certainly couldn't run or chase them. We improvised and devised a game where I was the permanent—but stationary—quarterback. I would sit in a chair in the middle of our dead-end street, and all the boys would run, play, yell, and scream, as I would call the plays, throw the passes, officiate the disputes, keep the score and the peace when necessary, and announce the action as the broadcaster.

Over a long period of time, my surgically reconstructed foot started to feel a bit better. Through it all we always kept to the street football games, the children never tiring of it. One day I was able to be the permanent but stationary QB while standing up. Later, as my health continued to improve, I was able to walk up and down the street, while the fast-growing children ran everywhere. Much further down the line, I was standing there in the street when one of the boys intercepted an errant pass, and as he was running for the game-winning touchdown, the other children starting to cry as their dad had let them down with a terrible pass, I took off running after the boy and caught him from behind, extending the game for at least a bit longer. And everybody stopped. It was the first time that some of them had ever seen me run. I couldn't remember the last time I had been able to.

And so it all began one more time—the long, hard climb back up the mountain. I slowly began to regain mobility, and the incessant pain began to fade away. Toward the end of my first year at Stanford, some of my classmates urged me to try spending some late afternoons down at the athletic fields on the Farm. They asked if I would play a very stationary first base on the law school intramural softball team. I eventually became mobile enough that we rotated our second baseman to a defensive rover position because I was able to cover the whole right side of the infield. In the beginning, at the plate, they allowed a runner for me for any ball that I put in play. Later I was slowly able to try it myself. We ended up winning the championship.

From there, my classmates urged me to try the same thing on the law school intramural basketball team. We played the short courts at Maples Pavilion. The spring-loaded floor there continued to be fantastic. We won that championship, too.

Back home in San Diego for the summer, I clerked at the longtime Stanford-influenced law firm of Luce, Forward, Hamilton & Scripps. They couldn't have been nicer, although I was hoping for more interesting work assignments. I did become extremely proficient at alphabetizing documents, or putting them in chronological order—I can't remember which. Or whether it really mattered anyway.

One of my fellow clerks, Tom Crews, coaxed me into playing on the firm's summer basketball team. We won that game, too.

—

As the summer wound down and we were heading back to Palo Alto for the second-year go-round with the law school, somebody put together a special game built around me and my newfound ability to play a little bit for the first time in many a year now. It was in Las Vegas—at Caesars Palace, out back in the tent pavilion where they were regularly playing all the big tennis challenge matches that always seemed to highlight either Jimmy Connors or John McEnroe, or both. The bleachers and lights were already in place. All they had to do was roll out a court and some baskets. We had what we needed.

They assembled a team of UCLA alumni. Our opponents were the UNLV alumni. We were coached by Walt Hazzard.

There were no locker rooms, so we dressed in our hotel rooms and had to make our way to the court and game through the casino. Henry Bibby kept getting waylaid at the craps table, and we had to keep sending people back to get him. I'm told that he only made it a table at a time. The promoters were getting worried. The game was not televised, I don't think, so it really was much more like a rock concert than anything else, with no official start time. We started when the fans showed up, the show was sold out, and I do remember that Henry did get there by tip-off.

Sports Illustrated covered the whole thing and made a big splash of it. Coach Hazzard was under strict orders from the doctors—Tony Daly and Ernie Vandeweghe—to play me only sparingly, and in short spurts.

Once we got going, we would always get out to big leads, and then I would go to the bench for my prescribed rest, and the old-time Rebels would fight back to take control. When I came back in, UCLA would again surge to a dominant position, and then I would have to go out. This cycle repeated itself throughout the long hot night in the desert. We had some NBA refs who had flown in from Los Angeles. They sure acted like they were well aware that UNLV was their host and meal ticket.

We were playing to win, but in the end we couldn't get the job done. And we lost. I think Henry left with a few minutes still to play, something about him needing to get back to the games inside.

I was happy simply to have played at all. We had lost, but it was fun, and my foot held up to the limited but real basketball.

———

Back at Stanford, I just kept feeling better and better. I couldn't resist the pull of what could have been. And, while still a full-time law student, I worked it out with the Clippers to let me try to play for them once a week. I would go to school all week long and kept up my very full schedule, including the Keystone late at night with Jerry, John, and Hunter. And then on the weekends I would fly down to San Diego and play an NBA game for the Clippers, returning to class immediately following the game, always studying in the airports, on the planes, in the locker room, wherever I could grab a quick read.

After the first semester of my second year, we went home to San Diego for the holidays. It was there that I tried to start playing more and more often. First it was twice a week, one day of practice, then a game three or four days later.

When that seemed to go OK, I moved it up to three days a week, always with at least a day of rest and recovery in between. Then every other day.

When it was time to go back for the second and final semester of my middle year of law school, I decided that I wasn't going back. I called Jack Friedenthal and sadly told him that I was going to chase this NBA dream one last time. He said he understood. I'm not sure that he really believed it all. He knew more than anyone how valuable that precious slot was that he had given me—by taking a chance on the unknown.

But I was feeling better, and I had to try.

I never did go back to Stanford Law School.

I did return to the NBA, though—against all odds, and the dire warnings of the doctors. This was my life, and I had been given another chance.

—

Back in San Diego full-time again, I fell into as good a rhythm as I could hope for, except that the team was awful and all the problems that plagued every part of the franchise remained, and really were inexorably worse. The wildly rotating carousel of executives, coaches, and players continued at a dizzying pace.

While I was able to keep playing, and more so all the time, it was never without problems. Every now and again, and with maddeningly frustrating regularity, Drs. Daly and Wagner had to keep going back in to continue the endless string of surgeries on my feet. Always cutting, carving, sawing, and chiseling—every couple of months. I generally had three to five foot and ankle surgeries a year, every year. I never successfully finished a single season without having to have more surgery, starting the vicious cycle over and over and over again.

—

In 1984, at the end of my fifth season with the Clippers, the team pulled up stakes and moved to Los Angeles. By this point I was playing well and fairly regularly, but still to no avail at the gate or in the standings—it never did work for me over any realistic stretch of time with the Clippers.

All the while, the business of the Clippers was devolving in a dysfunctional, crazed, mad rush to the bottom, yet the exact opposite was happening elsewhere in the NBA. With the simultaneous rise of Jerry Buss, David Stern, Phil Knight, Nike, ESPN, and now Michael Jordan and agent David Falk, the NBA was experiencing a boom that changed the whole world of sports—forever.

It was a world that I wanted to be a part of, but couldn't get into as part of the Clippers. I had had enough. I quietly asked for a trade, something I'd been hoping for through the last few seasons.

But the Clippers wouldn't do it.

I should have simply quit the team at the end of that fifth season, when the Clippers abandoned San Diego, but I still believed that I was good enough to get the job done. Being eternally optimistic, I held out hope that it would and could work.

When you're injured as much as I have been, you have a lot of time to think—about everything. And whether it was in the hospital, in the weight room, at the doctor or physical therapist, walking the beach, riding my bike, wherever, I often thought of what would have happened if only one of my dreams had come true. What if I had been able to play at my previous MVP level? Or what if Donald Sterling had somehow, implausibly, become Jerry Buss or Red Auerbach?

Neither miracle ever came close to pass. And in my sixth season with the Clippers, things only got worse. Nothing improved on the court, and I was done, spent, fed up, and had come to the end of the line with all things Donald Sterling.

It didn't help that in L.A., the traffic, the dirt, the noise, the crowds, the pollution, the losing, and the failures were all beating me down. It wasn't for me.

While in L.A., I did get to spend quite a bit of time with Coach Wooden. Sadly, most of it was at the hospital. Nell, Coach's one, true, and only light, was fading fast. The slide down was long, hard, painful, and very tough. I was there when the light finally went out. None of us had any idea where we were headed.

I had to move on, from everything. I started calling around. Jerry West and the Lakers were not interested. They had just beaten the Celtics for the title, and Jerry wanted no part of me.

I called Red Auerbach in Boston. I found out later that when we connected on the phone, Red was in his office having a meeting with Larry Bird about the future of the team, after having just lost to the Lakers in the NBA Finals. When I told Red that I wanted to become a Celtic, he asked me to hold the line a second. He cupped the mouthpiece of his phone and looked across the desk at Larry. "It's Bill Walton on the line. He wants to come to Boston. What do you think, Larry?"

I'm now aware that Larry told Red right there and then, "Go get him." Although at the time I had no idea that Larry was there, much less aware of my call or even who I was.

When Red got back on the line, he said, "OK, we'll do it. But please, Walton, please let me do everything. Don't you say a word to anybody about anything."

The Clippers dragged it out all summer—endlessly.

Red kept telling me to be patient, but it was hard. All the children were now school-age, and something had to be done at some point. I had just spent the last six years living in the weird, bizarre, alternative reality of Clipperdom and Sterling World. But like the Blazers six years before, the Clippers were being ridiculous in their requests—demanding everything that I wanted to go to Boston for.

—

When Red finally told me that he had been able to strike a deal, I was ecstatic.

I went into the Clippers' office to sign the papers.

Sitting across the desk was Donald Sterling. He looked at me impassively. Expressionless.

He said, "Walton, you really want this, don't you?"

I reiterated how it was time, that I had done my best, and that there was nothing more I could do for him or his team.

He responded that that was not true. From behind his ornate desk, perched high on his ostentatious throne, he leaned in and leered in his reptilian style that for this deal to go down, and for me to go to Boston, I would have to leave all the deferred compensation that I had accumulated over the years as a Clipper with him.

Deferred compensation was a big part of the NBA's financial model at the time. For me, it was a ton of money. It was all the money that I had in the world.

This money and the contracts involved had already been litigated many times. But I learned the hard way that this was Donald Sterling's way—sitting fat on a mountain of cash, with a stable of lawyers on staff to keep suing people to whom he owed money.

I reached out across his desk, took hold of his pen, and signed the document as boldly, powerfully, and confidently as I could.

I walked out immediately without ever saying a word, and I never looked back. It still sits alone at the top as the best money I ever spent.

CHAPTER 13

I Need a Miracle

HERE COMES SUNSHINE

We used to play for silver,
Now we play for life.

Having been a lost sailor, away at sea for far too long, I was now a Celtic. Or so I hoped. Two big mountains still loomed: I needed to convince center Robert Parish that I was only trying to help and that I was not trying to take anything from him as I sought permission to be his backup, and I still had to pass a physical. Robert said he was cool with it. But there is no way that I've ever been able to pass a physical of any kind. And things were not looking any better this time.

As I lay there on the examining table in a good-size room at Massachusetts General Hospital, on the east end of Storrow Drive, in downtown Boston, with my X-rays and medical records all over the room and pinned up on the LED-lit wall screens, I could hear the doctors whispering to each other. "What are we going to tell Red? There's no way that we can pass this guy. Look at his feet. His ankles. Look at his knees, his wrists, his hands. Oh my gosh—look at his spine. Look at his face."

All of a sudden, Red burst through the double swinging doors—smoking his cigar—in the hospital. He looked around, perplexed. He bellowed, "Who are you guys? And what are you doing with my player?"

The doctors covered their mouths with their cupped hands and murmured while drawing attention to the X-rays on the screens. "Red, look at his feet. Look at his face. There's no way we can pass this guy."

Red waved his arms, signaling for silence. Then he walked over to me, still on the table.

Looking down at me, he said quietly, "Walton, can you play?"

I looked back up at him with the sad, sorrowful, but hopeful eyes of a man who just wants another chance—in life. And I said, softly, "Red, I think I can."

Red stepped back, taking it all in. He took a huge drag on his cigar. It would have made Jerry Garcia proud as can be. He held his breath, as we all did, too, for a seeming eternity. And when he finally did exhale, I swear the smoke was green—and that there were shamrocks and leprechauns floating in it up against the flourescent lights.

Red's face went from concern and uncertainty to a cherubic smile as he proudly declared, "He's fine. He passes. Let's go! We've got a game!"

—

Whatever Red didn't take care of, David Halberstam did. David found us a house in Cambridge, right near Harvard—it was previously owned by Timothy Leary. David found the right schools for our children. He and Dick Trudell reconnected us with the Kennedys. David showed us how to ride the subway to the games.

The team was fantastic. I knew it would be good, but I had no idea just how good until I was there. Red had created a culture that was very much like UCLA, where we were expected to win everything, every day, forever. Like UCLA, we had better players at every position—Larry Bird, Kevin McHale, Robert Parish, Dennis Johnson, Danny Ainge—all the way down to the bench, the coach, the staff, the bosses, and the fans. We could win a power game or a finesse one; a fast game or slow one. We could win with shooting, passing, rebounding, offense, defense, or with any kind of combination of players. And at the end of the day, we had Larry Bird—and nobody else did.

Our Celtic practices were works of art, and things of beauty, due in no small part to the culture that Red and our coach, K. C. Jones, had put in place. K. C. was the perfect coach for our team, and the most like John Wooden of any coach I ever played for. We loved K. C. and we would do anything for him. We were a team that was superbly self-motivated, and K. C. knew that and respected it. He kept our practices short, to the point, and always focused on what was important. It gave guys more time pre- and post-practice to work on what they needed, on their own, one-on-one, or in small groups. And it kept practice moving, fierce—and fun.

We would start at 10:30 a.m., beginning with some easy running drills, three-man weave and the like. We would quickly transition to shooting games, then to the Three-on-Two Conditioner—the drill that Coach Wooden had invented, although you could say that about most every drill in basketball. And then we would scrimmage. Sometimes half-court first, then open it up to full.

Scrimmages always put the first string, who wore the white jerseys in practice, up against the bench, or the "Green Team" of Scott Wedman, Jerry Sichting, Rick Carlisle, Greg Kite, Sam Vincent, David Thirdkill, and me. Everything was always extremely competitive, and there was a steady stream of trash talking at the highest level. And as we got into the season, with K. C. not doing much substituting in the real games, the first string would often come in tired and beat up from the previous night's game, when they had played consistently big minutes. That left our "Green Team" fresh, rested, and hungry for whatever we could get done against our starting five, the "White Team," whom we always referred to as the "stat team." Invariably, Larry needed to have the last word, win, and everything else—even if it meant dragging out the practice.

One day early on, K. C.'s two assistants, Chris Ford and Jimmy Rodgers, who always "reffed" the scrimmages, kept making horrific call after horrific call, all in favor of the "stat team." After a particularly unjust string of terrible calls, I'd finally had enough. I grabbed the ball and stormed over to K. C., who was standing on the sideline taking it all in with a very serious expression.

I got right in K. C.'s face and demanded to know how he, as a man of impeccable character, integrity, and credibility, could stand idly by as his "refs" made such a travesty of the rules.

K. C. looked puzzled for a moment, then looked at me with a wink and a slight turn of his lip and said, "Come on, William. You know full well that we can't get out of here today until Larry's team wins a game. Now get back out there and do something."

The young guys, like Carlisle, Kite, Vincent, and Thirdkill, were always trying to prove themselves and impress the coach. Wedman and Sichting were great veterans and all-NBA-level players who always knew exactly what they were doing. I was just trying to hang on and make it. I hadn't finished a basketball season still able to play in nine years now, and two of the three seasons before that. And here I was, having already had more than two dozen orthopedic operations, constantly fighting off the rigor mortis that seemed to be creeping into my life and body forever. I was the backup to the Chief—Robert Parish—which was basically like following a Brink's truck down a bumpy road after they forgot to close the back doors. I wouldn't be playing a lot, and wouldn't be playing at the start or end of the games. And, as a bench player, I'd be playing against second-tier players mostly. I could not wait to do whatever I could.

—

The team became incredibly close, on and off the court. We did everything together, including taking long bus rides all around New England for games, promotions, and events of all sorts. Harvard law professor

Alan Dershowitz would jump on the bus whenever his schedule allowed and would move from friend to friend all up and down the aisle for the most interesting conversations about everything.

We opened the season on the road in the New Jersey swamps, at the Meadowlands. The game is worth mentioning for only two reasons: it was my first real game with the Celtics, and I was terrible. I could not do anything right, could never find any sort of positive rhythm or flow, and when we ended up losing—in overtime—I was the reason we lost. Larry wanted to know why we even bothered having me on the team. He was right. He always was. It was about this time when Larry would get so mad when I wasn't able to get it done out there he would demand of K. C., "Coach, you can either take Walton out of the game or me. It's your choice." K. C. was a brilliant decision maker.

Fortunately, things got better as I quickly remembered how to play, and the team found its stride. Every one of our games, both home and away, became memorable for something; it was a unique team.

In our first game against Washington, as we're getting ready in the locker room, Larry comes in, excited and animated as can be. He had just come back from his pregame shooting ritual, where he had witnessed Manute Bol, a quite tall fellow from the Sudan who was trying to make it as a pro basketball player. None of us had ever heard of him before. But Larry warned that whatever happened tonight to make sure that Manute didn't block your shot, because if he did get you, ESPN and *SportsCenter*, still in its infancy, would never let anybody forget.

We had all played against some really tall guys before—Tommy Burleson and Chuck Nevitt—but Manute, at 7'7", was in a whole different league.

Sure enough, when I was in early, the ball was swung to me on the left wing about fifteen feet out, with the perfect angle for a bank shot. I was wide open, so I let it fly, only to have Manute—who was totally out of position under the basket at the time—take a couple of long strides and elongate endlessly to swat my jumper out of the air.

Larry went wild, and to this day he has never let me forget it.

Later, Larry called us all together and said that we all had to put

$100 into a pool, and that the first one to dunk on Manute would get all the cash—$1,200.

When nobody was successful in throwing one down in Manute's face the next time we played Washington, Larry announced that we were going to roll it over, and keep it rolling over until somebody did successfully throw one down on the big guy. And that each game would require another $100 contribution per man from our entire Celtic squad of twelve guys—until it happened.

Now, Washington was a terrible team we never had any trouble beating, but all season long nobody on our team could get a dunk on Manute, and the pot of cash kept growing. Kevin McHale was most intent on getting it done. Kevin was the second-best low-post player I ever played against—after Kareem. Like Kareem, Kevin worked endlessly on getting better position before he ever even received the ball. And also like Kareem—for the opposition it really didn't matter anyway—they were both simply too good. So one game, after the Manute money pool had grown quite large, Kevin just kept going at Manute regardless of what the game or play called for. Manute was blocking every attempt by Kevin, who remained completely undeterred. Manute might have set a record that night for most shots blocked on an individual opponent in any one game. Later, I came up with a defensive rebound and threw a long outlet pass to Larry, who was all alone at half-court, on the left side. There was nobody between Larry and our goal. But instead of driving in and making an uncontested layup, Larry stops, cradles the ball on his hip with his left arm, and points at Manute, who is still down at his own basket and completely out of the play. Larry is waving frantically for Manute to hurry back on defense so that Larry can go in and try to dunk on him. Manute was clueless to our little game within the game, but he dutifully hustled back, and when Larry came flying in, Manute sent him and the ball back one more time.

Our great coach, K. C. Jones, was up off the bench, extending his hands and arms as if to say, "What is going on here?"

We went on to win the game quite easily, but neither Larry nor

Kevin succeeded that night. It was the Chief who finally got the throw-down in Manute's face, and ultimately a very large sum of cash.

Larry's wager on Manute epitomized some of the brilliant things about that Celtics team. In every game, Larry found a way to make it endlessly interesting and entertaining—for us as his teammates, and for everyone in the crowd watching. And when he was in the building, all eyes were definitely on him.

When you're a good team, you're supposed to, and do, win all your home games. We went an NBA record 40-1 at home that regular season, then undefeated in the playoffs. The Boston Garden was electric every night. It was the greatest show on earth. The fans would fill and rock the joint like never before. They would buy tickets for seats that you couldn't see the game from. The Boston Garden had opened in 1928. The construction capabilities of the day left massive columns inside the interior-seating bowl. They put seats right behind these columns where your face was right up against the pillar. It didn't even matter to Larry's fans, who simply had to be there. They came to witness, to pray, to honor, to offer tribute, and ultimately to celebrate—chanting "Larry! Larry! Larry! MVP! MVP! MVP!" until the massive scoreboard suspended over the floor was bouncing.

As grand as it all was, it was the road games that were the most fun. They always are. They require the most effort to win.

Early on after an embarrassing loss in Indiana—Larry's home state—I hounded K. C. into letting Larry and me stay there for a cou-ple of extra days so that I could make a pilgrimage to Larry's hometown, French Lick, down in the southern part of the state.

We traveled late at night, but still, people came out from every-where to pay their respect. Word travels fast when Larry's in town. We eventually made it to Larry's mom's house in time for breakfast. It was surreal to be there, where it all began for Larry. I pestered his mom, Georgia, for stories about Larry as a boy. I asked her if this was indeed the house where Larry grew up. When she confirmed it, I asked her if the driveway basketball court that I could see through the small kitchen window was the court where Larry learned to play. When she confirmed that as well, I asked her if she had an extra empty canning jar around the house. And she did, gladly giving me one.

I went outside, got down on my hands and knees, and started rubbing lots of the Larry Bird driveway dirt all over me. When I was done, I scooped up some of the loose, moist earth and filled the jar, closing the lid tightly when it was full.

I put the jar with the Larry Bird dirt in it in my Celtics game bag and carried it with me all season long, along with my tape cutters, jump rope, silly putty, hand squeezers, and shoes. It was awesome. Larry and Georgia thought I was nuts. But they weren't living with the Curse of Coach Wooden's Stolen Penny hanging over them like an unrelenting dark cloud—to say nothing of the Philippine witch doctor and his curse.

Whenever things got rough on the road that season, I would always reach into my game bag and rub just a little more dirt wherever I could—one more time. I would do anything to try to break that curse. I eventually sprinkled the last of the dirt on my own backyard court at my parents' home in La Mesa.

—

Larry Bird was a most remarkable player. I have never seen a player—any player—inspire the home crowd the way he did. He was an even better person, who always seemed to know everything about everybody on the team. I never knew how he knew, but whenever anybody was having trouble—marital, financial, personal, a sick child or relative, whatever—Larry knew. And then he would quietly go to Red, and Red would always fix everything, without ever saying a word to anybody. Nobody ever knew a thing about it—except the person whom Larry and Red would help.

Larry was extremely popular on every front, and all the businesses and companies in Boston and around the country were clamoring for Larry's endorsement and seal of approval and acceptance. And while he did do some of the commercials and sponsorship deals, it didn't really seem to be his thing.

But that didn't keep everybody from constantly asking. This one guy in particular, Harry I believe his name was, kept coming around all the time and bugging Larry to do an advertisement for his local restaurant, the Scotch 'n Sirloin, just a few blocks away from the Boston Garden. Larry kept telling the guy no, he wasn't interested. But Harry would not take no for an answer, telling Larry that if he did the ad, it would put Harry over the top, his restaurant would make it, and the sun would shine bright and warm—on everybody.

Larry was a firm no, but the guy would not give it up. And finally one day, Larry said, OK. I'll do it.

Harry was overjoyed—ecstatic, beside himself with glee. Larry Bird was going to endorse his restaurant. But then Harry came to the realization—oh my gosh, what am I going to have to pay this guy? This is Larry Bird. The King.

When they came to talk price, Larry said that he didn't want anything for the deal. Harry was stunned. Larry said that the only thing that he wanted was for each of his teammates—there were eleven of us—the three coaches, the trainer (Ray), and the guys who ran the locker room (Wayne and Corky) to be able to come into the Scotch 'n Sirloin anytime, bring their families, and eat for free—but that we would all leave a cash tip, and if the tip wasn't big enough, to be sure and tell Larry, and he would take care of it.

Harry jumped at it. Little did he know that Rick Carlisle would eat every meal there all season long. Rick already had one nickname, Flipper, for the enormous size of his feet, considering that he was just a guard. Larry soon took to calling Rick "Teriyaki Chicken" for the humongous amounts of teriyaki chicken that Rick put away at the Scotch 'n Sirloin on a daily basis.

It was one of the coolest things ever. We went there all the time. After almost every game, the whole team would go to this very nice restaurant just down the street and eat and drink all night long. Each player and their families would have their own table. And at the end of the night, Larry would quietly check to make sure that the plates were clean and the tip was the right size. And if you were coyly observant, you could usually catch Larry discreetly dropping some very-large-denomination bills on most of the now empty Celtic tables as he tried his best to make his way quietly out into the night.

And we'd be on our way—until the next practice, the next game, the next victory.

—

One morning, as we're getting ready to start practice and everybody is warming up, I am off to the side getting ready when, all of a sudden, Kevin and Larry are there at my side.

"What's going on?" they wanted to know. I asked them what they were talking about. "Come on, you know. What's going on here?" they demanded. "There's lots of new people all over town. They all have long hair, they're all wearing those colorful shirts that you always wear, and everything smells really funny. What's going on here?"

With all the seriousness I could muster and as straight a face as I could find, I told them I had no idea what they were talking about.

They pounced. "Are the Grateful Dead in town?"

I told them that the band was indeed "on their way."

"Is there going to be a concert?" "Yes."

"Are you going?" "Yes."

After a long pause: "Do you think that we can come, too?"

"I think we might be able to work something out."

So the whole team met at Larry's house, everybody except Danny Ainge, whose wife wouldn't let him come. Larry had arranged for a fleet of limousines. And we all went, as a team, in formation.

When we got to the show in Worcester, we were all backstage, and I was making the introductions. Jerry—Larry. Chief—Bob. Phil—Kevin. BK—DJ. Scotty—Mickey. Brent—Jerry. And on down the line. We were all having a high and fine time back there when Ram Rod came and told us it was time to get on with the show.

We, the Celtics, went up first. Now, when I asked crew members Ram Rod, Robbie Taylor, Big Steve, and Kidd Candelario about bringing the team to the show, I explained to the guys that these Celtics were true legends and that they would not have a good time if they were out in the crowd, where I always liked to be. The crew rolled their eyes and explained that they were not rookies—and that they would take care of things.

When we got up onstage, the crew had constructed a masterful space just off to the side, all curtained off so that nobody could see in. It was better than perfect.

And there were very nice, comfortable seats for all of us. As we took our places for the upcoming ceremony, Ram Rod and Steve brought over some extremely large coolers full of our favorite drinks—most likely milk and water, as near as I can remember.

The concert hall was all abuzz with the excitement, anticipation, and euphoria of a Dead show that was about to start. And with the lights now down, Jerry finally stepped into the shaft of golden light, as the place was just about ready to blast off. And as he fiddled with his foot pedals and stepped to the front to make sure that the microphone and everything was exactly perfect, Jerry turned to us, the Celtics, safe and secure in our little enclave to his right.

He made eye contact with Larry Bird. And he nodded. And winked. And then he mouthed to Larry, "THIS is what WE do."

And then he turned and the band blew it out and open for the rest of the night. And all the people never had such a good time.

When it was over—much, much later—and the lights came back up, all the Celtics turned to me, now with their kaleidoscope eyes spinning, and exclaimed, "WOW! Can we come back tomorrow?"

And go back we did, gratefully for many happy and fun years. And the Grateful Dead came to us as well, stopping by now and again for practice and the games to meet the guys and to see what we were able to do together on our stage. When K. C. would come onto the court to find Jerry, Bob, Phil, Bill, Mickey, and Brent there in all sorts of everything, he looked around in wonderment, asking anybody within earshot who these new guys were and what they were doing here. Somebody muttered something about them being friends of mine from out of town. K. C. always said, "Fine. OK. Whatever." And we all got on with it.

—

When you're a really good team, you win in a variety of ways. Most often it happens from an accumulation of successes over the course of the entire game, generally starting with the opening tip. And as these add up, it usually results in commanding separation that leaves no doubt at the end as to who the better team is. But sometimes it comes down to one play at the very end, and that is when you really need to have the single best player in the game to get it done. And we had Larry Bird. And nobody else did.

So there we'd be, needing one more big play to win the game, and we're all standing there in the huddle surrounding K. C. And he has the clipboard, and he's stroking his chin, tapping the board, and figuring it all out. Now, before K. C. could let us know his plans, Larry would reach right in and start pointing emphatically at the board himself.

He would lean in, tapping the board with his crooked right index finger, and tell our coach, at this critical juncture, "Just give me the ball right here. I'll make the game-winner, and we're out of here."

K. C. is listening patiently to all this, then he shakes everybody off. He looks up and firmly commands, "Shut up, Bird. I'm the coach here."

We all pause for a second, then K. C. looks up at us again, now with a real twinkle in his eye, and tells us, "Guys, we're going to give the ball to Larry Bird—right here," tapping the same spot that Larry had originally demanded.

Larry stands up a bit straighter now, and then he would go out and tell the other team, in advance, what the play was going to be, and how he was going to beat them, and where.

And then he would do it—exactly as he told them, and us, that he would.

There was nobody like Larry Bird—ever.

—

The Celtics would regularly go on these long and extended road trips, sometimes for two weeks at a time. Larry had gotten into the habit of predicting how the team and he individually would do on any given stretch away from Boston. Average a triple-double. Win all the games. Set scoring records. Take over first place. Whatever he felt like. Larry had high standards and expectations. And he was generally able to back up almost all of his proclamations.

Toward the end of one arduous West Coast trip, where Larry had been playing flawlessly, the reporters asked him after yet another masterpiece what else he had in store, what else could he possibly do. He announced right then and there that he was bored and that he was going to play the next game left-handed, or at least for the first three quarters, and that if the outcome was still in doubt, he would go back to playing right-handed to make sure that we won.

Some people thought he was kidding. Poor Jerome Kersey and the Portland Trail Blazers certainly wished he had been. Larry did play the entire game left-handed, and he put on an absolute clinic. Now, he didn't have the range on his left-handed jumper, but he played a different, more controlled and disciplined game that night in Portland. A midrange, driving, running, back-cutting, rebounding, passing, and slashing game for the ages. All left-handed. And there was nothing anybody could do about it. Including an All-Star-level player like Jerome Kersey.

As the season marched on, we found ourselves in Atlanta one night for a really big game. When you're on the best team, all the games are big. And for the other team, it's always the biggest game of the year. So with the Hawks fielding a most formidable lineup that included Dominique Wilkins, Kevin Willis, Tree Rollins, Reggie Theus, Doc Rivers, Spud Webb, and Antoine Carr, and all coached by Mike Fratello, this was a particularly competitive matchup for us. They had a record crowd at the Omni that night, and the fans came for blood. The Hawks were flawless from the outset, and we couldn't seem to get anything right. We were way down and hopelessly out of it at the half. Their fans were going wild, and the Hawks players themselves were all trash-talking to no end, with the exception of Dominique—who knew better and had too much class.

We limped into our locker room at the midway break, our tails dragging between our legs. K. C. walks in, looks at us, and shakes his head in embarrassment, disappointment, and shame. He looks around, finds the cooler in the corner, walks over and grabs a cold one, and goes and sits down in a chair off to the side and pounds it down. When he's done, he looks at his watch, looks at us as we're sitting there still down and dispirited, and goes back to the cooler for another one, which he pounds down as well. When he's done, he looks at his watch, looks at us, and goes back to the cooler for another one. Finally, he looks at his watch, stands up, and quietly says, "Let's go."

We're back out on the court now for the start of the third quarter. Larry is waiting to take the ball in from out-of-bounds to start the second half. And as the ref comes over and hands the ball to him to get things going, Larry takes the ball and shoves it right back into the startled ref's midsection and won't let go—of either the ball or the ref. Completely caught off guard, the poor, unsuspecting ref has no idea what's going on here. And then Larry looks right into the guy's soul, deep and burning through his now bulging and scared eyes. And Larry—serious as can be—tells the ref right there, "Hey, we're down big here. But we're not going to quit. You make sure that you don't, either!"

Larry went absolutely wild in the third quarter—made every shot he took, including an astronomical number of three-pointers. Whatever Larry didn't do, Scott Wedman did. Scotty was the second-best player on the planet that night, held back only because he played behind and in support of Larry, and no matter what, on this team he could never get the minutes he needed to be at the top.

By the end of this most remarkable quarter, we had come all the way back to tie it up. We won the game, at the end, in overtime. We didn't need a plane to get home that night.

It didn't always go so smoothly, though. As we rolled into Dallas toward the end of the season, it was not lost on anybody that the Mavericks, still a fairly recent expansion team, had never beaten the Celtics. And we are on fire. Larry is having a really, really big game, and has 48 points after three quarters. He knows he's hot, we have a huge lead, and he decides to keep going for it in the fourth. Except that he goes ice cold, and momentum shifts wholly to Dallas. Larry misses every one of the many shots that he takes in the fourth, making only two free throws, and Dallas comes back to beat us in the end. The Mavericks and their fans are overjoyed. We are stunned.

Most of the few games that we lost that year were to the worst teams that we played. This was no exception. In the locker room after the game, I walked by Larry on the way to the showers. I told him, "You might have scored fifty points tonight, but you were the worst player in the game." He had his head down as he mumbled, "I know."

He more than made up for it the next day. He always did.

The Mavericks made and sold countless copies of the video recording of their win.

—

On the rare occasions that we did lose a game that season, K. C. didn't say much in the locker room right after the game other than to direct us to "go take a shower and wash that mess off yourselves, and we'll talk about it all tomorrow."

When tomorrow rolled around and it was time to go again, K. C. would bring up the debacle from the night before and explain that he had spent the night lying awake trying to figure out how this supposedly great team could have possibly lost to "those guys." And as he was trying to understand it, he told us, his thoughts were interrupted by the phone ringing in his room. It was Bill Russell, and Russ said that he had seen the Celtics' loss on the satellite TV earlier that night. He was so embarrassed by our performance that he wanted K. C. to give him the team's mailing address so that he could send all of his eleven championship rings back. K. C. told us that John Havlicek called not too much later, and had also seen our miserable performance that night. And John was so ashamed that he wanted to know how he could have his retired No. 17 Celtic uniform removed from the rafters of the Boston Garden. And on it went through the night. They all called. The entire Celtic family. All the Hall of Famers. All the great champions. All the legends.

They were through with us. They all wanted to disassociate themselves from what we had just done.

We would go out and obliterate whoever was next—for quite a while.

—

Being part of a great team makes the locker room a very special place. When the team is lousy, that same room is dreadfully awful. This Celtics team had so many dynamic and diverse personalities, the locker room scene became a story all its own.

Dennis Johnson, DJ, in the right corner locker near the showers, hated wasting time and waiting around. He always kept his own schedule, preferring to arrive as late as humanly possible and still get there before the game actually started. He loved to eat just before the game, wolfing down food even as he was getting dressed, taped, and filling out the myriad of ticket requests.

Kevin, in the corner to DJ's left, loved the social aspect of always having someone there to listen to him. He enjoyed recounting the weirdness of the daily news, and would regularly read the day's tabloids out loud to anybody within earshot, which meant all of us.

To Kevin's left, Chief liked to focus on his fan mail. Sitting next to him, right in the middle, where the centers always are, I had the privilege of living his dreams alongside him. Robert would get all these letters that were doused with perfume and stuffed with pictures and all sorts of enticing invitations. Chief and I regularly discussed temptation.

Danny, in the far left corner, could never keep still. Always up and down, bouncing off the walls, and nonstop chatter—usually about golf, money, and how great a player he was—at everything. Which was mostly true.

One day, Danny was whining more than usual, about how Kevin would never pass him the ball, and that Kevin was the ultimate black hole—you threw it in there, and it never came back out.

Kevin took it all in quietly for a while, but finally he blurted out, "Enough! Corky, Wayne, get me the stat sheet. Right now." They do, and Kevin starts going up and down the list, reading it out. Here is Danny shooting 50 percent from the field for the season while being left unguarded the entire time, because every team had to put two or three guys on Kevin; and here's Kevin shooting 58 percent, near the top of the league, being totally surrounded by the other team all game long— including Danny's man. Then Kevin turned to Danny and, looking around the room at all of us for affirmation, asked him, "So tell me, Danny, with these facts and stats, why should I ever pass you the ball?"

The question was met with stone silence, as Danny quickly went off in another direction. The rest of us—Scotty, Jerry, Rick, Greg, Sam, David, and me—kept still and quiet. We were the cannon fodder for one of the great teams in sports history.

And then there was Larry. He was always so meticulous in his preparation and attention to detail. He was also constantly burdened by the responsibility of being the best performer and the leader of the band, all at the same time. In that spot, you're never really allowed the luxury of being happy. The obligation isn't easy, and Larry never took it lightly.

He was always one of the first to arrive, often hours before game time. He immediately took the court and started running and shooting. Always near the basket at first, and then as he found his rhythm and touch, he would slowly add distance to the practice shots. Larry generally had three men, all hired by the Celtics, there to feed him the ball. Not little children but grown men, who, like Larry, were all very serious in this warm-up session that lasted quite a long time. When he felt ready for the game—and only he knew when—he would head straight to the locker room, already completely drenched in sweat. He would strip down, take a hot shower, and then go and lie down in a dark, quiet space and get a full body massage from Vladimir, the first full-time massage therapist in the history of the NBA. Red always said do whatever it takes, and he'd take care of everything from the business end. And he did.

Vladimir is still a Celtic today, as we all are—because of Red.

When it was time, Larry would come out into the locker room, get dressed in his game uniform, get taped, and then sit there quietly by his corner locker off to the left of Chief, Scotty, and myself. He wouldn't put his shoes on until the last few moments. And as he sat there by himself, head down, deep in thought, analysis, concentration, and everything else, he would start chewing on his thumb. The earlier and more furiously he started chewing on that thumb, the more urgent we all knew the situation to be.

We ended the regular season with the third-best record in the history of the NBA. Most of our losses were to the league's worst teams—twice to the Nets, then once each to Indiana, Cleveland, Chicago, New York, Detroit, Sacramento, Phoenix, Denver, Washington, and Dallas. But now none of that mattered—nothing did. It was a blank slate, it was the playoffs, and the golden road to the championship was just getting started.

—

We started the playoffs against Chicago, who didn't have a very good team at all. But they did have this young player named Michael Jordan, in just his second year.

Michael had missed almost all of the regular season with a broken foot. His own team management didn't want him to play at all, but he said he was ready. And he went for it.

In life, there is always the retrospective analysis with anything that later turns out to be great and special. When Michael first joined the NBA, this was a league that was owned by Kareem, Larry Bird, Magic, and Dr. J, and the Celtics, Lakers, and 76ers. It was also an era that was not dominated by hype. Like how today if you make a basket, they immediately stop everything, call you the new greatest player ever, make a movie about you, and put you in the Hall of Fame before the ball is put back in-bounds.

So when Michael Jordan first joins the Bulls and they're in their first training camp, they don't even have any press coverage at all. And after the first few days, the Bulls coach, Kevin Loughery, finally meets a few of the assorted media that have come by to check on things. Somebody eventually gets around to asking how the new guy, Michael Jordan, is doing.

Coach Kevin, himself a fine NBA player in his own day, takes a beat, then a breath, and quietly deadpans, "He's better than we thought."

That same thing happened to us.

In the first game of this best-of-five series with Boston having the home-court advantage, we won easily, but Michael went for 49 points. We didn't think much of it, figuring he'd never do that again.

In the next game, also in Boston, Michael went for 63 points, an NBA playoff record that still stands, fouling many of us out in the process. Fortunately, Larry stayed around and pulled us through to victory in double overtime.

After the game, talking among ourselves, we readily agreed that "this guy" was really "pretty good" and that maybe we should "pay attention" to him.

And so we came up with the strategy that no matter what happened in the next game, now in Chicago, every time Michael got the ball—WHEREVER—we were going to double-team him and make him give it up. And we would take our chances on having Michael's teammates on the Bulls—Orlando Woolridge, Charles Oakley, and Dave Corzine—see if they could beat us.

We routed them and sent them home early. Michael was worn down and out and never really got going that day, reinforcing the notion that even if you're Michael Jordan, it's not ever really how good you are, but rather the quality of your teammates.

And that's what we, and Larry Bird, had.

—

We moved on to face Atlanta, whom we had not lost to all season long, despite their plethora of talent, size, and strength, and the magnificence of Dominique Wilkins.

The first two games in Boston were both wins, notable only for how well we kept playing, getting ever more focused as we homed in on the title. There was a growing circus over how well we were playing, and more and more people and media wanted to come and watch. But there was simply no more room; the Garden was always packed full, if not overflowing. So around this time, someone on the operations side of the Celtics decided they could squeeze another row of seats into the joint, if they just cut most of the length of the legs off the chairs and then put them in front of the existing front-row seats. More people, even closer to the action—the Garden crowd was never more intimidating. When Larry saw this, he immediately noted that Red must have gone over to Jerry Sichting's house and taken all the furniture.

Down in Atlanta, we won the first game to go up 3–0, and then the Hawks finally managed a win in Game 4. No one could remember the last time they'd beaten us, but we just didn't play well enough at all to get it done on the road. I was unable to play in either of the games in Atlanta. I had badly hurt my knee in a tough collision in one of the games back in Boston and I couldn't go, despite the nonstop medical treatment and therapy.

Now, back in Boston for Game 5, we and our fans were more than ready. It was one of those magical games of perfection that this Celtic team was regularly bringing now.

I was able to play a bit again after my knee injury. But this game was over from the opening tip. We would go on these incredible runs where we would score on almost every possession, and the Hawks rarely scored at all.

At one point in the second half, with our crowd going predictably wild, Danny made another in a string of great plays, and Tree Rollins, the Atlanta center who had a long and bitter history with Danny, took the ball out-of-bounds after our made basket. Instead of throwing it in to his teammate to bring the ball up the court, a frustrated Rollins wound up and threw the ball right at Danny's head—as hard as he could, from near-point-blank range. Tree was not the first—or last— guy who wanted to do that. But in the midst of an electrifying run for the Celtics, now everybody came to a complete stop, figuring something was about to explode—and none of it was going to be good.

So while we were all standing there waiting for the refs to come in and do something to put the fire out, Danny, quick to realize that the play had not yet been whistled dead, raced to the other end of the floor, where the ball was resting quietly, all by itself. He picked it up and dribbled it furiously back up the court, while everybody else thought that the action had already been stopped by the refs. And just a couple of strides across half-court, and still with his live dribble, Danny pulled up and shot another really long three, which went in. Everybody else was just standing there watching.

The refs called the play good, and Atlanta's Coach Fratello had to call one of his few remaining time-outs. Our crowd never stopped roaring with glee for us—and disdain for Tree and the Atlanta Hawks—the entire night.

We won by 33 points to send the Hawks home for good. Fratello, when asked after the game what he thought was needed to have made a difference in this game and the series, quipped softly, "We were unable to make any trades or sign new players during the game."

—

With our early and easy disposal of Atlanta, and while waiting for the series on the other side to be decided between Philadelphia and Milwaukee, we had way too much time on our hands, but there was nothing we could do about it.

After the Hawks series, we were out, probably at the Scotch 'n Sirloin, toasting yet another Celtic masterpiece when somebody came up with the seemingly brilliant idea that, we're getting really close here, guys, why don't we all make a vow and commitment tonight, right here and now, that none of us will take another drink until we win the championship—just to make sure that we don't leave anything to chance.

And everybody jumped aboard, raising our glasses and toasting with the loud proclamation, "Yeah! I'll drink to THAT!"

Then Kevin, always the voice of reason and perspective, quietly asked around the table, "Hey, guys, we're going to win the championship this year, aren't we?"

And everybody chimed in one more time, "YEAH! I'll drink to that, too!"

Milwaukee beat Philadelphia. And when the games finally did start again, right before one of the first two games in Boston, there was an on-court pregame presentation where the NBA awarded me the league's Sixth Man of the Year trophy.

When the game did get going, I stunk it up big-time. We won handily—we always did. And when Larry was asked after the victory what it meant to the team to have me win this Sixth Man honor, he laughed.

"Sixth Man? Of the NBA? Bill Walton? Are you kidding me? This is a farce. Tonight he was our worst player out of twelve; and he was Milwaukee's best player all at the same time! Sixth Man? Bill Walton? Spare me. Please."

And he was right.

—

Milwaukee had no chance against us. This series was not going to last very long. Everybody knew it, so the NBA and CBS scheduled Games 3 and 4, both in Milwaukee, to be played back-to-back on Saturday and Sunday afternoons, so that they could get Larry and the Celtics on TV twice before it was over.

In the first game in Milwaukee, on Saturday, we suffered a very tough loss. Scott Wedman got hurt. Late in a game that we controlled throughout, Scotty got caught in a tough spot defensively as the Bucks' huge, powerful, and mighty forward Terry Cummings came driving across the lane. And as Terry planted his foot and exploded to the rim, his knee drove into Scott's back; Scott had gotten turned around on some defensive rotations. Cummings was so big and strong, the collision broke Scotty's front ribs. Scott lay on the ground motionless for quite some time. It was very scary, and a terrible loss for our team. Scott Wedman was a great player for us, in immeasurable ways.

When they asked Larry about it after the game, when it was known that Scotty was not going to be able to play the rest of the season and any of these playoffs, he immediately piped in with a reference to 1984: "Well, the last time Scotty broke a bone in the playoffs, we won the championship, so I think we'll be fine."

The gathered reporters didn't want to write stuff like that, but that was Larry. So they gave him another chance and asked Larry to be serious here for a minute and to please give them a quote that they could use and that showed the seriousness of Scotty's injury, and his value to the team, and what it all meant going forward.

Larry looked at them like they were wasting his time. He took a deep breath, bent down to tie the laces of his shoes, straightened back up, cleared his throat one last time, and muttered as he grabbed his game bag and headed out the door to walk back across the street to our hotel, "Better him than me!"

The next day at Milwaukee's Mecca, for Game 4, we had to tighten up our rotation, as Scotty was unavailable, but our starters overpowered the Bucks regardless. Even without Scotty we had a more complete squad than them. And we had Larry Bird.

As the game was winding down, we had the lead, we were playing well enough, and we were going to win. But we still had to keep scoring and keep the clock moving. It was far from over. One of the real strengths of our team was that there was very little dribbling—ever. And as we would move the ball around the perimeter and then inside and back out, the ball inevitably wound up in Larry's hands—which was always a good idea.

And with just a couple of minutes to go in the game, and the series, the ball came through Larry on the left side of the court about halfway between the three-point line and the midcourt divider. Larry swung the ball through his triple-threat position to clear some space for himself, as he always did, but instead of continuing the play with either a pass or a dribble (he was too far away from the basket to shoot it) Larry uncharacteristically held on to the ball, and put it to rest on his hip.

We were totally unsure what he was doing here, so we kept moving through our patterns as we always did. But Larry just kept looking—at us, at the Bucks, and at the shot clock.

K. C. got up from his seat on the bench to see what was going on, the crowd came somewhat alive at this very unusual turn of events, and everybody just kept looking at Larry. And this keeps going, with the shot clock ticking relentlessly down, and still nobody can figure out what's happening here.

Finally, with just one or two seconds left in our timed possession, and we're all still in futile motion, Larry takes the ball from his hip, swings it up into his shooting motion, and delivers a thirty-plus-foot three-pointer that swishes through the basket.

The next time down the court for us, the same exact scenario develops, with the ball on Larry's hip until a second or two is left on the shot clock. Again he rises up and drains another thirty-plus-foot three-pointer.

This happened at least four times in a row down the closing stretch. I would like to say it was the most remarkable thing I've ever seen in a basketball game—but this was Larry Bird. And with Larry, the unthinkable, the impossible, the incredible, the unimaginable was commonplace—every day.

And that was all for Milwaukee.

—

Here we were, exactly where we were supposed to be—the NBA Finals. We were facing the Houston Rockets, whom the Celtics had defeated in the 1981 Finals but who were now sporting a completely different lineup from that '81 team. The Rockets were now coached by Bill Fitch, who had been the Celtics' coach in that previous matchup, a U.S. Marine who always seemed to have a scowl on his face. Larry loved him. I didn't get that same sense from the rest of the guys.

The Rockets had impressed down the stretch, toppling the reigning champion Lakers in the previous round. With Hakeem Olajuwon, Ralph Sampson, Rodney McCray, Robert Reid, Craig Ehlo, and Jim Peterson, they had a deep and formidable front line that was young, explosive, and talented.

But we had Larry Bird and K. C. Jones.

Their backcourt had been decimated earlier in the regular season when their lead guard, John Lucas, had been kicked out of the league for substance abuse issues. The cliff came for John and the Rockets the night the Celtics beat them there in Houston during the regular season. John Lucas, who had a real tough go that night, one that didn't stop with the end of the game, never really recovered to be the top player he could have been. Fortunately, John certainly has been able to get the rest of his life together, and today does exemplary work on every level of his life.

The Finals began right where we left off—with the Celtics as a team playing spectacularly. Larry continued to play like a man possessed, and Kevin took it upon himself to personally destroy Ralph Sampson, Hakeem, and anybody else that Coach Fitch tried on him. Neither of the first two games in Boston was close at any point.

Shifting to Houston for the next three games leveled the playing field somewhat. Game 3 went down to the wire, and we bobbled too many of the closing moments, giving the game away with sloppy, careless execution at the end. Game 4 was a thriller, and Larry made some monumental plays. It all came down to a dagger three-pointer in the closing seconds that Larry nailed to give us an insurmountable 3–1 series lead.

Game 5 saw the Rockets at their worst, as Sampson started a fight with our little Jerry Sichting—who might as well have been Delilah. Ralph had at last two feet in height and probably one hundred pounds of body mass on poor little Jerry. Order was restored quickly, but we did not play with enough emotional commitment to even make a game of it. We gave them the victory without a fight or exacting any price, and left embarrassed and disgusted by our performance.

The plane ride home to Boston was very quiet, solemn, and reflective. As we were coming into the airspace around Boston, they told us that so many Celtic fans had come to the airport, it was not going to be safe or possible for us to go through the regular terminal. When we landed, we were taken to a remote airport location and then transported home with police escorts. Our fans were ready. They did not like the way things had turned out in Game 5, where we were pushed around down in Texas by a desperate opponent on their last legs, grasping to hold on to anything as they were going down. And our fans were not about to take anything for granted.

The city of Boston and the entire New England region was very tense as we approached game time on yet another Sunday morning on CBS. My brother Bruce, as he had done in Portland nine years earlier, showed up with more of his friends—just to make sure that everything would turn out right. He insisted on seats as close to Ralph Sampson as was legally possible.

The guys who ran the locker room, Wayne and Corky, called everybody on Saturday and told us that we would not be able to get to the Garden as we usually did, because of the crowds that were already gathering. We all had to meet at our practice court at Hellenic College and the police were going to have to escort us in, on a bus—to our own home game.

We rode silently in on the magic bus. Red was with us. He sat in the front seat opposite the driver. He was smoking his cigar. It was all very serious—and quiet. Even Kevin and Danny were silently still—in a relative way. We couldn't get to the Garden—the crowds were so thick. The Boston police had to clear a path, and our fans were wildly fierce, with hours still to go before tip-off. The bus took us up the back ramp right inside the place.

When Larry came in from his individual pregame shoot-around, he got all of our attention immediately.

"Guys, it's an hour and a half before tip-off, and our crowd is already in their seats, and they are ready—as ready as I've ever seen anyone. They want blood, guys, and right now the blood they want is the blood of the Houston Rockets. But I'm telling you guys right here and now that if we don't deliver today and get this done, they're going to want *our* blood. Now let's make sure that we bring it."

When we came onto the floor, it was surreal—the fans would not let up. They wanted the Rockets, and they really wanted Ralph Sampson. There was this little, tiny, and very old lady. She was right up close, and she had hand-painted a sign that was bigger than she was. It read something like, "Hey, Ralph—I'm 5'2" and eighty years old. Do you want to fight me, too?" And this little old lady wanted Ralph. She kept trying to run onto the court and go at him. And she kept shaking her clenched fists and her giant sign right in Ralph's face. She was ready to kill him. And she was one of the calmer ones that day.

The game was Larry's self-acknowledged greatest game ever.

On this day, in a game that had all kinds of winners of the genetic lottery—Hakeem, Chief, Ralph, and Kevin, all playing above the rim all day long—Larry did everything. He made every shot. Stole every pass. Set everybody else up perfectly. And as great as he had been all season long, this was another whole, stratospheric level of perfection. With all these giants soaring the entire time, Larry was still gathering every rebound. And the offensive ones: instead of just putting them right back up from underneath the basket, Larry would dribble the ball out to the three-point line and let it fly. He didn't even wait to see if it went in or not. As soon as the ball left his hand, he was running back downcourt on defense with his raised and crooked finger in the air.

The Rockets, and particularly Ralph, didn't offer any resistance at all. It wouldn't have mattered anyway. We were the Celtics. We were at home in the Garden. We had Larry Bird. And we were now officially the champions.

With a couple of minutes left on the clock, the Boston police had to come and take us off our own home court and get us to the safety of our locker room. I don't even know what happened to the poor guys K. C. left out there to finish out the last ticks of the clock. The crowd was just swarming everywhere, it was quite the celebration, and everybody was very, very happy.

When it was finally time to leave the Garden, we had to take the bus that had delivered us there many hours before. And as we're all aboard—Red, K. C., his assistants, and the twelve players—Kevin remarked that he would finally stop asking Rick Carlisle why he and Ralph Sampson had never won the NCAA title when they were teammates at Virginia. We all went to K. C.'s restaurant out in Framingham and everybody had a high time. There were many family members there, and things went well into and through the night. I woke up to what I think was the next day with Rick Carlisle's shirt on. And that was just the beginning.

With the entire region in on the celebration of the Celtics' sweet six-teenth championship, they clearly knew what they were doing in making sure that everybody had lots of fun. Within the next few days, when the city of Boston hosted a parade for the team, millions of people had poured into the city. And the pouring was just getting started.

They had us on these large elevated military assault vehicles that allowed us to get through the immense throngs of people who were all very happy with the way things had turned out. The city officials had to have police officers and dogs to keep the motorcade going. The fans loved the team, and we them. So it was quite natural for the raucous crowd to get as close as possible to share the love. There was not a lot of supervision or organization. And that was fine with everybody I saw and knew. At one point our general manager, Jan Volk, came up to me as we were all sharing the love of and with Celtics Nation. He was preaching caution, civility, and human decency. I poured what was left of the communal beer that I was holding over his head, and told him that this is what we lived for. Then I threw the last remaining droplets back to the roaring and appreciative crowd. There are few things on earth like a championship parade. I highly recommend them—as often as possible.

—

That summer, Larry and his wife, Dinah, came out to San Diego, and we had a delightful time. The children were in heaven. I was ecstatic. We played everything; basketball, tennis, beach volleyball, and swimming were just the start.

As I said before, I get up and start early. So I was already in the garage weight room after an early-morning run on the beach when Larry first came out. Early on, he wanted to play one-on-one on the garage court just out in front of the weight room.

I torched him. He was very upset. It's a center's court, walled in, and there's not the unlimited space to keep backing away to spread the floor. Larry didn't have the room he needed to free himself from the size, strength, and length of my defense.

He asked where the gym was. I took him down to Muni in Balboa Park, less than a mile away. He was very impressed when he walked in. It was still AWESOME, after all these years. Three side-by-side full courts, now with glass backboards, drinking fountains, and chairs and small bleachers to rest on between sessions. And open all day long, starting early and closing late.

We played every day for long stretches. One-on-one. Two-on-two. And all the way up to full-court five-on-five. Greg Lee played with us a lot. Larry insisted that Greg always be on his team.

As we came to the end of Larry and Dinah's stay with us, Muni had become our nexus. Our day started and ended there. And on our final day, at the close of our session there, after playing every kind of basketball possible until we literally could no longer stand up because we were so tired, we came to yet another moment of truth—the last one-on-one head-to-head matchup.

We had done all our drills, our shooting games, our two-on-two, five-on-five, and Larry always had Greg on *his* team. It was like the Memphis State game from 1973, in that my guys could never quite figure out that trying to help out on Larry was the worst defensive strategy in the history of the world. Larry, Greg, and I would just laugh hysterically at the futility of it all.

But now it's just Larry and me, one final go-round. And I'm on fire. The game is to 11, by ones, winner's outs, win by one. And I've got him. I'm on my way. There's no stopping me. I'm up 10–1, with the ball. I look at the poor guy, bent over, grabbing his shorts, out of breath, and say to him, "Larry, I feel bad. Here you are, coming all the way out here—you and Dinah, as my guests—and I'm beating you badly in this last session. I tell you what, Larry; I'm going to give you a chance—but only one. I'm going to give you the ball here, one time only, and let's see if you can do anything with it."

Larry took the ball and proceeded to hit ten straight shots in my face. And with each succeeding make, he was talking more and more trash. I was playing with everything I had. I was pushing him, grabbing him, hacking him, fouling him, tackling him, everything. And with each new attempt Larry kept stepping farther and farther back, away from the hoop.

By the final shot he was near half-court. And even that desperation heave—with me draped all over him—still swished through the basket. He went running, yelling, hooting, and hollering all around the gym in ecstatic glory, arms extended over his head in celebration.

And then, sadly, he was gone.

—

With time running short, the new season about to start, and the children's school year fast approaching, we headed back to Boston. All the guys were trickling back into town from their summer days and summer nights, and we would gather at our practice court at Hellenic for fun and games. I frustratingly broke my little finger on Chief's shooting elbow in a pickup game, as Robert hit the game-winner in my face. So as training camp started, I was limited to the weight room and the stationary bike. Larry and Kevin would carry on this running one-way trash-talking conversation with me about me not playing, being soft and a sissy, and getting beat and broken by Chief in the process. There was nothing I could say or do.

As I was getting ever closer to the point where I could start to play again, Kevin stopped by me on the bike one day, and we got right into the whole trash-talking routine. Eventually I bet him that over the long haul, I would play in more NBA games over the rest of my career than he would in his.

A couple of days later, while pounding out ever more of the endless hours and miles on that stationary bike, the deep burning pain in my foot returned—the same pain that had derailed so much, for so long, and on so many different occasions.

It was now back, although this time—it was in my other foot.

I was never able to play again. And I lost my last bet with Kevin.

—

Just like all the other times, I tried everything, but with no success. My one "good" foot had now gone bad.

I started having operations quite regularly. I tried to play. Ultimately, from this point forward, I had more orthopedic surgeries than basketball games that I could play in. A lot more.

The year became a blur. The fun, joy, and games were gone. The Celtics were still great. They still had the best record in the East that year. But I no longer felt like part of the team. I would occasionally get into the games for a spot appearance—but I couldn't run. I had a broken foot, and every time I tried to run or play, it would break more.

The team's injury problems were not confined to just me. When one regular player gets injured and can't go, that puts a heavier burden on the guys who are still able to carry on. And so with me being out, Larry, Kevin, and Chief all had to play too much, and then they got hurt, too.

But despite all the problems, with Larry's back and elbow wearing out and Kevin's foot breaking down and Robert's ankle giving him all kinds of grief, the Celtics still had a chance to win it all.

The regular season and the first round of the playoffs were workmanlike performances—putting in the time. The Celtics swept Chicago in the first round, but then needed seven games to beat both Milwaukee and then Detroit.

We made it to the Finals. And here we were now, matched up against the L.A. Lakers. It was supposed to be the greatest moment of my life. I had dreamed forever of playing against Kareem—anywhere, everywhere, and particularly on the grandest stage of all, the NBA Finals.

It was all right there; except that I had a broken foot and couldn't play. All I could do was sit there with my feet and lower legs submerged in a deep tub of ice, trying to freeze them so that I could get out there and do something to help our team. It was as low a point for me as I've ever had. To have everything come together, to have a chance, and then to not be able to do your part. It turned out to be no chance at all.

We couldn't win in L.A. I couldn't move, run, or play.

Back in Boston during one of the games, late, with everything on the line, the Celtic crowd started chanting my name. "WALTON! WALTON! WALTON!"

The chant reverberated through the Garden, making the place shake. Like if only I would try harder, then everything would be fine, as if it were a matter of effort. I couldn't play. My foot was broken. My team needed me. I needed my team more.

The chant continued endlessly. I didn't know what to do. There was nothing I could do even if I did step on that court. I was so terribly alone and sad.

"WALTON! WALTON! WALTON!"

K. C. and all the guys were looking to me. Waiting. Hoping.

Finally, DJ came up to me, standing on the edge of the huddle.

He put his arm around my shoulder. He had been there in Portland in April 1978. He stretched up to my ear, and he whispered softly, as my friend, "Don't do it, Bill. . . . Don't do it."

We lost our chance at the championship because we couldn't get one defensive rebound off a missed Laker free throw. But we really lost it much earlier, with all the broken bones in our feet and our bad backs, elbows, and ankles. Had that not been the case, we would have won handily. It would not have been close. All I could do was sit there, alone with my feet and ankles, frozen and blue, in a large tub of ice.

—

I would spend the next three years in the hospital with Dr. Daly and Dr. Wagner doing surgery after surgery after surgery on my foot and ankle. Big, huge, giant ones. Medium-size ones. Little ones. All trying to solve the lack-of-mobility problems in my feet that had plagued me my entire life.

When the Finals with the Lakers were over, I headed straight to Dr. Wagner's office back in Whittier, where he and Dr. Daly tried to do the same complicated surgery they had done on me five years before, just before I went to Stanford. This time it was on my other foot and ankle.

I tried to recover and come back one more time, in time for the playoffs of the following year. And as the season progressed and moved toward spring, I went back to Boston to give it a shot. I was able to participate in some of the practices, but I couldn't run, jump, or play.

When the team finally reached the point where they had to submit their playoff roster, Red came up to me and asked me one more time the same question that had put it all in motion: "Can you play?"

This time, I had to tell him, "No, Red. I'm terribly sorry. I can't." I just couldn't run or move.

I went back to San Diego. In the next few years there were many more surgeries, more procedures. I tried everything that I could to climb the mountain one more time.

One day I was in the garage weight room. It was February 1, 1990. My mom's birthday. My foot had been broken for more than three and a half years. The music was blasting. I was in the zone. I was sure success was imminent. I could feel it. I knew that I was right there, and that I would soon be back out there playing once again. Now it would be against the new generation of giants—Hakeem, David Robinson, and Patrick Ewing. They were my new sources of inspiration, as Kareem had retired after twenty years, alone at the top of the highest mountain.

I was pounding away on the gleaming steel. Pushing. Pulling. Driving. Doing it all. Dripping wet with sweat. The Grateful Dead were on fire on the stereo. I was out there, on the edge, all the way to eleven— and beyond. I had it all. One more time. I was going to make it.

I finally finished. Drenched. Hot as can be, but cool inside. And I closed the gym down. I took the short walk across the backyard over to the main house. Halfway there, I had to stop. I had to go down to my hands and knees. I could no longer walk. I had ground the bones in my foot and ankle down to dust. The tibia was no longer on top of the talus. It had slid off the back.

I crawled across the ground the rest of the way into the house and to the telephone. I called my friend. I asked him to please come over to my house and find my crutches. I was no longer able to walk.

CHAPTER 14

Eyes of the World

MARCH 15, 1990

Sometimes the songs that we hear are just songs of our own.

I woke today . . . in Whittier, California.

In the hospital. I just had my ankle fused.

As I was going down with the IV drip, fading to black, Drs. Daly and Wagner were there by my side. They told me that this was going to be tough. And that it was going to hurt. I looked at the side of my hospital gurney. The tables and trays were fully loaded with what seemed to be all the tools for a major construction project—scalpels, hammers, saws, files, drills, knives, scissors, bolts, screws, protractors, levels, screwdrivers, and much more.

When they were inside me, they took a big electric saw and cut all the ends of the bones off in my foot and ankle. They then pushed all the raw, bleeding bone into a big ball, held the stump of it at a right angle, and then went around it with a big power drill and bolted everything together.

What they didn't fuse surgically that day has fused on its own over the last twenty-five-plus years.

They then put a huge cast on my leg. It must have weighed eighty pounds. It went from my toes to my hip. Then they hooked me up to a morphine drip and pump. Every time I woke up, they came by my bed and put me back to sleep.

I was in the hospital for a week. I don't remember a thing, other than that it really hurt.

Every time I turned even the slightest bit, I could feel the loose bones rattling in the stump on the end of my leg. Everything was still loose—and settling. It was all moving, grinding, and grating. And it all really hurt. They weren't kidding about that.

And this was the easy part.

—

I had been out of work for so long now that after the past few years, I now had nothing. And here I was starting the long, hard climb one more time, with no dream, no vision, no plan, nothing.

I was in the cast from my toes to my hip for two months. Then in one from my toes to just below my knee for another month.

And then a new beginning. One more time.

I now knew that I would never play ball again—ever. I knew that I would never again be in the game, in the huddle, on the bus, in the locker room, or with the guys. Basketball had always been my life. The game was my religion; the gym my church. I would never again be barking at the refs, or my coaches and teammates.

From the darkness—it crystallized. The light started to grow and glow. The lightning-bolt flash of inspiration seared across the smoking crater that is my mind one more time. I finally realized that when you're 6'11"; have red hair; a big nose; freckles; a goofy, nerdy-looking face; a lifelong stutterer; and are a Dead Head—television is the only career possibility for the future.

—

That I could even consider television, when I had once been such a stutterer that I couldn't even get a single word out, was testament to Marty
Glickman, whom I'd met through Ernie Vandeweghe in Southern California back in the early 1980s, when I was trying but failing to play for
the Clippers. In a remarkably simple twist of fate, Marty changed my
life forever.

Marty had been a world-class athlete in his youth, only to have his
dreams smashed when he was denied participation in the 1936 Berlin
Olympics because he was a Jew. He and Ernie became great friends in
the 1950s when Marty was broadcasting in New York and Ernie was
playing for the Knicks. Marty was an outstanding speaker, and a most
remarkable spirit and force. When I met him for the first time, I couldn't
talk—at all. I literally could not say a word. I had never been able to.
Marty immediately looked right into my soul through my pained and
embarrassed eyes and said, "You're a stutterer, aren't you?"

I couldn't respond. I tried to, but I was stuck on the first sound of
whatever word I was trying to say. That's the way it had always been.
And I was sure that it would be that way forever.

Marty wasted no time, cutting off my futile attempts right away
and gesturing for me to follow him over to the corner of the room. We
ended up behind a potted plant.

And in a five-minute, one-way conversation, he laid it all out for
me. He explained how speech and communication were skills that had
to be learned, like any other skill, which meant they required discipline,
organization, persistence, patience, and a plan.

He instructed me to chew sugarless gum to strengthen the muscles
in my neck, jaw, mouth, and tongue. He then urged me to slow my
thoughts down and to concentrate completely on the one word that I
was trying to say at that moment—not three or four words, not phrases
or sentences down the road. Then he directed me to read out loud in
front of the mirror, to practice saying the words so I would get used to
seeing myself as others would, so that I would eventually learn to like
what I saw and was doing. He also told me to find written passages
that had lots of the sounds that gave me the most trouble—for me

that was easy: it was all of them. Then, after this practice, I should take the whole show out and into the world to become a teacher, first to young children, who wouldn't care about my mistakes and problems, but who would be ecstatic that someone actually cared about them at all. And then to move on, forward and further, to everyone, whether they wanted to listen or not.

As he came to the end, he encouraged me to take all the techniques, methods, and practice procedures that my great basketball coaches had taught me and apply them to speech. I should incorporate Coach Wooden's Four Laws of Learning: demonstration, imitation, correction, and repetition. Just as I'd learned how to pivot, change direction, pass, rebound, shoot, and dribble, Marty thought that I could develop the skills to speak. And if I did all of this with the commitment, enthusiasm, and passion I had used in becoming a successful basketball player, I might have a real chance to learn how to talk.

And that was it. I was on my way. Marty stayed with me and kept refining things. But much like how Coach Wooden told us before the games that it was now up to us, Marty let me go, with the freedom to fly and chase it all down.

He ultimately encouraged me to study the people who were on TV all the time, and to study and learn from and about them the way I did my basketball heroes, role models, and opponents. I chose Jay Leno.

Marty Glickman taught me how to learn to speak. It is my greatest accomplishment in life—and everybody else's worst nightmare.

Once I started to learn how to speak, and with the dogged encouragement of some friends, particularly Charlie Jones and Pat O'Brien, I started down this fateful trail. The only problem was that I couldn't get a job. Anywhere. They'd all look at me and say, "Are you kidding me, Walton? We're not putting you on TV. You'll get up there and start stuttering and spitting all over everything and everybody. Then you'll start talking about Jerry Garcia, the Grateful Dead, Bob Dylan, and Neil Young. We can't have that. Now get out of here and don't come back. Quit bothering us!"

With every rejection and shutdown, I became more determined. I came back to Coach Wooden's final tool to overcome the adversity that he knew would one day come our way—the discipline, persistence, and perseverance to get what you want.

Now, when you look like I do, and when you struggle with speech and communication like I still do, you hear the word *no* a lot. And I was up against things here. It was not looking good. I had no Plan B, and I was just hoping against hope for something positive to come my way.

I was in church late one evening in 1990, praying for a better to-morrow, and I met Lori, this incredible angel of mercy. She's intelligent, skilled, articulate, kind, fun, happy, and cute as can be. She has everything that I need, and she's excellent at all the things that I like. Rest assured that she's been there the rest of the way with me. I can't speak for her, but it has been better than perfect for me—marrying this wonderful, caring, loving, interesting, and talented goddess of the night.

It felt like a new day, but I still needed a job. I should have gone back to Stanford. But the children were older now, and I didn't want them to have to keep moving all the time, after the bouncing back and forth for too many years now. I was up against things, time was short, and everybody kept saying no.

But then one day, I got my first broadcasting job. It made no difference to me that it was a CBA minor-league game, on the radio, from Bakersfield, California, on Christmas Day, for no pay, with the team and the entire league folding the next day. But I got to call the game. And I was on my way—in the business of sports.

I had no idea what I was doing. Or what I was getting myself into. But my friends were incredibly supportive and encouraging, and it kept on growing. I started doing all kinds of small events. Local news and remote hits from the shopping malls, and at grand openings of pizza parlors, car dealerships, whatever was happening that day. I elbowed my way in as a guest on countless radio shows around the country. I started writing articles and columns for whoever would publish them, pay me, or buy my next meal. I took any and every opportunity, often for no pay.

In Los Angeles, I met Don Corsini, who at the time was running

Prime Ticket, a fledgling cable sports network that Jerry Buss and his Lakers were behind. Don gave me my first TV game, then some games at UCLA and around the rest of the Southland.

Then I stumbled into Ralph Lawler, the voice of the Los Angeles Clippers, at a convenience store by the beach in San Diego. He asked me what I was up to, and I brought him up to speed on my latest efforts. Soon after this chance encounter, Ralph called me with an opportunity to work with him on the Clippers' local TV package in Los Angeles. I ended up doing Clipper basketball games with Ralph for the next thirteen years. It was easily some of the worst basketball ever, and Donald Sterling's "business practices" were shoddy, despicable, demoralizing, depressing, and basically immoral, if not illegal. I got fired every year, sometimes multiple times. One go-round, I got the boot four times during the same season, including once at halftime.

But Ralph and I became best friends, and I couldn't wait to get there every day. Ralph is pure genius. As smart, kind, and generous as anyone I've ever known. He was able to make evil and weirdness fun. Working with Ralph was like playing basketball with Larry Bird and being coached by John Wooden—all at the same time. It was like making music with the Grateful Dead. He is a remarkable performer and teacher. And he's the best friend a guy could ever hope to have.

The opportunities started to come. Roy Firestone was responsible for lots of them. Even though his Up Close studio was in a most difficult part of L.A. to get to—Hollywood—it allowed me to spend countless long and late nights with varying combinations of Jerry Garcia, Bob Dylan, Timothy Leary, and George Carlin. When Lori was still there after a spectacularly unending run, I thought I might have a real chance there. I had a run for a while as the announcer for the Dallas Mavericks. I was brought in by CBS for their NCAA March Madness and Final Four programming. I got to work with true legends and heroes, including Bob Stenner and Sandy Grossman. Eventually I was given a contract with NBC, where I spent ten years teaming up on one of the great broadcasting squads ever. Greg Gumbel, Tom Hammond, Snapper Jones, Jim Gray, producer Kevin Smolen, director John Gonzalez, and all-around Mr. Fix-It Jeff Simon were a band of brothers beyond description—as was our life together.

I later followed the NBA media rights package to ABC and ESPN.

In the early 1990s I got to follow Bill Graham as Father Time for the Grateful Dead on New Year's Eve. Bill died in his helicopter, which tragically crashed on his way home from work late one night. It was a most solemn duty and responsibility—very much like following Kareem at UCLA.

—

All the while, the children were growing up fast. I got them ready for school each morning to the joyous rock-'n'-roll beat of our lives, and I would write on the boys' lunch bags an endless variety of Coach Wooden's maxims. The boys were so embarrassed, but when I would drop them off at school, all their friends would be waiting to see what I had written that day. Our boys would roll their eyes, and maybe the other youngsters did, too. As the children got out of the car, I would always say, as loud as I could, "I love you!" They pleaded with me to stop saying it in front of their friends. But that just encouraged me. Then they would ask me if I would please drop them off a block from school so that I wouldn't embarrass them. They were all very happy when they started driving themselves.

We had our living room set up with the dining table positioned perfectly to watch basketball games in the evening. Michael Jordan was the main attraction, and he never failed to deliver. We scheduled our lives around the 5:30 p.m. (local time) Jordan tip-off. We never missed it. Nor did he.

It was all completely unlike my own childhood. My parents were not into sports. We didn't have a TV. There was not a single night of my childhood that I can remember, or think of, that both my parents were not there for dinner—often first to the table. The thought of scheduling anything, much less dinner, around somebody else playing a sport on television is as far from the reality of my childhood as you can get. But that's how good and reliable Michael was. And a real measurement of how much the times had really changed. As a master teacher and performer, Michael Jordan was more than worth it.

As my broadcasting and business career began to take off, I was on the road more and more, at a time when our children needed me more than ever. When I would start to pack for yet another trip, the muffled and pained refrain from the boys invariably came down to, "You have to leave town again, Dad?"

In my absences, the children were now starting to find their own way, which, as anyone who's ever had boys knows, meant that I was now responsible for enforcing the discipline that the boys lacked. They complained that I was always saying no, and that I was the worst dad ever. Their final option in our disagreements was, en masse, to threaten to go to Notre Dame.

I tried to explain to them that I would love to say yes, but they were always asking me the wrong questions. And if they wanted me to say yes, then all they had to do was ask, "Dad, can we go to bed now? Dad, can I do the dishes? Dad, can I turn off the TV now? Can I go outside and play?" I tried to teach them about the importance of self-discipline, and that the culture of yes is built on a foundation of no.

As the gorgeous afternoons of San Diego turned to dusk, the boys often found themselves on the backyard garage basketball court. I had always encouraged them to play sports for fun, health, and to learn life's greatest lessons. I did not want to be their coach. I wanted to be their dad. And I told them that if they wanted me to be their coach, they would have to ask me to do that—but they needed to be aware that I am a tough coach.

Too many times, as the evening would be coming on, some of the boys would come inside and start whining and complaining about how things were not going their way on the court out back. They would regularly ask me to call Larry and Magic to come over and help them with their games. One afternoon, Little Luke came inside crying. He said his older brothers, Adam and Nate, were cheating him and beating him up and keeping him from winning. I had lived that whole deal myself forty years ago with my own older brother, Bruce—so I knew that it was all true. But that's also part of how you learn. I told him to get back out there and work it out. He came back soon, crying some more and rubbing his arm. He told me through his tears that they were unrelentingly mean out there, were cheating on the score and the fouls, and they kept knocking him to the ground. And now his arm was really sore. I told him to put some ice on it, that he'd be fine.

Luke was still complaining about his arm the next morning and wanting to stay in bed and miss school. I wasn't buying it, and again I told him to ice it. When Luke got to school, the school nurse called Lori and asked her to please come pick Luke up because he had come to class with a broken arm.

—

Without basketball in my life now, I was riding my bike whenever the surgeries and my health allowed me to. I couldn't run or jump or hike—still can't. But I can ride my bike, and I've made the most of it. And now that I was back in Los Angeles for business more often, I was able to spend a lot more time with Coach Wooden. I also began learning and studying classical piano, something I could do sitting down for the rest of my life. My dad was proudly ecstatic, although my practice habits—as often as possible, starting well before the dawn—drove Lori and the boys crazy.

I was still finding my way as a TV and basketball announcer as well. In one of my first NCAA tournaments, there was a Florida State player who'd had a mercurial first half but looked awful down the stretch. Late in the game, we were told at the table that it was due to an upset stomach. And as my broadcast partner, Sean McDonough, was wrapping things up before sending viewers back to the studio, a flash of inspiration hit me one more time. So I leaned in for a final comment: "If this was me, I'd have taken that guy with the upset stomach down into the locker room, put a finger down his throat, have him puke it back up, and then get him back up here on the court and get going!"

Sean looked at me, aghast, as if I'd just committed the worst atrocity in the history of the world. And he says good night to the world, and we're off the air. I thought he was going to kill me.

At every broadcast table in those days, there was always a telephone. The ringer was silenced so as not to disrupt the show, but it had a red light that would light up when a call came through. As soon as I stopped talking, the phone lit up like the Grateful Dead stage at the start of the second set. Sean McDonough suggested that it was probably for me.

When I picked up the phone, the stern voice on the other end started right in. "Hey, Walton! My name is Neal Pilson, and I'm the president of CBS Sports. And Walton, if you look at your watch right now, you will note that it's the dinner hour in New York City. Now, Walton, I'm here to tell you straightaway that we at CBS do not talk on our air about PUKING during New York City's dinner hour. Got it?"

He hung up before I could even say anything.

I was beginning to make progress, but I still too often mistook activity for achievement. Flailing and grasping would best describe my efforts. But then I got a huge break: the chance to call a big game with the incomparable Dick Enberg.

It was a big stage, and I was scared to death. I kept asking myself, What am I doing here?

I was warming up with everything I had—everything Marty had taught me. I was chewing and chomping on my gum. I was reviewing everything, going over in my mind how it was all going to play out. I was writing everything down. I was memorizing all that I could. But I was petrified that I would freeze up, start stuttering and spitting all over everything, and be unable to get a single word out.

And now Dick and I are out there on the court, on our stools, the moment before the moment of truth—and it's more nerve-racking than anything ever. I'm sweating profusely, nervous, anxious, and our producer starts his countdown in our ears: 10 . . . 9 . . . 8 . . .

I look over at Dick. He's having the time of his life. Waving to all the beautiful people, signing autographs. He knows that that red light is going to come on in a few more seconds and he's going to love talking basketball for the next couple of hours.

Dick looks over at me—just a wreck—and he's quite taken aback. "What's wrong with you, Walton? You look terrible."

I tell him, "I can't do this, Dick. I don't belong here. It's just too hard. I'm going to start stuttering and spitting all over everything. I can't do it."

Dick reaches over and pats me on the thigh. The countdown's still going: 5 . . . 4 . . . 3 . . .

"Don't worry about a thing, Billy. That red light's coming on in one more second, and there will be countless millions of people hanging on every word you say!"

Thanks a lot, Dick. We were on our way.

—

In the years that followed, I had some amazing opportunities. I called the NBA Finals and the Olympics. I got to travel the world as part of the NBA's program to develop the game of basketball around the world—Istanbul, São Paulo, Israel, France, Germany, Italy, Spain, Holland, Sweden, and beyond—running clinics with Jack Ramsay, Hubie Brown, and Calvin Murphy. I was inducted into the Basketball and Academic All-America Halls of Fame and the Grateful Dead Hall of Honor. And for years I got to follow Michael Jordan's Bulls, Hakeem Olajuwon's Rockets, Stockton and Malone's Jazz, Ewing's Knicks, and Shaq and Kobe's Lakers as they battled for the top of the mountain.

There were times when I had to be escorted in and out of arenas by large contingents of armed police officers in cities where the local fans didn't like what I'd said about their teams. Players and their family members would confront me at the games over the same issues. My hotel in Seattle was surrounded by an angry mob chanting for my head late one night after the game.

We took outrageous space-jam odysseys through Australia after the Sydney Olympics and journeyed by boat down the great unknown of the Grand Canyon and the Colorado River—twice.

In 1997, the fiftieth-anniversary year of the founding of the NBA, I was most fortunate to be named one of the 50 Greatest Players in NBA History. They brought everyone together, a real gathering of eagles, over All-Star Weekend in Cleveland. On the night of the All-Star Game itself, there was a big ceremony at halftime, where we would be officially introduced to the crowd and the world on live television.

We were all gathered in this one anteroom, all of the greatest players in the history of the NBA in a single space. At the beginning it was just us—no photographers, no agents, no handlers, no press, no posses, nobody—not even NBA commissioner David Stern. It was a perfect lovefest. Everybody was going around high-fiving one another; hugging; laughing; yelling; cheering; signing autographs; taking pictures. It was so much fun—even Kareem was having a good time.

While everybody was milling around and celebrating, Wilt and Michael Jordan were off by themselves, seated at a side table. They were arguing vociferously about who the greatest of the 50 Greatest was. And they were going back and forth. Nobody paid them any mind, as it was like, Come on, let's go, we're here, and what could be better?

Every time I looked back at Michael and Wilt, neither one would give it up.

Finally David Stern comes in—with his list. And he starts lining everybody up in TV order to make it just right, the way the NBA always does things. As David is going about his business, he keeps glancing over at Wilt and Michael, who are still going at it. And David is getting exasperated, since this is going to be a live TV event that will wait for no one. So finally, up against the moment of truth and the clock one more time, David gets sternly serious as he barks at Michael and Wilt, "Come on, guys! Enough! Wilt! Michael! Come on, we have to go, NOW!"

So these two timeless and epic giants finally do cut it off and slowly rise to their feet—and start their solemn walk to their rightful and designated places in line.

Suddenly, Wilt stops and pivots backward to face Michael and all of us. The room becomes eerily quiet, because we all know that Wilt always had to, and did, have the last word.

"Michael," he says as he looks a young, little Michael Jordan skeptically up and down. Then he pauses as he looks up and down the line at all of us. Everybody is holding their breath.

"Michael," he says so all can hear, "just remember. When you played, they changed all the rules for you to make it easier for you to dominate!"

Then Wilt glanced up and down the line one more time. He closed it out: "When I played, they changed all the rules to make it harder for me."

Wilt, now satisfied, proudly went and took his place, and we all marched out to take the court together.

—

Just two years later, we got the tragic news that Wilt had died. We were stunned. Wilt was indomitable, indestructible—and now he was gone. He was as great a champion as I've ever known—and an even better person. He would do anything for anybody, and yet he would refuse to ever let anybody talk publicly about his kindness or generosity. He lived to a higher standard than everyone else. And when I look back at Wilt's numbers, they dwarf everybody else's. So much so that when I point them out to the new guys, who weren't there, they shrug and say that they don't count—because he's Wilt. He did the impossible. It may be the case that he's not the greatest basketball player ever—how can you ever say who that one person might be? But there has NEVER been a single conversation about the greatest basketball players ever that didn't have Wilt Chamberlain at the center of it all. Right where he belonged.

Death was taking a terrible toll on my friends, heroes, and role models during these years—it has no mercy on this land. I have learned over time to never rank, rate, or compare children, coaches, championships, concerts, or congratulations—they're all to be enjoyed in their individuality.

The same forces that abhorrently try to drive and promote the individual over the team end up trying to minimalize and trivialize friendships, accomplishments—heck, all of life.

So in 1995, when Jerry Garcia died—after giving us so much joy, and singing directly to and for each of us, for so many years—what were we to do? Like Wilt, Jerry is in a league all by himself. He was an authentically great leader in many classic ways: He made life fun. He made it fair. He made it real. He made it cool. He made you want to come back for more— forever. And then he was suddenly gone. We were left all alone, and nothing was going to bring him back, and things were never the same again.

A few years later, we got the terrible news that Chick Hearn had passed away. He, too, had been omnipresent in our lives forever. He had been the Lakers' broadcaster and the voice of reason, clarity, sanity, authority, and our moral compass for the past forty-two years. He was my best friend. And he was the same for everybody else who ever came into his universe. In many ways, it was his voice and spirit, so many years back, when I was just a child, that pulled me to basketball and started my endless dreaming beyond my own small life. Like with Jerry, whenever I stumbled, failed, and fell, whenever I was down, it was Chick who always kept me going.

—

Our own boys were now finishing high school and heading off to college, chasing their dreams and building their lives. Adam was a top student in high school, and a strong basketball player on a good team. But we realized too late that there was something horribly wrong about the coaching decisions on and off the court. We tried our best to come to a positive resolution with the school and its administration, but I will always carry with me that it was something I couldn't do anything to change. We had time to find a different school and coach for Nate, Luke, and Chris—but Adam was a graduating senior when it all came down. He was already halfway out the door to LSU with Dale Brown, which luckily ended up being a great opportunity for him. Adam eventually went even farther south to play professional basketball in the Latin American leagues of Mexico and beyond.

By then, Nathan was choosing colleges, ultimately deciding on Princeton, a most exciting adventure for him. He learned so much from coaches Pete Carril and John Thompson III, as well as Athletic Director Gary Walters. It also helped a great deal that David Halberstam was able to make some important introductions for Nate—teachers, professors, writers, business folks—all people who have been phenomenally helpful to Nate as he's built his adult life. And because I was in New York and Philadelphia so much for work, I got to see many of Nathan's college games on Friday and Saturday nights—more than those of any of his brothers. Years later, when Princeton did a historical retrospective of the greatest moments ever in its Jadwin Gymnasium, one of Nathan's performances was No. 9 on the all-time list. I can proudly and forevermore say that "I was there!"

Luke, up next, chose Arizona and Coach Lute Olson. He made his choice on his first recruiting trip, when Arizona was the reigning NCAA champion. He met Richard Jefferson, another high school recruit from Phoenix, on his visit, and he came home afterward and immediately canceled all four of his other allowable recruiting trips. He and Richard Jefferson had both made up their minds that they were going to be Wildcats and spend the rest of their lives together. When things got going in their games at the McKale Center, it was surreal beyond description to hear the crowd chant "Luuuuuuuuuke . . . Luuuuuuuuuke . . . Luuuuuuuke," just as the Blazermaniacs had done for Big Luke in Portland so many years before. There were tears of joy and unremitting pride streaming down my cheeks as I immediately speed-dialed Maurice and held the phone up to the heavens so he could hear and feel it, too.

Our youngest son, Chris, had a tough time growing up, in that his older brothers would pick on him, beat him up, and tease and taunt him to no end. Chris was the neat and tidy one of the bunch. Sleek, lean, and clean as could be, Chris liked to keep his room spotless and totally organized. He had to lock his door all the time to keep his brothers out and his stuff safe. If Chris ever forgot to lock that door, his brothers would move right in, trash the place, sleep in his bed, eat their meals in his bed, wear all his clothes, and use all his stuff. He would get so mad.

Chris got his big break in the eighth grade when he found a top academic school in Rancho Santa Fe with an excellent basketball coach. He joined his cousin, Kam, Bruce's only son, there—in the same class. And they fell in with a terrific group of boys, all under Coach Dave McClurg, who transformed those young people's lives the way that Rocky, Gordon Nash, and Coach Wooden did for me. They became quite the team, playing and living like Coach Wooden's teams, and winning all their games. Bruce arranged for Coach McClurg to spend a surprise day with Coach Wooden at the Mansion on Margate, with all the surrounding amenities.

When it came time for college, Chris chose San Diego State, where my mom had gone to college, and just a mile from where we'd grown up and where my mother still lives in our family home today. Coach Steve Fisher had just been hired to build from scratch a program that was so far down, it was below sea level. It has taken a while, but Coach Fisher has now impossibly done what Lute Olson did so many years ago in Tucson. And now Coach Fisher has the second-best program in the western United States—after the Arizona Wildcats. Chris was one of Coach Fisher's early, foundational recruits, and it has been a pure thrill to see the program rise with him at its core. I couldn't be prouder—of Chris, Luke, Nathan, or Adam. I'm the luckiest dad in the whole world.

—

I eventually had the privilege and honor of broadcasting basketball games on television that each of our four sons have played in. But one that comes to mind today was in 2001, in the NCAA Regional Final, when Luke's Arizona team played another heavyweight team, Illinois. The winner was going to the Final Four. And both teams had a real chance of winning the championship that year.

I'm calling the game with Dick Enberg, and it's a back-and-forth, epic confrontation. Everything is up for grabs. And in the closing moments, with the fate of the known world in the balance, Coach Olson gets up from his seat, looks down the bench, and motions for Luke Walton to get in there. Luke makes some nice plays, helps his team play better, and at the end of the game, ARIZONA WINS!

The Wildcats are celebrating. They're running up and down the court, arms and their "No. 1" index fingers pumping to the sky in full extension, cutting down the nets and mussing up Coach Olson's hair and all—no small feat. Now Dick and I are already off the air, having given the show back to Greg Gumbel in the CBS New York studios. Dick and I are standing quietly back in the shadows, soaking it all in, basking in the happiness of these young people enjoying the grandest moment of their lives.

Little Luke Walton, right in the middle of it all, sees us out of the corner of his eye and breaks away from the fun and festivities. He comes to Dick first, now a great family friend, and says that it's good to see him. Dick, in his effervescent and bubbly style, starts pumping Luke's outstretched hand, encouraging him to go for more, to go for it all. That it was all out there in front of him—right now.

And then Luke turned to me—his dad. The dad who just hadn't been able to be there enough for him throughout his young life. And Luke looks up at me with the sad and soft eyes of a young boy who only wants more from his dad and from his life. He puts his hand up and out to me. And looking right at me, Luke softly says, "Thanks for coming, Dad. Thanks for coming."

I pulled him in as close as I could and hugged him. I was crying— tears of joy, happiness, and pride streaming down my face. I told him that I was the luckiest and proudest dad in the whole world.

—

With time, all the skeletal problems that I had were worsening. Yes, my fused right ankle gave me a whole new start in life, in that it took the pain away and allowed me to keep going further and forward. But now the other ankle had been ground down to dust, too, and in July 2001, I had to have that one fused as well. I was down and out for another nearly nine months or more. My bad left knee continued giving me all kinds of problems, too. And by now all these lower-extremity problems were working against my spine, a recurring issue since I broke my back in 1974 playing for UCLA. I could still get around a little, but it wasn't easy, painless, or pretty.

—

At the top of the list of the best parts of my life is that I was born, raised, and live in San Diego. And as my life has always borne out, the best also plays into the worst. Eighty percent of the television households in our country are east of Chicago, and everything in the world of sports television is about the East. San Diego is as far across the country as you can get, which means a lot of wasted time bustling around and flying back and forth to get to work—often way more than 600,000 domestic air miles a year.

But we kept after it, all the while experimenting and exploring all kinds of new things in the technological revolution of media. This included a one-of-a-kind, award-winning, rock 'n' roll satellite radio show in the early days for Sirius and their leader, Scott Greenstein. Like the Grateful Dead, the show had an amorphous start time, although it was regularly scheduled for Saturday night. It ended when we were done, often four, five, or six hours later. We covered a lot of ground. It was not a show for kindergartners. And I was there at the beginning—one more time.

—

In my TV world, as I was putting my 2002 Spring Calendar together around the NBA playoffs, in talks with NBA and NBC, it was increasingly clear that I would be out there, on the edge, literally the entire time. Our children were all gone now—in college and beyond. We decided that it might be best for me to just stay out on the road the entire run, and make it a tour that would allow me to go to the games as a fan, even when I wasn't broadcasting.

I like to tour, whether it's with the Grateful Dead, Bob Dylan, Neil Young, the Rolling Stones, or on my bike—I've been doing it my whole life. Now it was with the NBA playoffs, too. We called it "The Love It Live Tour."

For the first thirty-one days of the playoffs I went from San Diego to Sacramento to Los Angeles to New Jersey to Charlotte to New York to Boston to Seattle to Portland to Salt Lake City to Indianapolis to Los Angeles to Detroit to Sacramento to Los Angeles to Sacramento to New Jersey to Orlando to Dallas to Boston to Dallas to San Antonio to Sacramento to Los Angeles to New Jersey to Somewhere to Sacramento to New Jersey to San Diego.

Games every day. A young NBA superstud on the business side, Aaron Ryan, came with me and did all the really hard work. All along the way, I wrote one of the world's first sports blogs, similar to the journals that I had kept from my other great adventures. This one was posted, published, and updated by the hour on NBA.com, supported by pictures new and old.

We rarely slept. We were constantly on the move, powered by love, adrenaline, and some cool tie-dye shirts that the NBA had made up. The Love It Live Tour turned out to be one of the best things I ever did with my life. And by the end, we had flown over 40,000 miles, written over 55,000 words about it, and taken countless pictures. On the last night David Stern and Adam Silver gave me a signed and bound hard copy of the whole story.

With the end of the Love It Live Tour also came the end of an era. Dick Ebersol and NBC parted ways with the NBA. And in the ever-changing business model of television and media, ESPN and ABC came in and bought the NBA rights package in 2002.

Fortunately for everybody involved, ESPN and ABC had some fantastic people at the top, particularly George Bodenheimer and Mark Shapiro, two young, dynamic, and passionate leaders who understood that this whole deal is about fun and entertainment. And we jumped right on board this new bus and kept ramping everything up.

The next season, ESPN and the NBA turned our Love It Live Tour into one of TV's first reality shows, calling it *Bill Walton's Long Strange Trip*. And it was true to its name.

We covered a remarkable amount of territory on the show, including the first national broadcast of LeBron James's basketball career, when he was still in high school. We spent days trying to explain Western civilization and life to Yao Ming, who had just arrived from China—all through the prism of the Grateful Dead. He was very kind, but I'm not sure he was able to really put his arms around it all. In Florida, I stopped in to see Larry Bird. Our conversations and show were centered around a chess game. Every time Larry fell behind, we would just swing the board around, changing sides. After seven or eight pivots, I was unable to mount a final comeback, and Larry walked off in triumphant glory—one more time.

Because of my speech impediment, limitations, and communication challenges, I am terrible and awful on taped shows. But the NBA TV crew and producers, particularly Dion Cocoros, did everything they could to help me out. Even though we forgot about the time, sadly we did not keep the whole thing going long enough.

The year 2003 brought both wonderful news and sadness to the Walton family. It was the year of Luke's NBA Draft. All of us, Luke and friends included, watched from our house together. He had just gotten back after a rough senior season at Arizona, plagued by injuries, and he said that he had no idea where or when he might go in the meat market. After the first round passed without Luke's name being called, the room was eerily quiet with growing tension. With each guy chosen before him, all of Luke's brothers, and Richard Jefferson, John, and David—who grew up with us and were Luke's lifelong friends, schoolmates, and teammates—would jump up saying, "That guy's no good. Luke, you're so much better than him, and all these other guys, too. What are they thinking?"

Luke said nothing, just sat and watched. The second round started, and after a few teams made their choices, the NBA's Russ Granik stepped to the microphone and announced that "with the thirty-second pick of the 2003 NBA Draft, the Los Angeles Lakers select . . ."

Russ paused for what seemed an eternity. We all held our breath. "LUKE WALTON!"

There was immediate pandemonium. And things were never the same again.

—

Lori and I went to Luke's first NBA game that season at the Staples Center as proud parents. I wore a gold tie-dyed T-shirt. It couldn't have been a better scene. The Lakers already had one of the great teams of all time, and they'd just added Karl Malone and Gary Payton. As the game unfolds, Phil Jackson has Luke in there with Shaq, Kobe, Karl Malone, and Gary Payton. The fans are having the time of their lives. And the Laker fans have already picked up the chants of "Luuuuuuke . . . Luuuuuuuke . . . Luuuuuke . . ."

Luke has the ball in the middle on the break. He looks off Kobe on one wing, then Gary on the other. Then he lays off a no-look drop pass to a stampeding Karl Malone trailing the play, and Karl goes in and throws one down with a thunderous explosion.

The crowd is going wild—dizzy with possibilities about what the future holds for this great team. "Luuuuuuke . . . Luuuuuuuke . . . Luuu-uuuuke."

I am quietly but proudly clapping politely when my laser focus on the moment is disrupted by a gentle tap on my shoulder. I turn to see a smiling James Worthy. He tells me that he's now seen it all. Me, in a gold T-shirt, in the Staples Center, cheering for Karl Malone and the Lakers.

There is nothing like the pride of a dad.

———

We had the privilege about this time of being part of Yao Ming's triumphant return to China, bringing with him all his new friends from the NBA and the Western world of business—all spearheaded and orchestrated by David Stern. *Awesome* does not even come remotely close to describing how great it all was. When everybody else immediately went home from Shanghai and Beijing, Lori and I stayed for three more weeks. Yao Ming connected us with everything we could possibly ever need as we traveled to the enchanted lands of Shangri-la, Lijiang, and eastern Tibet.

We also started making regular bike trips to Death Valley with our chief adventure officer, Chris Kostman. His AdventureCORPS outfit was able to take us places that we could never get to on our own.

It was also this year, though, that my own dad's body was failing him. He and I had a great relationship, and with him just ten minutes away in La Mesa, I spoke with my parents or visited them every day—and had for years now. I would just lie down on the carpet with our dogs, stretch it all out, and go over all the issues of the day with my mom and dad. Visiting my parents was very much like visiting Coach Wooden, except that they didn't try to tell me what to do as much as Coach did. And at the end of every visit or phone call, my dad would always say to me, "Thanks, Bill, you're a wonderful son." And I would return his love and kindness with a line from Jerry Garcia, when I would say goodbye or good night myself: "Dad, I'm a lucky old son."

Every time I would say that "I was a lucky old son," my dad would counter with "Frankie Laine!" one of my dad's favorite singer-songwriter-entertainers, who sang the same song. And I would come back with "Jerry Garcia." It was a ritual that we did to the end. And the end was now here.

Toward that end, my dad was in and out of the hospital down the street all the time. And it was here that I failed my dad one last time. He knew he was coming to his own end. He wanted that to come in his own house, the house that he had built for us. He made me promise him that I would not let the doctors and paramedics take him to the hospital to die.

I was there with him when the ambulance showed up one final time. My dad was on the stretcher, with me at his side and holding his hand. He squeezed my hand and looked up longingly at me, telling me, with tears in his eyes, to not let them take him away from his home anymore. He reminded me that I had promised him.

I was the one who closed the ambulance door for the last time.

As the time came, we all gathered there together—Mom, Bruce, Cathy, Andy, Lori, and me. The doctors and nurses at the hospital could not have been nicer or treated him better—but all the same, he hated having to be there. I went out on my bike to clear my head, and I rode slowly and silently all around our town. To all the places that had meant everything to me and our family. I stopped at every one of them, from the first places that my mom and dad had lived in the earliest days; to the church where my parents got married; to the Prado in Balboa Park, where my parents had their wedding reception; to all the places that my dad worked; to our schools and church; to Muni and through all the parks that my dad used to love to take us to; to the beaches, lakes, libraries, concert halls, music stores, and museums that I always used to go to with my dad; to Rocky's house; and finally to the house where we all lived in La Mesa.

When I got back to the hospital, my dad's body had begun shutting down. We all sat together with him, and he took his last, quiet breaths. When it was over, I hugged and kissed him. I whispered thank you, and told him that I loved him more than words could tell. And then he was gone, forever. I'm not sure that he heard me.

—

As you get older, each year seems more miraculous, more remarkable, more worthy of celebrating. And as Coach Wooden neared his ninety-fifth birthday, a lot of people wanted to celebrate his life and the influence he's had on all our lives. ESPN and HBO both did specials on Coach, though he was very reluctant and did not like any of this.

The ESPN production ruined and ended my friendship with one of Coach's favorite players and people from the early days—Rafer Johnson. The ESPN producer was on me constantly, endlessly, and relentlessly to deliver Coach and our UCLA guys for the show. When I did everything that he asked, and everybody was there, on time and ready, the producer said we had too many guys. He then made me tell Andy Hill and Rafer that they were not needed for the show—this after Andy and Rafer had completely rearranged their busy schedules. I never should have done it. It was one of the lowest points of my life. I should have walked out myself. Rafer has not spoken to me since.

At the premiere of the HBO special, at the Bruin Theatre in Westwood, the same place we used to go to the movies while students almost forty years before, I was walking Coach Wooden to his seat. He had his right hand on my elbow for balance. He started tapping me on the leg with his cane in his other hand.

I leaned down to hear his hushed question. "What do you think, Bill?"

I asked him what he meant. I didn't understand his line of thinking.

He picked it right up. "Do you think that they'll say nice things about me?"

I told him that this was a documentary movie, that they could do whatever they wanted—but that I was pretty sure he'd come out OK.

I had no confidence that it would be the same for me.

The lights went down, and for the next hour, there was not a sound to be heard other than the show. It was a dazzling production. When they brought the lights back up, everybody was so happy, proud, and relieved.

Afterward, Coach Wooden was asked if he would kindly say a few words. Coach reluctantly agreed.

He stood at his theater seat and spoke from there. He started slowly. He was in his late nineties. A couple of minutes in, he found a groove and hit his stride. And as he started rolling, he was looking around and seeing all his players, family, and friends who had come out for this glorious moment of reflection and gratitude, everyone staring up at him in appreciation, love, and respect—he just broke down and started crying.

None of us had ever seen this before. With all that had gone down, over so many years and so many moments, Coach was simply and finally overwhelmed by it all.

—

Consumed and overwhelmed were the overriding emotions for all of us when Ram Rod called with the news that he had cancer. Every great team has real and true elements of purity to them. That was Ram Rod—to the Grateful Dead, and to everybody else he ever came into contact with. It was fast, brutally painful, and tragically sad. As much as we all tried, there was nothing we could do. And then it was over, with nothing left—forever. Robert Hunter's eulogy was as brilliant, powerful, and moving as anything he's ever done.

Over the last nearly three decades, I was most fortunate to be David Halberstam's friend. It is hard to imagine anything in life being better. When he called in April 2007 saying that he would soon be in California on his next project, after having just turned in his self-acknowledged greatest work, I was mad and sad that I would be out of town on business and unable to connect. Imagine my sorrow and burden when David died suddenly and immediately in a car crash on his way to work that day—a day when I couldn't get there to help. It all turned indeed into the coldest winter.

As I continued to fly endlessly across the country, my body was really suffering from this life lived in a world built for preschool children and an unrelenting and overwhelming workload.

One of the many things I love about my life is all the fantastically cool things that I get to do all the time. And how my calendar and schedule is always full. I got to be part of the Martin Luther King Memorial groundbreaking ceremony on the mall in Washington, D.C. I was honored and humbled to be named one of the top ten pundits in all of media; one of the top twenty sports business representatives around the globe; and to be named one of the Top 50 Sportscasters of All Time.

But about this same time, Mark Shapiro left ESPN, and that brought an end to my calling the games. Instead, I was assigned to the endless, mind-numbing, maddeningly repetitive, sterile, context-free studio shows out of ESPN headquarters in Bristol, Connecticut. Bristol is about as far from me and my life as you can possibly get. It takes more than thirteen hours on the clock to fly from San Diego to Bristol. It is easier to get to China. I took an apartment in West Hartford, but with the bitter cold, rain, ice, and snow, coupled with the uneven terrain, I just started to shrivel up and die. The nerve pain from my spine that had plagued me for most of the past thirty-five years steadily worsened.

Even so, I still had an extensive business side of my life with all the NBA and ESPN sponsors and advertisers. I was also working the corporate speaking circuit. I was still flying across the country two to three times per week—in both directions.

In the icy frozen world of the ESPN mothership, unable to move or warm up, working incredibly long and late shifts, there was no way for me to stretch it out or move forward—in anything. The ever-increasing, burning nerve pain forced me to take to bed with me as many ice bags as my freezer could make. I could not put the fire out. And before I could even fall into a state of semi-sleep, it was time to get up and go back for more of the endless studio shows. I couldn't eat, sleep, move, or think.

On Monday, February 25, 2008, I was in Bristol, leaving to fly home to San Diego to see Lori, the dogs, the plants, the sun, and the glowing warmth of the Golden State. When I parked the car at the Hartford airport, there was a beautiful bluebird that had missed its trip south and away from the numbing cold. She huddled under my temporarily warm motor, begging me to take her with me. More than thirteen hours later, when we landed in San Diego, I could no longer move. I went to the ground and couldn't get up. My spine had collapsed and failed.

And, sadly, the song that the morning always brings went deadly quiet.

CHAPTER 15

Knocked Down—
It Gets to Wearin' Thin

THEY JUST WON'T LET ME BE

February 2008

I was on the floor, and I could no longer get up. Burning, radiating nerve pain coursed through my entire body. I couldn't eat, think, sleep, or move. I had nothing.

When I couldn't show up to work that week, my eighteen-year broadcast partner, Jim Gray, asked the rest of our team where I was. When he found out about the collapse of my spine, he called every day. He would urge me to hang on, to not give up, and he constantly reminded me that, yes, I could make it back.

Jim would ultimately find Dr. Steve Garfin at the UC San Diego Health System. He found NuVasive for me, a remarkable group of visionary humanitarians and entrepreneurs who have created over the last dozen years or so an innovative spine technology company based here in San Diego that has pioneered lifesaving, life-changing procedures, techniques, and equipment that have all revolutionized the terrifying world of spine health.

But I knew nothing of any of this, nor what lay ahead for me. I was on the ground, incapable of anything. I went through all the stages: I'm going to die; I want to die; and the worst stage of all—oh my gosh, I'm going to live and this is what I'm stuck with—forever.

I tried everything I could: physical therapy, acupuncture, chiropractic adjustments, alternative medicines, meditation, massage, yoga, core strengthening, medication, injections. And *nothing* worked. I was a hopeless, helpless, and pathetic ball of flesh.

I had to eat my meals lying on the floor, facedown. I couldn't get dressed. I couldn't reach for anything.

When I had to go to the doctor's or anywhere else seeking relief, Lori had to round up the people in our neighborhood to push, pull, drag, and carry my lifeless body into the car. Then they would pack me in ice and give me all the medicine they could find. During the car ride, I would tell Lori that it was over for me. And that she should go. Get out now, while the getting's still good.

She stayed. She worked so hard to make it and me better. She gave up everything in her life, including raising her beloved service dogs, to try to save mine. Before she chose to try to save me, Lori had raised eight of those precious dogs that went on to give life to so many others. She and my longtime physical therapist, Bruce Inniss, ultimately saved my life.

I have held off talking about Bruce Inniss until now. Bruce, like me, grew up in San Diego, down in the South Bay. He has been my physical therapist and master healer for the last thirty-five years. He doesn't like me to say that, since he hopes that his patients get better and move on. But I keep coming back, and I'm very frustrating to him.

Bruce Inniss has been there for me since the early days of the San Diego Clippers. He has seen it all. He has done it all. He brought me back from all my operations, including both my ankle fusions, and kept me going when all seemed lost.

But this time we couldn't break through. No matter what we did, I kept getting worse.

I tried all that I could. I met regularly with the spine surgeon, Dr. Garfin. He was very quiet and subdued, very much like Coach Wooden. He was also from the Midwest, from Minneapolis, and had come to San Diego in the late 1960s to build his life while saving others. He was calmly impressive and guardedly laid everything out for me. But spine surgery was the last thing that I ever wanted. I had never talked to a single person who ever had anything positive to say about spine surgery. And after the news got out and I disappeared from the scene, I was bombarded with calls, letters, people just showing up—all warning of the horrors of spine surgery. None of it was encouraging.

I tried to wait it out.

I tried to work it out.

I tried to think it out.

I tried to wish it out.

I tried to pray it out.

I thought about the Philippine witch doctor.

I tried to ignore it.

No matter what I did or tried, everything just kept getting worse. Here I was, up against the wall—and with no spine to even hold me upright. After an interminable purgatory, I finally made the decision to have Dr. Garfin try to surgically fix my broken body. I had no other choice—other than death.

When I went to the hospital for my preoperative exam and final instructions, I couldn't make the fifty feet from the car to the examining room. I was all crumpled over. I was having trouble breathing. They thought I was having a heart attack. They turned the hospital sirens on indicating an emergency medical crisis was in progress. Through the tears, gasping, and grimacing, I struggled to tell them that it was my spine.

There are few places that I've ever been in my life more depressing than the waiting room of a big-time, high-level spine surgeon. Dr.

Garfin is a great healer. He and his team heal in many ways. They are so good that their crushing workload is overwhelming. His patient list is the worst of the worst. And there is an endless line out the door of people who will do anything to get in to see him—for a chance to get better.

All the broken, crooked, and crippled bodies and lives. The wheelchairs. The external halos. The walkers. The canes. The pain. The sadness. The desperation. And then there are the spouses and family members who get sucked down into this agonizing cauldron and lose everything themselves.

Fortunately for us, Dr. Garfin's amazing assistant, Dr. Liz, took all our frantic phone calls and patiently tried to calm us down, what with our endless questions, anxiety, and uncertainty.

My surgery was on a Sunday morning, early. I was the only patient that day. Dr. Garfin pulled together the best of the best for his team.

I was lying on the hospital gurney. Dr. Garfin called for the drip to begin, the sedation that would put me to sleep. I have had the drip far too many times. I know what it's like. I know what it means. I knew that I didn't have any time left.

Dr. Garfin was standing by my side, trying to reassure me. With my last bit of anything—life, breath, strength, whatever—I weakly reached out and grabbed his forearm as he stood there at the side of my bed.

I looked up at him. The anesthesia was taking me away. I could hear a faint countdown in the background.

And I begged him, through my tears, "Please fix me. Please give me one more chance. Please let me play in the game of life one more time. Please let me climb on the mountain once again. Please let me ride my bike one more day."

And then I was gone.

—

Spine surgeons, when they're inside you, try to do five different things, all based on what is necessary for any particular case. They take junk and broken stuff out. They decompress the spinal cord. They straighten and align the spine. And then they stabilize it with all the equipment, devices, technology, and hardware that NuVasive makes.

I'm told that the surgery took eight and a half hours, and that there were four incisions—one on my side and three on my back.

I don't know when I woke up. When I did start to become cognitive of things, I felt as if I had been run over by an eighteen-wheeler. And after that giant truck first ran over me, the driver went up the street, turned around, and came back and did it again. And then it was as if they called in the steamroller to finish me off.

I hadn't told anybody that I was having spine surgery, other than the people who absolutely had to know. That Sunday, February 8, 2009, Luke and the Lakers were at LeBron and Cleveland, playing the NBA Game of the Week on ABC. Before the game, Luke was chatting with my friend and former broadcast partner Mike Breen, and when Mike asked Luke how I was doing, Luke told him quietly that I was having my spine reconstructed that morning. During the game and broadcast that day, when the conversation turned to Luke and his play for the Lakers, Mike mentioned on the air that I was having spine surgery at that very time.

My mom had no idea of any of this, other than that I was home quite a bit lately. Ever the librarian, my mom has no interest in sports. But ever the proud and loyal grandmother, she never missed one of her grandson's Laker games. When she heard Mike Breen say that I was having spine surgery right then, she got very concerned. Fortunately, brother Bruce was able to calmly reassure her.

There was a lot of pain medication involved. I just slept for a very long time. People tell me that they came to the hospital to visit me. I have no idea. I don't remember.

I was in the hospital for a week. They told me that I would need a wheelchair, a walker, and a cane. Because of my size, weight, and length, Darren, an engineer who for years has made a lot of the special parts for my custom Bill Holland bikes, had to fabricate new and extra-long extensions for the adaptive tools and equipment that all seemed built for preschool children.

The hospital's physical therapy staff was having a real hard time getting me up from the bed. Because of my two fused ankles, my bad knee, my hands and wrists, my size and weight, and my spine, it is very difficult for me to get up and down.

I need my hands and arms to do it, and to turn over in bed as well—and have for a very long time now. But I was severely limited in their use and availability because my hands, wrists, and forearms were jammed and covered with IVs, needles, and bandages as the entrance portals for all the medicine that was constantly being delivered.

Bruce Inniss, with his then thirty-plus years of experience with all my challenges and limitations, had to come across town and get me up and out of bed. And whenever I did get up, I had to wear this huge, cumbersome, and very uncomfortable brace.

Walking is the basic therapy for spine patients. But with all my leg problems, walking is extremely difficult for me. And I certainly don't or can't do it for exercise. Function and need—yes. But I have learned the hard way over time that what is good for my spine is bad for my legs. And the opposite is true as well. What is good for my legs is bad for my spine. Every day is a balancing act.

I finally made it home after the first week. I was not allowed to go in a car for three months because of the vibrations and movement that would work against the fusion attempt in my spine that Dr. Garfin was trying to get to solidify. He said it would take a minimum of six to nine months, if it worked at all.

—

Greg Lee would come over to try to lift my defeated spirit and help the time pass more quickly. The vagaries of life were at play, though, as that brutal metronome just would not change the beat. When you're down and you want time to speed up so that you can move on, it just seems to slow and drag on endlessly—forever. When you're up and you want that ticking of the clock to slow down so that you can enjoy the ride and savor every moment, it just races away, before it's already gone.

Greg had been having life-threatening, life-changing health troubles of his own. For the previous ten years, Greg had been in a nightmarish downward spiral of one health crisis after another. It had started in his spine, went into his heart, went back and forth between the two, and then moved to his blood, skin, nervous system, elbows, hands, fingers, feet, eyes, and any and all other parts of his body. Today, sixteen years after this tragic turn of events for Greg, he is completely disabled, he is in and out of the hospital constantly, he has had endless surgeries, he hasn't been able to work or drive for years, he has to take massive amounts of daily medication just to stay alive, and his entire life has fallen apart. Other than that, he's fine. The fact that Greg is even alive is a miracle in and of itself.

And he was coming over to cheer me up.

Lori was starting to leave me little Post-it notes: on my pillow, on my tray of food, on my clean clothes and linen for the day. They were little words of encouragement.

"Today, you turned over in bed by yourself."

"Today, you were able to sit up on the edge of the bed."

"Today, you were able to feed yourself—a little bit."

"Today you went from your wheelchair to your walker."

And those were the good things, and signs of progress, that were happening in my life.

The first big step was the hardest one—the first time I was able to walk, with my walker, from the bed to the other bed. And then eventually from that other bed to another bed. And then to the couch, and chair, and patio. And then to the tennis court. Greg was always there. Over an extremely long and frustrating period of time, we finally made it out the front door. Then eventually around the quiet cul-de-sac block that is our neighborhood.

One of the new neighbors, who had no idea about Greg's and my earlier lives together, commented rather strongly to Lori one day how these two really old and broken-down guys were slowly walking—shuffling, really—around the small block where our home is, and how it looked quite painful even to watch. When that same observer was told that both Greg and I are Hall of Fame, former champion and professional athletes, she was shocked and flabbergasted, and asked what had happened.

Lori had put a hospital bed in our living room. She had to do everything for me, including put my compression socks on. I've had to wear them for a very long time now, what with my fused ankles and all the circulatory problems that I have in my lower legs. It was very hard just to get them on and over the bulbous stumps. But she did it all and never complained—about anything. As bad as she had it, though, nobody had it worse than the nurse who had to try to get my bowels working again.

And that was the good news.

More Post-it notes:

"Today, you could go outside."

"Today, you could sit with your face in the sun for a few moments."

"Today, you could bury your face in the flowers and smell the garden."

"Today, you went from your walker to your cane."

"Today, you could take your brace off for a few minutes."

"Today, you could take one less pain pill."

———

One day we were back at Dr. Garfin's office for a checkup. Lori was in the corner of the examining room while Dr. Garfin and Dr. Liz were huddled over and attending to me. They both kept preaching patience and moderation—the two worst qualities of my character. The three of them were carrying on in a casual, social conversation as I was just in a daze, wishing that it would all be over. Lori was trying to stay upbeat in what was an incredibly depressing existence, and she noted, just in a conversational tone, that although she had read about how stressful this whole process was on the spouse and caregiver, she was holding up well and hadn't broken down yet under the pressures and burden. Dr. Garfin and Dr. Liz, who seemingly had their total focus and concentration on my pressing needs and their backs to Lori, immediately both stood up, turned, and chirped in unison, "Oh don't worry, that breakdown will come."

And then they quickly returned to their duties over my broken body.

—

Thirty days after my operation, Lori had her birthday party. She had a small circle of her girlfriends over to the house. She rarely left my side during these trying times, and when she did, she always arranged for somebody who knew what they were doing to be right there in her place.

I was lying in my hospital bed in the living room. The girls were having their party across the way, laughing and cackling on and on. I was struggling; the life-draining and spirit-zapping drugs and pain medication were still coursing through my veins.

The phone rang. I answered it. It was my boss, with the news that ESPN had fired me.

I still had a year and a half to go on my contract. Before my spine failed, I had never missed a day of work in eighteen years. I had volunteered for every assignment possible. I took every red-eye flight. I showed up first and stayed until last. I missed my children's and family's lives—for a job. A job that I thought was important. And then when I got hurt doing that job, I got fired. Not even a thank-you, or an "I'm sorry." Just fired, hung out, and hung up on.

Lori's birthday party rolled on unabated. I didn't—couldn't, really—tell her the news for two days. I didn't want to ruin what little fun she was having, for the first time in who can even remember how long.

With me losing my job and income, I also lost my health insurance. My dignity and self-respect were next to go.

My friends and family, including Jim Gray, Mickey Hart, Bill Kreutzmann, and Bob Weir, would call every day. They would urge me to not give up; tell me to hang on; that I could make it. But I no longer believed. I had given up. It was just too hard, hurt too much, and took too long.

Lori kept up with the Post-it notes:

"Today, you could pet the dog."

"Today, you could put your own T-shirt on."

"Today, you could go to the bathroom by yourself, and the nurse didn't have to go with you."

—

Seventy-three days after my surgery, Dr. Garfin said I could stop taking the medicine—all of it. He told me that I could try to put my own compression stockings on. He wanted to watch me do it the first time, to make sure that the stress on my spine was not too severe. My hands, fingers, heck, my entire body was trembling and shaking in pain. It must have taken nearly thirty minutes that first time to get my own compression stockings on. How could I tell? It took everything that I had.

When I got home, by the time I got inside, Lori had already posted a new note.

"Today, you were able to put your own shoes and socks on."

I don't know who was happier—me or her.

But still, it was just too hard. And the whole thing took forever. What was the point, all this pain for these tiny, minuscule gains?

Dr. Garfin was worried about me, said he could see the sadness and pain in my eyes and face. He sent me to one of his doctor friends. I told him through the tears that I just wanted it all to stop, and that all I wanted was my life back.

Without a job, without health or insurance, with no signs that I was ever going to get better, without hope and without the dream that tomorrow had a chance of getting any better, I didn't think that I was going to make it. I didn't want to leave Lori with a big mess. We moved out of the big house and put the place of our dreams up for sale. We settled, temporarily, into the little guest caretaker's house on the west end of our property.

—

At the four-month mark, now into May, Dr. Garfin said that I could go into the pool, although very slowly and carefully. And it had to be at a pool with better disability access than what we had at home, where I had normally just dove in after a long, hard, hot day of whatever. I didn't want to go. People like me in a state of poor everything—sadness, loss, depression, and denial—always have an excuse and explanation as to why they can't do something. My initial one was that I still could not drive and therefore could not get there.

My brother Bruce came and dragged me to the Mission Valley Y, ten minutes from our house. They have a very large indoor pool, enclosed in a glass greenhouse-like structure, bigger than a basketball court, and heated to 90 degrees. The place was full of other Dr. Garfin spine patients.

When I first got there, I was still all bent over and using my cane. I was making my way slowly and gingerly to the steps to lower myself into the warm, healing water.

This elderly but very fit dude came bounding by me, with all the confidence, spring, and bounce of a champion—which I found out later he was. He turned and looked at me as he glided effortlessly by. He looked right at me. And he stopped.

"Don't do it!" he said. "Don't do it. I can see it in your face. Don't do it."

He went on to tell me that his name was Mike, and that he was a world champion swimmer. And that he had a friend who years ago was going to kill himself because of his back problems and pain. But Mike had convinced this friend to get into the water, and that the water would save him. This friend had spent years lying on the floor, and within reach he had a bottle of pills, a bottle of whiskey, and a gun. He never knew which one he was going to reach for, because nothing ever worked for him.

Mike said his friend did indeed slither down into the water and was able to eventually work it all out, and went on to climb back up and out, to live a productive life for another twenty-five years.

Mike finished his story, and then was on his way to the pool himself with the parting admonition, "Don't do it. I can see it in your face. Don't do it."

When I first got into the warm water, I struggled to find my balance, equilibrium, or anything else. It took me about three days of going to the water to figure out what Dr. Garfin and Mike meant by the value of going into the warm water. They have not been able to keep me out of the water ever since. The Mission Valley Y opens at 4:30 a.m. I was there waiting for them to open the doors. I don't swim, I just move. I don't like to put my head under the water. I just work out all the kinks, all the stiffness, all the limitations that I have in the air, all the things that are not factors in the warm water.

One day I spent eight and a half straight hours in that pool. I got to know all the lifeguards on a first-name basis. The facilities are fantastic and state-of-the-art, the location—perfect. But it's the electric amalgamation of people and patrons that makes the place rock from the daily opening of the front door. Every day, countless scientists, visionaries, engineers, artists, technology kingpins, dancers, doctors, inventors, police officers, hippies, entrepreneurs, lawyers, wealth managers, dreamers, teachers, nurses, social workers, librarians, firefighters, beekeepers, space explorers, judges, musicians, pilots, paramedics, beatniks, military personnel, truck drivers, technicians, yoga masters, investors, bohemians, day laborers, stage actors, students, writers, movie stars, financial planners, mechanics, professional athletes, and politicians all pour through the doors with the singular purpose of making themselves better so that the team can ultimately be better. Today the warm water and the pool are the foundation of my spine's health. The first thing I do every morning when my feet hit the floor is head to the Mission Valley Y and its wonderful 90-degree pool.

This journey was long and arduous. With all my other injuries combined, I had never been through anything like this. It was so hard, and it still hurt so much.

Even though I was now off the medication, I could still taste it, as I would do for another two full years—that blue metallic, bitter taste of poison, with every breath, smell, gulp, and swallow.

—

I also had permission now from Dr. Garfin to slowly return to the weight room. Dr. Garfin's repetition of words like *slowly, patience, easy,* and *moderation* reminded me so much of the early days at UCLA with Coach Wooden. I had no choice this time around. My body really didn't work anymore, and I was starting over from nothing, from below the bottom.

In the beginning on my long, hard climb back up, the weight room was sometimes little more than a destination where I would stop to rest from the exertion of getting there. I would often not have enough left to do anything other than lie down on the massage table and wait and hope for all the bad stuff—like fatigue and pain—to go away. The weight room is in our garage, just a few short strides—for an able-bodied person—from the house. But when you can't move, those few short strides can be as formidable as the Grand Canyon or the escarpment of the eastern Sierra.

Bob Dylan and Neil Young had both recently come out with new releases. And it was like they were written just for me, as I was trying so desperately to even begin the long, hard climb back into the game of life. *Together Through Life* and *Fork in the Road*—I played these two discs constantly in the weight room—just looped them over and over and over, every day, every moment I was in there.

The new music kept me going. And when Dylan and his band came to town for a summertime show on their Never Ending World Tour, I was, amazingly, able to go. It was my first time out. I got to bathe and bask in the music, the warmth, the glow, and the love—for the first time in who knows how long.

Not long after, Bob Weir and his RatDog band came to Humphreys. After the show, Bob came out and sat with me, as it was all I could do just to get to the show.

—

Back home, I still hurt constantly, and I still had nothing really going in any part of my life. Everything was just stuck. There was no light, but I still kept going to the pool and to the weight room. It was more rote than anything of substance or direction.

In early September, now seven months after my surgery, I was in the weight room on autopilot. On the stereo, Jerry was singing Bob Dylan's "Visions of Johanna," the most beautiful song—about the hope and dream of a better tomorrow. And it was in that moment that things turned for me.

I will never forget. Dylan's words were washing over me in Jerry's voice and guitar. And I knew at that instant that I was going to make it. The daily tears of sadness, loss, and desperation now turned to joy, happiness, and hope. I was going to make it. I could feel it now.

I turned off the stereo, shut down the weight room, went back across the yard, and told Lori, this time through tears of happiness and joy—

"I'm going to make it. I can feel it deep inside. It just turned. For the first time in forever, I know. I know that I'm going to make it and that tomorrow is going to be better."

I was so happy, and so relieved. I was going to make it, and I knew it.

A couple of days later, I decided to go out on my bike, for the first time in so long I couldn't even remember. As always, for so many years, whenever I left the house, Lori would walk me out with the same parting words: "I love you. Please be safe. Please be careful."

I was still all bent over. I could barely turn the cranks. But I was riding my bike. And I could feel the wind. I could feel the sun. And I could feel the thin film of sweat on my skin—sweat from actual activity. I was riding my bike. Easily, gently, and just rolling around our wonderful and perfectly flat neighborhood, where all the streets are either dead ends or cul-de-sacs.

I had been out for only a few precious minutes. I didn't want to overdo anything. So I turned and headed for home. As I came around the last bend, I was starting to slow down in front of our house. There on the far street corner were all the neighborhood teenagers—enjoying just another perfect San Diego summer day.

When they saw me, they were stunned. "Bill! You're on your bike! We haven't seen you in forever, Bill! How's your back? It must be feeling better, Bill! This is great, Bill! We are so happy for you! You're riding your bike!"

I was nodding and signaling acknowledgment, gratitude, and appreciation back to them. I was slowing down, pulling up in front of our house, getting ready to dismount.

The fourteen-year-old boy who lived next door had a couple of beautifully fine California beach girls with him, all decked out in their bikinis, beads, and flowers. He apparently didn't like the fact that everybody's attention had momentarily shifted from him to me.

So this young neighbor boy jumps up, grabs his Tony Hawk skateboard, and comes out into the street to put on a show and bring the focus back his way.

Except he lost control on takeoff. And he plowed right into me. Knocking me off my bike and to the ground. Leaving me broken and helpless on the pavement, lying on the asphalt for a seeming eternity in my blood and tears.

All the children ran. Just gone. Evaporated. Like dust in the wind.

I looked back. My bike was broken.

I reached down. My pelvis was broken.

I reached back. My sacrum was broken.

I was all alone. And I couldn't get up off the street.

CHAPTER 16

Once in a While You Get Shown the Light, in the Strangest of Places If You Look at It Right

All the Things I've Tried to Do But Only Did Half Way
Please God, Don't Let Me Die, There's So Much Left to Do.

With everything broken—again—I was back on the ground—one more time—and starting over again.

But my spinal fusion and all of NuVasive's hardware had held together through my crash. Initially that didn't seem to make any difference. I couldn't move due to the pain. Every breath I took. Every time I tried to turn over in bed. Every time I tried to get up and down. Every effort to get dressed. Every step I tried to take. Every movement that I tried to make. There it was. That burning, radiating, debilitating, excruciating, unrelenting pain was back.

I could not differentiate the pain from the new bone fractures in my pelvis and sacrum from the nerve pain that Dr. Garfin had seemingly fixed in my spine surgery, now more than seven months gone by. I was back to using my walker. Lori started up with the Post-it notes—again, one more time.

—

I was back at the doctor's office, the last place any spine patient ever wants to go. I told Dr. Garfin that I couldn't do it all again. I just didn't have it in me.

He looked at me with those soft eyes, those eyes of someone who has seen so much, and has been here before. He asked me if I was familiar with Coach Wooden's Pyramid of Success. I was in no mood to think back to those days. Back when I could run and play the game I loved. I was so mad, I didn't even respond.

He kept going—asking me if I remembered the foundation that Wooden had laid out for us all those years ago. I sat there with silent tears.

He kept going. He laid out the fifteen human attributes and personal characteristics that make up the Pyramid. I silently nodded.

He laid out Coach's Seven-Point Creed. I had my head down. I couldn't go on. But he did.

He laid out the Two Sets of Threes and reviewed Coach Wooden's maxims—none of which were making any sense at all to me now.

He started into the tools that Wooden gave us to overcome the adversity that he knew would one day be needed—again, one more time.

I finally looked up, and sadly, through the tears, said, "Please, what does any and all of this have to do with me? I just want all this pain to stop. I just want my life back. Why is this still happening?"

Dr. Garfin looked right through me, with all my failures and limitations and the broken body, spirit, and life that I had and seemingly would have forever.

He calmly and softly said, "Bill, I have two words for you here."

I didn't want to hear it. Nothing made any sense anymore.

He continued. "Bill, Coach Wooden spent fourteen years working on those fifteen building blocks in his Pyramid. He moved things around. He massaged, pondered, and reconsidered it day after day after day, always trying to get it just right. He has so much in there: industriousness, enthusiasm, friendship, loyalty, cooperation, intentness, initiative, alertness, self-control, commitment to the team, skill development, physical fitness, poise, confidence, and competitive greatness."

I told Dr. Garfin that I knew all this stuff. That I had lived it. That I had memorized it. But still I was hurting—again. And everything was broken. And nothing was working. And all he or anybody else had for me was words.

Dr. Garfin had been there himself before. With the calm serenity of someone who has seen so much, who has done so much, he slowly and methodically soldiered on.

"Bill, I've got two words for you. Years after Coach Wooden finished the Pyramid, he went back and added two external words at the top. And that is the medicine that I have for you today. Just two words, Bill—*Faith* and *Patience*. Do you believe? And are you willing to put in the lifetime that this is going to take?"

And then he was silently off to his next patient—who had his own broken body, his own broken spirit and dream, his own broken life.

—

The ticking of the relentless metronome and the turning pages of the calendar have now brought me here to today—a today when I am all better. Today, I have no pain. Today I take no medication. I had no idea what life was like without back pain. What has happened to me is a miracle.

And how do you ever even begin to thank the people who have saved your life, who have given you your life back?

All because of people like Dr. Garfin, Dr. Daly, Dr. Wagner, Bruce Inniss, Coach Wooden, and the countless others who spend their lives trying to help others live theirs better. Today, I have the great fortune of good health. That is a privilege. With privilege comes responsibility and obligation.

During my long, hard climb back, I reconnected with Rolf Benirschke, a lifelong friend and former NFL kicker for our Chargers who, after his own near-death battle with ulcerative colitis, has dedicated the last thirty years of his life to his Great Comebacks project, supporting patients with Crohn's disease, ulcerative colitis, and colorectal and bladder cancer. With Rolf's and NuVasive's help, we have started our own program, the Better Way Back, to help spinal patients and the entire world of spine health understand the possibilities for a new life ahead and to begin the eventual climb back up and into this great game of life one more time—just as I've been able to do.

Today, I spend hours, every day, on the phone, face-to-face, and online, working for and with NuVasive's Better Way Back program trying to help people who are going to kill themselves because their spine and bodies simply hurt too much. Every day, I talk people into putting the gun down and taking a step back from the edge of the cliff. I am an ambassador and advocate working constantly with doctors, hospitals, insurance companies, government regulators, policy makers, medical-device manufacturers, the FDA, the IRS, and any and all players in this huge world of people who are trying to make a difference, to save lives, to give life to people who think there is nothing left to live for, and who ultimately think that they'd be better off dead.

I've also now had the chance to become a volunteer for the Challenged Athletes Foundation (CAF). We buy wheelchairs, prosthetics, and adaptive sports equipment for people who don't have arms and legs so that they can participate in the game of life through sports. We provide friendship, mentoring, programs, and leadership to people who are struggling. Some of the groups of people that we help are veterans coming back from our wars in Iraq and Afghanistan, blown up and thinking that their lives are over; or young children who have been born with a serious birth defect or health crisis—children who never had the chance that so many of us too often take for granted; or people who have been in a terrible accident and lost their health and parts of their bodies, and are now faced with a seemingly impossible climb on an insurmountable mountain.

I know that road all too well. Among my myriad of problems, I am always sick—sick of something or somebody. But I now know that I can always go to a CAF event and I'll be better when I leave. Participation in sports, being part of a team, and music are my medicine. The CAF allows me to immerse myself in all of those at the same time, and to be there with all my teammates who are also trying to rebound and rebuild. We are all challenged athletes. Some of you just don't know it yet.

At the CAF, we ride our bikes, with a purpose. We are driven to changing lives, one turn of the crank at a time. My bike is the most important thing that I have. It is my gym, my wheelchair, and my church all in one. My bike represents everything that I love and believe in. My bike is a combination of science, technology, engineering, the team, discipline, organization, repetition, goals, practice, preparation, and so much more. My bike gives me freedom and independence. My bike is my ultimate tool and friend—it allows me to go places that I cannot get to on my own. Now, through the CAF, every turn of that wheel represents a difference in somebody else's life, a difference that some folks can no longer make for themselves.

Early on, I was off with the CAF for one of their signature events, the Million Dollar Challenge (MDC), which is a dream to annually raise a million dollars or more by riding our bikes down the coast of California from San Francisco to San Diego over the course of a week. We stop for the night along the way in Santa Cruz, Big Sur, Pismo Beach, Santa Barbara, Santa Monica, and Dana Point, before rolling into San Diego.

One hundred riders, and an incredible support team, and we're off.

This was going to be a really big challenge for me, still only eighteen months after my spine surgery, which, in the world of spine health, is the blink of an eye.

The night before we started, at the orientation in the hotel in San Francisco, the CAF asked me to say a few words.

I spoke about my health challenges, particularly with my spine reconstruction. I tied in the anticipation of a big ride, challenge, and event, with being part of a special team, and everything I had learned about the climb from Coach Wooden and the Grateful Dead. I weaved in the story of me stealing Coach Wooden's Lucky Penny and how I thought I was finally breaking free from that curse. I sang selected lyrical phrases of "The Wheel" throughout. You'll have to ask the audience if any of it made any sense.

Then we got to ride, and every time we stopped during the course of our trip, other people on our journey would quietly come up to me and express their sadness and sorrow for my predicament—with the Curse and all. And then they would reach into their pockets and pull out a small coin, present it to me, and say that hopefully this replacement coin might do the trick in helping to break the Curse.

As we rolled down the coast, I accumulated quite the collection of new lucky coins, including one that I am never without to this very day. It came from Chris Self, who had been severely injured, losing his leg fighting for us in Iraq. He gave me one of his Special Forces coins after I nearly got him killed again, this time when I got us lost and everything got away from us. Chris and his tandem teammate, Gil, who had been blown up in Afghanistan, ill-advisedly followed me off-course for some extra and most beautiful mileage on the ocean side of the Palos Verdes Peninsula. When I missed a turn, we ended up in the urban jungle and traffic nightmare of San Pedro and Wilmington. As we were navigating the gridlock, Chris and Gil got out in front of me, where they were hit and run over on their special bike by a negligently out-of-control car driver who was making a forced left turn in way too much of a hurry— going who knows where.

The earlier riding, farther north, was fantastic, but the weather was awful. It was bitter cold, wet and raining, and windy. And on the second day, the weather got even worse. It was now freezing, the wind was gale force, and the rain was coming down sideways. I'd decided that we needed some songs to get us through, picking out Jerry Garcia's "Mission in the Rain" and Bob Dylan's "Chimes of Freedom."

So we're with a small group, rolling through the farmlands of Monterey County heading toward the incredible splendor of Carmel, Pebble Beach, and the 17 Mile Drive—on our way to Big Sur. When and where everything should have been perfect, it was simply miserable, as the weather could not be worse if we were in Antarctica—or Portland, Oregon, or Bristol, Connecticut.

With the terrible conditions, people are crashing, going down all over the place. Flat tires are slowing everybody down, and it is all just awful. I'm trying to teach our group the lyrics to "Mission in the Rain"—"some folks would be so happy to have just one dream come true." When they were thoroughly confused and dispirited from the disastrous conditions, I shifted to "Chimes of Freedom"—"and for every uptight, hung-up person in this whole wide universe, we gaze upon the chimes of freedom flashing." I was trying to pick things up, but nothing was working.

And it was all getting worse—if that was even possible. We were blue from the cold. We were soaking wet. We were battered, bruised, cut, and covered with mud, muck, fertilizer, manure, and worse. I couldn't feel my hands or feet.

I kept asking myself, "What are we doing? Why are we out here in this miserable mess?"

I looked to my right. There was my friend Tommy, with the biggest grin on his face, having the time of his life. I looked to my left. There was Brad. He was even happier. Tommy looks at me and yells out, "Come on, Bill . . . We're riding our bikes . . . Here we go! The coast of California . . . 'Mission in the Rain' . . . One dream, Bill. One dream, one time!"

Brad took it up. "Let's go, Bill. Ring the chimes of freedom. We're right there, far between sundown's finish and midnight's broken toll. Come on!"

I looked back to Tommy. He has one arm.

I looked back to Brad. He has one leg.

I realize—as the rain's flying sideways into my face—that I'm the luckiest guy in the whole world, and there's no place I'd rather be.

—

I have learned over time, and the hard way, that health is everything—the most basic element in our goal to be happy. It's rivaled only by love.

It is hard to be happy in life without being happy in love. I'm lucky—I now have both, when forever I thought that I would have neither.

My wife, Lori, bless her, embodies all the goodness in the world that I am constantly searching for. Lori has done so much to help me and others. Through fifteen years of training service dogs, she has given much of her life so that others can have a better one. Every day I'm amazed to have her in my life, right here, within arm's reach.

Our boys, too, have grown all the way up and embarked on amazing lives, starting families of their own. I miss them more than words can tell, but they're out there chasing their own dreams now and building their lives. One of the things that I am most proud of as a dad is that the boys seem to genuinely like each other, and appear to be happy for each other's successes, as different and varied as all their lives are.

Christopher, the youngest, got married first, on July 12, 2008. He made a point of telling us that while he was always the youngest and the last, he was going to be first here. He married Gina, from Orange County, his college sweetheart and captain of the soccer team at San Diego State. Chris and Gina got married at the big, huge Immaculata Church at the University of San Diego—ten minutes from our house. High on a hill, the church offers some of the best views of all of San Diego—from downtown, across the sweeping vistas of the bays and ocean, to Point Loma, and all the way north to La Jolla. It was beautiful and very formal. And they even let me play in the band at the reception. Today Chris and Gina have three children, Olivia, Chase, and Parker. They live near Gina's family in Orange County.

Adam was next to get married—to Tracy, on July 12, 2010. Tracy's a native angel from San Diego. Adam said that since he and Christopher had been born on the same day, albeit six years apart, it was Adam's responsibility that he and Tracy get married on the same day as Chris and Gina did, this time two years after Chris. Adam and Tracy got married in Hawaii, at Olowalu—a sacred point jutting out into the ocean on the leeward side of west Maui, in the shadow of the West Maui Mountains. It was fantastic—one of the most perfect places I've ever been. We had the best time, even though I'd initially put up a fuss about having to fly out so far so soon after my spine surgery. We stayed at Don Nelson's incredible beachfront compound in Paia. The day after the wedding I was up with the sun, and then after wading into the ocean I climbed on my bike and rode the thirty-six miles up to the top of the Haleakala Crater. The numerous climate zones that I passed through were minimal compared to the emotional ones. It was long and hard, but I made it. And now, every time I'm in Hawaii, I make a pilgrimage to the wedding site, calling out to Adam and Tracy and reporting back that all is well—and how proud, lucky, and happy I am for them. I also try to get back on that really big mountain, on my bike, every time. Adam and Tracy now live thirty minutes north of us, in Encinitas, with a daughter, Avery, and her new little brother, Patrick.

Then it was Nathan. He married Ali, from Grafton, Wisconsin, about thirty miles north of Milwaukee. We flew in, as did a lot of other people from around the world. Nate has been on the move since leaving home for Princeton—and people showed up from all of his stops along the way: New Jersey; France, where he played professional basketball; Africa, where he worked for the United Nations; Wall Street; Boston, and the Celtics, where he worked for a while; Stanford, where he graduated from Phil Knight's business school; and Los Angeles, where he works these days in the world of high finance and lives just a few turns of the cranks from the beach in Santa Monica.

Ali's parents and family spared no expense, and left nothing to chance, or any detail unattended. Their family's farm is beautiful—nice big lake; trees, open space, lots of cornfields; adorable old farmhouse, barns, and outbuildings. After a punishing rain the day before, on the wedding day, July 28, 2012, we woke to perfect weather. Sun, blue sky, no wind, no humidity—which then transitioned to a beautiful full moon that night, as the wedding band rocked. I don't know if they ever did stop. I had to go to bed. It was amazing, though I think that I was the oldest person there—something that happens more and more these days.

And then there was Luke, the last one. Luke had just had a spectacular few years, winning two championships with the Lakers in four trips to the Finals. He married Bre, his college sweetheart from Tucson. They wanted to have a destination wedding, too—in Aspen, Colorado, which is not an easy place for me to get to, especially since I had just had my knee replaced, a full forty-six years after I first hurt it in 1967. I made the same argument against destination weddings as I had earlier, but I lost this one, too. Brother Bruce's daughter, Harmony, a queen in the wedding world and beyond, certainly helped to change my way of thinking by pointing out that there was going to be a big pro bike race starting in Aspen two days after the wedding. The wedding was on August 17, 2013, on the top of Aspen Mountain. We were high in the Rockies, and on top of the world in many respects. People had come from all over—from San Diego; from Tucson; from Los Angeles; from the Lakers, Cleveland, and the NBA; and beyond. It lasted for days, and was an endless lovefest of fun. Today Luke and Bre and their new baby boy, Lawson, live in Northern California, where Luke is starting a new life as a basketball coach with the Golden State Warriors.

After the wedding, I was able to join the bike race and ride along in Chris Carmichael's pay-to-play program with the professionals, as close as you can be during the big races. At the end of the ride, my body, and my new knee, felt better than I could ever remember, dating back to elementary school, with that wonderful thick rubber pad that Drs. Joe Jankiewicz and Peter Hanson left in between my new titanium endcaps after they cut my leg open, sawed off and removed my old, mangled knee, and drilled and glued in a brand-new one. With that new knee and rubber pad, life was like living on a trampoline.

A lot of other things were bouncing back in other ways as well. Almost two years after my spine surgery, I slowly and a bit reluctantly went back into broadcasting. First with the Sacramento Kings, thanks to Gavin, Joe, and the rest of the Maloof family; and Jim Gray, too. Then it was gradually with the new Pac-12 Network and their brilliant and visionary leader, Larry Scott. I also ultimately expanded this to a new go-round with ESPN, now under different leadership. New ESPN president John Skipper has most certainly delivered on all that he said, after I initially turned him down based on my lingering distaste from getting fired a few years earlier. When I initially said no thanks, that I had moved on, John came to our house immediately and changed my mind.

So now as I'm getting back up myself, we were able to spend lots of time with Coach Wooden, just as he was settling down.

Shortly after Coach Wooden's ninety-ninth birthday, some group or organization gave him just what he needed—another award. They named him the Greatest Coach Ever. Not the Greatest College Coach. Not the Greatest Basketball Coach. They named him the Greatest Coach Ever. No. 2 was Vince Lombardi. No. 3 was Bear Bryant. No. 4 was Phil Jackson. No. 5 was Don Shula. No. 6 was Red Auerbach.

Coach Wooden wanted no part of any of this. It was not his thing. He was a teacher, a worker, and a giver. He was not into accolades, awards, or honors. He always questioned the methodology for determining anything so subjective. What are the standards? What are the measurements, benchmarks, and metrics? Under relentless pressure, he finally agreed to show up—on his terms, at one of his favorite local restaurants.

He didn't want a big deal made of everything. And he only wanted his family, friends, and players to be there. So after a dinner with those closest to him, they presented him with the award. And they rolled him up onto the stage, now in his wheelchair, and handed him the microphone. When you're ninety-nine, you've already used your best material, particularly when you're already preaching to the choir—family, friends, and team.

Coach started off by telling everybody there was no way that he deserved this honor. How could you tell who was the best? Then Coach turned the conversation around and said that he wanted to apologize, in that he had made a mistake—with his Pyramid of Success. Everybody was aghast. Coach had worked endlessly on that Pyramid for fourteen years. And now all these years later, and nearing the end, he was going to admit that he was wrong? We were stunned.

He told us that he had made a mistake by leaving the word *love* out of the Pyramid of Success. And that *love* is the single most powerful and important word in our language and culture. And until we allow the power of love to supersede the love of power, none of us has any chance of success at all.

There was not a sound in the room. Still. Quiet. Peace at last.

And then Coach Wooden turned the conversation one final time. He stared up slowly. He was looking around to everyone there—whom he knew everything about. It was his guest list, his party. He closed the whole evening down while making eye contact with everybody: "I also want to say that I'm sorry. I'm sorry that I have not been able to do more to help you in your lives . . . I'm sorry that I've not been able to do more to help you."

It was his last public comment.

—

As I was recovering from my spine surgery, as soon as I was able, Lori, Greg Lee, and I would drive up to see Coach Wooden for breakfast as often as we could. We would call a bunch of the other guys and all meet at VIPs, and Coach would just pick up with exactly whatever the conversation had been from the last time we were together. Wooden was magnificent at that, with a remarkable knowledge of history and trivia. By now, people had iPhones and the first iPads, and we would challenge him on some of his proclamations. He was invariably right. We would try to see him two or three times a week. Every week. Andy Hill, Jamaal Wilkes, Bob Webb, Marques Johnson, Kenny Washington, Mike Warren, Keith Erickson, Lynn Shackelford, Lucius Allen, and Greg Lee were all regular visitors.

One day in February 2010, we noticed a difference. For the first time in our lives, Coach wasn't totally on top of things. He couldn't get things together. And we knew that from here on, things would never be the same again. That day, back at the Mansion on Margate, I got Larry Bird on the phone for the Coach. I sat on the other side of the small room in Coach's house. He was trying so hard, but it just wasn't there for him. Larry carried the conversation. Coach had small tears running down his cheeks. They talked about Indiana, sports, life, and what a nuisance I was. And then they said goodbye to each other.

Coach and I said our own goodbyes that day, too. We both knew. Coach Wooden was tough as can be, all the way to the end. Even though there had been countless times over the last twenty-five years that Coach seemed to be at the end of the line, he always made it back. It was astounding. We took to calling him the Energizer Bunny. But this time was different. There were too many things that he could no longer do—things that he needed to be able to do to keep going.

Lori and I were on tour with the Grateful Dead up at Shoreline in the Bay Area when the call came. It was Andy Hill. He said it was time. And that Coach didn't have much, if anything, left. We grabbed our stuff and raced to L.A. We met Andy at the UCLA Medical Center. As we were getting out of the car, I still had my Grateful Dead laminate around my neck. I told Lori that I was going to bring it in for Coach, that he was going to need some help on his next journey. Lori shook me off; she said that Coach would be fine. I left it in the car.

When we got up and into his room, he already looked dead. He was just lying there on his back with his arms folded across his chest. He had no color. He wasn't moving at all. There were no signs of life in what was left of his skinny little skeleton. His chest was not going up and down with any of what could be called breath.

I walked silently over to his bedside. I bent down and kissed him. I whispered in his ear. "Thanks, Coach. I love you. And I'm really sorry for ruining your life."

He shuddered, his first perceptible sign of life since we walked in. He mumbled, "Who's that? Who's there?"

I leaned down one more time. I whispered one more time. "Coach, it's Bill Walton."

Coach sat up in bed, as much as he could. And he cried out, "I thought that I was through with you!"

And then he fell back onto his pillow—exhausted, spent, and now truly and finally through with me. I'm not sure that Coach ever realized that I had actually become the person he was trying to help me be.

—

Because of everything that was going on and the huge number of people involved, it took more than three weeks to have the memorial service for Coach Wooden. It was at Pauley Pavilion, and open to the public.

We went and sat toward the back with friends and teammates in what was a very, very sad and personal day—on a public stage. Coach was the glue that kept the disparate parts bonded.

Al Michaels, as master of ceremonies, was professional, polished, powerful, and impactful. There were some that day who weirdly spent their time onstage promoting themselves, trying to impress the crowd with how close they were to Coach and what they meant to him. But Dick Enberg and Vin Scully kept it very real with video tributes that were beautifully poetic, reflective, and extremely personal. Keith Erickson, Kareem, and Jamaal Wilkes spoke on behalf of the players and were all masterful, touching, insightful, and enlightening. I stayed with my long-held policy of never speaking at funerals. It's just too personal, and I choose to speak in life rather than death. Very little of any of Coach's service revolved around basketball—just like so much of our own lives with him. How hard it is to try to put into a few simple words on a grand stage what is so meaningful, so broad, so vast, and so all-encompassing.

When the memorial was over, a lot of the players stood in the back on the floor of Pauley, where we had spent so many of our formative years with our master teacher, coach, and, later, friend. It was very hard to keep it together, since we all knew, without speaking, that after so many roads, we would not be coming down this one ever again. This was the end. Our Coach had passed, and now we really were on our own, left alone to carry on.

—

Four months later, Maurice Lucas died—on Halloween, Adam's and Chris's birthday. We got the call from our Little Luke—from the Lakers' locker room. Maurice had been fighting his cancer for as long as I had been up against things with my spine. We had been visiting Maurice and talking on the phone as often as we could, trying to cheer each other up. We knew Big Luke was up against it, but still it came as a crushing shock. He had finally met an opponent he could not beat, or punch in the face. Five days later, on my birthday, Lori and I were in Portland to help bury the greatest Trail Blazer ever, the one who had always been able to step in during any time of trouble and calmly say, "I'll take care of this."

As hard as it is to climb back from a collapse—of your spine, your options, your hope—it is a most harrowing experience to see your friends and loved ones battle for life and not be able to help. Maurice was my greatest teammate, a true teammate, the kind who makes you better—as a player, a person, and in life. I'll always wish I could have done more for him—as he had always done for me.

—

Over the years, I've been a student of many unparalleled coaches and teachers, and a member of many remarkable teams and organizations. In our world of basketball, the end of the climb at the top of the mountain is the Basketball Hall of Fame. I have had the honor of presenting Larry Bird, Robert Parish, Jamaal Wilkes, Arvydas Sabonis, Jerry Tarkanian, and Spencer Haywood when they entered the Hall of Fame. When I chose my presenter, back in 1993, I chose Jack Ramsay.

Now, twenty years later, we got the tragic news that Jack was really sick and wasn't going to be able to win this game. Like many of the other key figures in my life, Jack spent his whole life working tirelessly to make other people's lives better—all the way to the end. And now, as I went back to the Hall of Fame one more time to present Jerry Tarkanian—as the greatest story ever told—I knew that there was not a chance in the world that I would ever have been there if it weren't for Jack Ramsay. He was as great a champion as I've ever known, and an even better man. Jack was a terrific and loving husband, a wonderful dad, and a remarkable teacher.

Too many of my master teachers have now passed away. Each time I've been flooded with sadness and grief, but also a drive and commitment—the same kind that they tried to instill in me so many years gone by.

Through their help and lifelong wisdom, I had now climbed back to the point where I was not simply doing better, I was actually doing well. I had my health. Our family was doing great, and it was growing.

When I started this latest climb, I first went to brother Bruce, requesting some San Diego business contacts for my new beginning. He introduced me to Ted Roth, Pat Kilkenny, Ron Fowler, and Jim Waring—all foundational pillars of the 200-plus-billion-dollar-a-year San Diego economy. I'm still with all of those guys today, and because of them, my business is better than ever.

Our nonprofit groups are making real strides. The Better Way Back continues to flourish. Lori has been able to resume her award-winning philanthropic activities, including her work raising, training, and helping service dogs and their community.

Through Lori's work with service dogs and the people they help, we have become best friends with U.S. Marine Lance Weir, who twenty-two years ago got hurt—real bad. He's been a quadriplegic ever since. After my spine surgery, when all I could do was lie there contemplating suicide, Lance would sit at my bedside, asking me how I stayed so positive.

Since we started with the CAF, Lance has been able to get a new, one-of-a-kind bike that enables him to get out there on the road with us. A great all-around athlete before his accident, Lance is currently doing things that no other person with his level of disability has ever been able to do. Today we refer to him as the ultra-endurance athlete of the millennium, and that is a conservative description.

Also through the world of service dogs, we now know Andy and Caroline Boyd, and their children—Chase and the twin girls, Izzy and Zoey. They epitomize the perfect Southern California family. When Chase was just three years old he was diagnosed with progressive muscular dystrophy. Andy and Caroline did everything they could to mainstream Chase's deteriorating life as his body progressively failed him. Everyone else did whatever they could to help.

Chase was the most remarkable spirit and force that any of us have ever known. With the biggest heart imaginable, he far exceeded his expected life span. Chase's light finally went out in early 2014, just after his nineteenth birthday. He lives on eternally in our recently organized Team Chase, as we all try to add lasting purpose to his endless efforts.

Ted Roth, of Roth Capital Partners, subsequently introduced me to his older brother Duane. Duane became my ultimate mentor. He was John Wooden, Chick Hearn, and Maurice Lucas all in one. He shined the light and illuminated the path forward, he delivered the message of a better tomorrow, and he cleared the space under the boards. Duane ran Connect, a San Diego–based nonprofit, business-accelerating trade organization. I volunteer for the San Diego Sport Innovators, the sports division cluster that complements Connect's sister organizations in wireless technology, clean energy, biotech, and the life sciences.

I recruited Duane into the CAF. He became a masterful cyclist and huge financial supporter. One day on a CAF ride on Mount Laguna, just east of San Diego, on top of his game, the mountain, and everything else, Duane went down on a turn and never got up.

Then Ernie Vandeweghe finally gave so much of himself for so long that he could no longer go on. And he was now gone, too.

And most recently Rocky, whose heart was so big that it beat for all of us, could no longer carry the load, nor answer the bell for the first time in forever.

Through all the devastation of the accumulating losses, I was continuing to improve from my spine catastrophe, getting better to the point where I could finally begin to dream and hope that I could work to help others and pass the efforts of Lance, Chase, Duane, Ernie, and Rocky along—trying to make everybody ever happier and better, starting the cycle anew as the wheel keeps turning.

I was out again, riding my bike—on a long, hard ride. Just the way I like it. And I was on fire. It was the end of another CAF Million Dollar Challenge. We were on the last day of the group fund-raising ride from

San Francisco home to San Diego. I've been able to successfully do this ride every year since I started with the CAF in 2010.

I love my bike . . . I love California . . . I love San Diego . . . I love the CAF . . . and I was having the time of my life.

We were getting close to the end. We were in Del Mar. It was a perfect day—maybe better. I knew I was going to make it. There was just one more climb—Torrey Pines. I was feeling great.

I sat up and backed off. I let the other riders go ahead. I wanted to be by myself. I just kept thinking how lucky I was. It wasn't that long ago that I had nothing. And now I had everything. I was riding my bike down the coast of California. The only way that things could be any better was if we were going to turn around and ride the whole course in reverse—and just keep going, looping endlessly, forever.

I kept reminding myself how many people had called when I was down. How they all kept telling me, "Don't give up, Bill. You can make it . . . Don't give up. You can make it."

Now I just have a few short miles to go. I glide down the groove toward Torrey Pines State Beach, across the estuary, and then the long, hard climb starts up and to the left.

I'm on the climb. I'm in the zone. It's what we live for.

I'm purposefully by myself. There's nobody else around. I make the halfway curve to the right. I look up, and there's one of our teammates riding by herself, all alone, on the last stretches of the last climb.

I can see now that it's Kelly Fox; she's a good rider, but she's having a tough final climb.

I'm starting to catch her. I'm going to catch her. Kelly's now struggling big-time.

Now, Kelly is just like you and me in so many ways, and beautiful as can be. But Kelly is paralyzed from her rib cage down. And she has just ridden her hand-cycle all the way from San Francisco and the Golden Gate Bridge, well over six hundred miles, to right here on the final slopes of the final climb.

As I'm coming up behind her, I start calling out to her. I start urging her, "Don't give up, Kelly . . . You can make it . . . Don't give up."

I start singing "Chimes of Freedom" and "Mission in the Rain." "Come on, Kelly . . . Ring those chimes . . . One dream, Kelly, one time . . . You can make it, don't give up."

Now I've caught her. I look down. She's on her last climbing gear, and has no easier ones to fall back on. She's not going to make it. And if she doesn't get that crank on her hand-cycle turned over one more time, she's going to start rolling backward down the mountain.

We're both crying. We are there together at the moment of truth, one more time. I keep urging her to continue. But it's not happening.

And then, from nowhere—nowhere but deep inside—Kelly does find it. She finds something from deep in her core that allows her to slowly, barely, get that crank to turn over. Once. Slowly. Barely. But it's over the top . . . Then again . . . and again.

And now she has it. And we find a rhythm. And we are able to make that final stretch of the last long, hard climb—together.

We crested the summit, and then soared like eagles down into La Jolla, where at the park there were countless little children and their families all running, playing, singing, dancing, and just having the time of their lives—on the beach, on the lawn. Most of the children—and a lot of the adults, too—were in wheelchairs, or with their prosthetics, or on crutches, or whatever.

It didn't matter. They were there. And they now had a chance—the chance to play in the game of life one more time. And they have all come to say "Thank you." As have I.

I Can See Clearly Now
I Can't Get Enough
Is It the End? Or the Beginning?

I am so looking forward to what's next for me. I have been at this for far too long.

I have a new spine. I have a new knee. And now I'm going off in search of a new life.

I want to become a student again in this great game. I want to read a book. I want to go to lectures and conferences. I want to watch a movie. I want to go to the theater, museums, exhibitions, and libraries. I want to listen to great speakers, and learn.

I want to go back on tour.

I want to live the Sunshine Daydream.

I want to go back to a life of substance and depth—and get away from the shallow sound bites and snippets.

I want to ride my bike.

I want to pay honor and tribute to my fallen heroes, mentors, and role models—Ernie Vandeweghe, Duane Roth, and Chase Boyd.

I want to ride my bike for a purpose and reason with our Team

Chase squad—the greatest team ever—with Lance Weir and our captain, Andy Boyd, Chase's dad.

I want to go to the park, to the beach, to the mountains, and to the desert.

I want to go back to the Mission Valley Y, and my weight room.

I want to go back to helping those who can't get by without help.

I want to go back to raising funds for the nonprofits that are doing work that matters.

I want to get on with my new business life based on health care, solar energy, sports technologies, education, finance, music, consumer products, and Azuñia Tequila.

I want to do right by and justice to my renewed media and broadcast partnerships at ESPN, the Pac-12 Network, and the NBA.

I want to continue to learn from and work with my new business mentors and partners—Pat Kilkenny, the Roth family, Ron Fowler, and Jim Waring.

I want to go back to my piano and drums.

I want to go back to my friends and my mom.

I want to go back to my wife and our children, and get to know our grandchildren.

I want to go back to my brothers and sister.

I want to spend time with all the people I love and care about.

I want to be with Cortez, whom we rescued from our son Chris. Cortez is now my service dog. He makes me happy. And he is the greatest dog in the history of the world.

—

I am happy again right now. Happy to be moving on down the road, looking forward to the next long, hard climb—one more time, with still so much more to do.

My history tells me that there's a crash coming soon.

But I know this time will be different.

I've got my family and my friends. And I've got Cortez.

I know I can make it through.

I can see clearly now.

Artwork © 2015 Mike DuBois

SONG CREDITS

Chapter Titles and Epigraphs

1. One Way or Another This Darkness Got to Give
   ("New Speedway Boogie," The Grateful Dead)

2. My Time Comin' Any Day, Don't Worry 'Bout Me, No!
   ("Estimated Prophet," The Grateful Dead)
   Epigraph: "Estimated Prophet," The Grateful Dead

3. Here Comes Sunshine
   ("Here Comes Sunshine," The Grateful Dead)
   Epigraph: "Can't Come Down," The Grateful Dead

4. Pleased to Meet You, Hope You Guess My Name
   ("Sympathy for the Devil," The Rolling Stones)
   Epigraph: "Sympathy for the Devil," The Rolling Stones

5. You Say You Want a Revolution
   ("Revolution," The Beatles)
   Epigraph: "Ohio," Neil Young

6. My Lightning, Too . . . The Music Never Stops
   Epigraph: "The Music Never Stopped," The Grateful Dead

7. Commissars and Pinstripe Bosses Roll the Dice, Whichever Way They Fall—Guess Who Gets to Pay the Price
   ("Throwing Stones," The Grateful Dead)
   Epigraph: "Deal," The Grateful Dead, and "Up to Me," Bob Dylan

8. New Morning
   Epigraph: "New Morning," Bob Dylan, and "Playing in the Band," The Grateful Dead

9. The Great Unraveling
   Epigraph: "Uncle John's Band," The Grateful Dead, and "High Time," The Grateful Dead

10. Feel Like a Stranger
    ("Feel Like a Stranger," The Grateful Dead)

11. Help on the Way
    ("Help on the Way," The Grateful Dead)
    Epigraph: "Terrapin Station," The Grateful Dead

12. Shadowboxing the Apocalypse
    ("My Brother Esau," The Grateful Dead)
    Epigraph: "Box of Rain," The Grateful Dead

13. I Need a Miracle
    ("I Need a Miracle," The Grateful Dead)
    Epigraph: "Jack Straw," The Grateful Dead

14. Eyes of the World
    ("Eyes of the World," The Grateful Dead)
    Epigraph: "Eyes of the World," The Grateful Dead

15. Knocked Down—It Gets to Wearin' Thin
    ("Truckin'," The Grateful Dead)

16. Once in a While You Get Shown the Light, in the Strangest of Places If You Look at It Right
    ("Scarlet Begonias," The Grateful Dead)

Main Text

Page 2: "The Wheel," Jerry Garcia

Page 4: "Uncle John's Band," The Grateful Dead

Page 5: "The Music Never Stopped," The Grateful Dead

Page 6: "The Wheel," Jerry Garcia

Page 12: "Truckin'," The Grateful Dead

Page 13: "Turn On Your Love Light," The Grateful Dead

Page 13: "Comes a Time," Jerry Garcia

Page 14: "The Music Never Stopped," The Grateful Dead

Page 15: "The Wheel," Jerry Garcia

Page 15: "Old Man," Neil Young

Page 64: "Ohio," Neil Young

Page 64: "Just Like Tom Thumb's Blues," Bob Dylan

Page 65: "Dancing in the Streets," Marvin Gaye, William Stevenson, Ivy Jo Hunter

Page 66: "Stella Blue," The Grateful Dead

Page 68: "Casey Jones," The Grateful Dead

Page 74: "Maggie's Farm," Bob Dylan

Page 79: "Like a Rolling Stone," Bob Dylan

Page 107: "Ohio," Neil Young

The credit for the photo of Bill Walton in front of the John Wooden statue in the first printing should have read "Photo by Erkki Corpuz."